More Books from The Sager Group

Labyrinth *of the* Wind

A Novel *of* Love *and* Nuclear Secrets *in* Tehran

MADHAV MISRA

Labyrinth of the Wind: A Novel of Love and Nuclear Secrets in Tehran
Copyright © 2021 Madhav Misra
All rights reserved.

Cover and Interior Designed by
Siori Kitajima, SF AppWorks LLC
Cover Art Adapted for Use by Permission of the Artist,
Motoi Yamamoto

Cataloging-in-Publication data for this book is available
from the Library of Congress
ISBNs:
eBook: 978-1-950154-31-9
Paperback: 978-1-950154-30-2

Published by The Sager Group LLC
TheSagerGroup.net

Labyrinth
of the
Wind

A Novel *of*
Love *and*
Nuclear Secrets
in Tehran

MADHAV MISRA

Artifex Te Adiuva

For my parents Dr. Prabha Misra and Mahesh Chandra Misra IAS,
who found true north

*After all, we make ourselves
according to the ideas we have of our possibilities.*

V.S. Naipaul, *A Bend in the River*

Contents

Cast of Characters

TEHRAN, IRAN

AYAN PATHAK, twenty-eight-year-old protagonist of this novel, chief financial officer of Iran Power, educated in Delhi and London.

GABY FABER, Ayan's girlfriend, flight engineer with Iran Air and supporter of Baader-Meinhof/Red Army Faction, German born, educated in Switzerland.

CAPTAIN BAHMAN, Gaby's friend and Iran Air pilot.

NADER OVEISSI, CEO of Iran Power, Ayan's boss, favored by the Atomic Energy Organization of Iran.

FIROUZ AKHBARI, closely connected to the Shah, special advisor to the Ministry of Energy.

KHANOM-EH MOHSEN, Ayan's landlady.

HAMID GHORBANI, Ayan's driver.

SHOLEH GHORBANI, Hamid's wife.

ADIL GHORBANI, Hamid's older son.

IMRAN GHORBANI, Hamid's younger son.

HEDAYAT, Hamid's friend, violent and unstable revolutionary.

COLONEL HEYDAR HOSSEINI, SAVAK, Shah's secret police, assigned to Iran Power.

CAPTAIN SALEHI, SAVAK interrogation officer.

DAVOOD AGHA, SAVAK heavy.

AREF AGHA, SAVAK factotum.

DARIOUSH, Ayan's best friend in Tehran, hotelier and owner of Cascades spa and restaurant, member of Ayan's tennis group at Club Veyssi, Key Club discotheque regular.

HASSAN KARIMI, Ayan's friend, industrialist, another member of the Club Veyssi tennis group.

FARIBA KARIMI, Hassan's cousin.

NICK STASNEY, CIA operations officer, completes the tennis foursome at Club Veyssi.

DELHI, INDIA

PADMA PATHAK, Ayan's mother.

JATIN PATHAK, his father. .

SHIV PATHAK, Ayan's older brother.

JAYA PATHAK, his younger sister.

VIKRAM RAI, Ayan's uncle, a mentor who introduced him to Firouz Akhbari.

RAVI RAI, another uncle and mentor.

LONDON, ENGLAND

REKHA ROY, Ayan's first love.

JACKIE SMITH, a freelance foreign correspondent.

OWEN ASHTON, a wealthy, forceful Welshman, Ayan's rival for Jackie's attention in days gone by.

CHIP de GROOT, Nader's South African contact, big-ticket arms dealer.

GENEVA, SWITZERLAND

LUC BOSSARD, senior relationship manager with Banque du Rhone, responsible for the Iran Power account and Alpine Global, Chip de Groot's Zug-based company.

WEST BERLIN, MUNICH, LAKE STARNBERG, WEST GERMANY

ANDREAS FABER, Gaby's father.

NINA FABER, her mother.

MATHIAS FABER, Gaby's younger brother.

KARL-HEINZ MULLER (CHARLIE), her childhood friend and adult suitor.

PART ONE

CHAPTER 1

Tehran, Iran, October 1977

Some succeed in grabbing the world by the scruff of its neck. His had been an insecure grip, but on this morning, he felt hopeful.

Ayan Pathak rested his weight on the rooftop railing of the apartment he rented in Khanom-eh Mohsen's high-country Tehran villa and looked north, away from the unmade, limiting city that meandered towards the Great Salt Desert. The Alborz, just emerging from silhouette, rose steeply above him. Shadows evaporated on Mount Damavand to the east, and the sunrise raced towards him along the slopes of the crescent range separating Tehran from the Caspian Sea. It was clear and crisp. The autumnal air built on Ayan's mood of renewal and anticipation the mountains had brought on, as they had ever since family holidays spent 6,000 feet up in the Garhwal Himalayas, at a far remove from Delhi's infernal heat. Hints of Gaby's perfume wafted up from his body, sending a frisson of excitement through him, reminding him of last night. All days should start like this.

A familiar voice, reciting the morning *Fajr* prayer, drew Ayan to the front of the villa. Hamid had arrived early, and his prayer mat was laid out beside the swimming pool, facing Mecca, infinity, a thousand miles to the southwest. He was sitting back, and his eyes were distant, focused on some sacred place.

The rumble of traffic cut through the mulberry and cedar trees defending the villa from the parkway. Ayan hurried back inside. His forty-five-minute commute to the Iran Power factory could turn into a two-hour nightmare if he lingered. He walked softly into the bedroom where Gaby still slept, pulled the covers over her legs, and kissed the top of her head. She smiled and reached out for him, then fell back on her pillow, recovering from the multiple flights on yesterday's dreaded "Shiraz Everywhere" assignment. Ayan placed her pilot's cap on the chest of drawers, hung her Iran Air uniform in the closet, and made room in the Kelvinator for the remnants of champagne she'd brought—"from the flight deck, pilot's perks." The fridge was stuffed with rice, *dal*, *gobi*, and *aloo matar*, four things he loved and knew how to cook, but not Gaby's first choice. She could fix herself a sandwich: He had eggs, smoked chicken slices, and cheese, and there was enough coffee and tea to get her going when she surfaced. He helped himself to some of her chocolate raspberry cake—"from my hometown in Bavaria, my mother's specialty"—and ten minutes later, he was dressed and moving briskly down the circular stone staircase that led to the carport.

Khanom-eh Mohsen was standing on the bottom step. Her hennaed hair was in rollers, and there was still sleep in her eyes. Her broad, handsome face did not look happy. She adjusted the top of her robe pointedly when their eyes met, amusing Ayan. Why did she imagine he was interested in looking down her cleavage?

"Ayan Agha! Keep your *dehati* driver off my property!" the Khanom said, pointing towards Hamid, who had folded away his prayer mat in the trunk and was waiting for Ayan by their Iran Power car. "Let him pray all he likes outside!

He is too insolent! In your country, do you tolerate such behavior from servants?"

Ayan looked at Kamran Street that ran past the house. Out there, the desert still ruled. Sand and shrub had already begun to reclaim recently paved areas. "Sorry, Khanom," he said with a shrug, "I'm not going to ask Hamid to pray in the dirt." He turned his back on her protests, stepped around her BMW, and folded his six-foot frame into the cramped Paykan, the Iranian version of the Hillman Hunter assigned to him. People like Hamid were probably an unwelcome reminder for his landlady that rustic Iran lurked beyond the confines of her villa. Well, let her tell him off directly, but that was unlikely. Not even Khanom-eh Mohsen would dare insult the dignified man of faith.

Hamid reversed out of the driveway and navigated the series of one-way streets as they entered the depressing, grey-white sprawl of downtown Tehran. He expertly avoided the increasing mayhem till they reached Pahlavi Avenue, then pulled up near a newsstand, ignoring honks and curses as cars swerved around them. The newsstand stop had become routine. Hamid deserved the shot of caffeine and break-fast before he took on the serious business of driving south through Tehran's traffic. His odyssey commenced at 5:00 a.m. and required two buses and a shared taxi just to reach Khanom-eh Mohsen's villa.

Hamid bought a copy of the *Kayhan International* news-paper for Ayan and hustled off to a small tea stall. *Dad must be on the last trek of the season, on the way back from Milam Glacier,* Ayan thought as he waited for his driver to return. He pulled out the letter he'd received from his father that was posted a couple of weeks ago from the base camp of Munsyari. It was a wonderful time to be in the region, his father wrote in his elegant handwriting, describing the canyons and gorges,

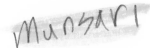

the forests and mountain views Ayan remembered well from their hike together two years ago. He closed his eyes and could still see Nanda Devi clearly, rising 26,000 feet into the clouds above, and hear the rapids of the Gori Ganga raging one careless footstep below. Ayan put his father's letter back into his briefcase. *I have to reply to it soon,* he thought as his eyes roamed over the headlines of the newspaper.

Hamid soon returned and stood outside, eating his flatbread and cheese sandwich underneath the tall graceful sycamores of Pahlavi Avenue. Around them, Tehran awakened. Old men, in a variety of tuque caps, open-necked shirts, and jackets drawn over thick sweaters, fondled their worry beads and chatted outside small bakeries interspersed with haute couture boutiques and branches of global brands. Men and women in smart business clothes made their way to work or stopped to breakfast on croissants and cappuccinos in stylish cafés. Commuters waded into the traffic, yelling "*Mostaghim! Chap! Rast!*" and waving their arms, pointing in the direction they wanted to travel; others, with nothing much to do, stood around slurping tea through sugar cubes placed behind their front teeth.

Ayan sat up in the backseat, trying to find a comfortable position. Having a car and driver was not bad for somebody only twenty-eight years old and definitely an upgrade from slumming it on the London Tube, but the Paykan was an underpowered shoebox. He was due for an upgrade to a Mercedes now that he was the chief financial officer of Iran Power, as Hamid frequently pointed out—saying it was embarrassing to drive a senior manager in the common Paykan. A substantial raise had also gone into the ether. His boss never gave anything away without a protracted negotiation, and Nader was a master, impressive to observe, but not when you were on the receiving end of his blizzard of flattery and threats.

Let's face it: He was outmatched in this country of hints and half-truths, of manners above all else. It had been hard to accept that people seemed to speak from their hearts, in the most poetic way, and then acted at a tangent to their promises. He was adapting to survive, uneasily aware that he had become more opportunistic but cloaking his intentions in niceties, compliments, and deference. Ironically, this made him more sophisticated in Persian eyes. People remarked that he was beginning to understand the Iranian mentality and learning how to play the great game of *taarof.* But he would never reach Nader's level.

They resumed their journey, Hamid showing the local disregard for anything that was behind him. Soon, they were passing the German Cultural Institute where, just days before, Gaby had leaned against Ayan amidst the overflow of a crowd of thousands defying the police presence. It had begun to rain, Ayan remembered, but Gaby had insisted on staying until the end, listening to his translation of the speeches and readings. All of them were caught up in the spirit of the *Das Sab,* heady with the challenge and freedom of the Ten Nights of poetry and protest organized by the Writers Association of Iran. Afterwards, he'd raced to catch up to Gaby's passion as they made love; he'd held her in his arms till dawn, and she'd talked about the fight to change Germany, alarming him with hints of involvement with urban guerillas, worrying him with her intensity.

Ayan saw an Iranian woman standing at the curb waiting for a break in the traffic. She was running her hand through her hair, and something about her reminded him of Gaby—of her long, delicate fingers gripping him, of her feet caressing his legs and locking around him—and he wished desperately he was back home with her. Gaby would be flying out again soon, off to the States or Europe, adding a few days to each trip to visit her family in Bavaria, making each separation seem endless. He felt lonely and restless when she was away, missed the reassurance of falling asleep with her arms wrapped around him, missed her smile and enthusiasm. So much had happened last week. He needed time with her to find out more, long stretches of uninterrupted time; perhaps then, she would tell him more about the storming of the hijacked Lufthansa jet in Mogadishu, why the death of Andreas Baader had enraged her, why she felt so strongly that the leader of the Red Army Faction should have lived, and why the head of German Industries had deserved to die. He should be spending the day hiking with her in Darband, then going to the Key Club for dinner and letting its music and atmosphere work their magic.

Hamid braked hard. They had run into traffic at the merge onto the Parkway and almost hit the car ahead. Ayan rolled down the window and heard yelling as Hamid got out to investigate the gridlock. The voices morphed into rhythmic chants that made Ayan uneasy, bringing back memories of being in the midst of a column of Shia mourners flogging their backs during Muharram. He was in a place he didn't belong.

Frenzied demonstrators began to run past the Paykan shouting, *"Marg bar Shah! Marg bar Amrika!"* One of them lagged, as if caught on the stretched edge of a rubber band pulling him back to his pursuers. He was just a boy, sixteen at most, a Persian Adonis, with delicate features and a tentative beard, and as he sprinted past the Iran Power car, looking back anxiously at the men giving chase, a crack in the treacherous road felled him.

Two men in track jackets and jeans threw themselves on the teenager and handcuffed him. One dug his knee into the boy's spine and repeatedly slammed his captive's face into the asphalt, while the other kicked him mercilessly.

The boy's mouth and forehead spurted blood. A kick caught his jaw and sent a shower of teeth and saliva onto the road. A dark wet patch spread out from his groin, down to the end of his jeans, and formed a pool by his sneakers.

Ahead, the shouting stopped. Engines revved and tires squealed as the protestors sped off. The impatient traffic began to move around the brutal tableau.

Ayan's fists clenched. He pushed open the door and yelled, "Stop!"

The man who had been kicking the boy pulled out a pistol.

Hamid reappeared and pulled Ayan back towards the Paykan.   *CIA*

"No! No! Ayan Agha!" Hamid said as Ayan resisted. "SAVAK! Please go back in the car! They will kill us too!"

The driver put his hands together and bowed to the approaching man. "Excuse us . . . please forgive us," Hamid said. "This Agha works for Shah, Iran Power . . . he is a foreigner, he doesn't understand."

The man pointed his gun at Hamid and then at Ayan, then at Hamid again.

Hamid dropped to his knees and continued pleading and pointing to the Iran Power logo on the Paykan as the man brought the gun to his forehead.

Cars behind them honked.

The boy on the ground stirred. The SAVAK man holding him down called to his companion.

The agent with the gun waved Hamid off contemptuously. He swaggered back, lifted the barrel of his pistol, and brought it down on the boy's head with immense force.

"Oh my god, the bastards," Ayan said, clutching Hamid's shoulder as the two SAVAK men dragged the still, bloody body off the road and onto the sidewalk.

Somehow

They made it to the Parkway in silence, escaping the city through the Touhid Tunnel and onto the Navvab Highway and the Behesht-e Zahra Expressway.

Ayan's stomach churned. His fists were still clenched. His heart raced, and his damp shirt clung to his body.

Hamid's fingers teased the scar that curved from his ear to his mouth.

"That boy's death is nothing for SAVAK, Agha Ayan," he said in Farsi, abandoning the hesitant English he practiced on the way to work. "They kill anybody, everybody, even Ayatollah Khomeini's son! These dogs martyred him in Najaf yesterday!" Hamid looked at Ayan in the rearview mirror, his voice rising. "They lie and say he died from sickness! The imam in my mosque, everybody, we all know SAVAK killed Mostafa Khomeini! For no reason! He was a just a scholar and a religious man. Shah and his family are immoral infidels! But Ayatollah's voice reaches us through his tapes and gives us courage. In forty days, there will be an *Arbaeen* to mourn the martyr Mostafa Khomeini—also for this boy they murdered just now. Many people will come."

Ayan broke eye contact and picked up the newspaper, reading desultorily. His chest felt heavy and constricted, his mind a swirl of images: the boy running, falling, dying; a father beating his chest in anguish; a mother collapsing on the floor, inconsolable.

"Ayatollah Khomeini is not afraid of anything because he is the Mahdi," Hamid continued with unerring conviction. "He is our twelfth imam returning to liberate us from Shah and his Amrikan and Israeli masters! As has been promised, *Inshallah. Alhamdulillah!*"

What to say to a man with such religious certainty? Nothing.

Ayan rubbed his forehead and looked out of the window.

The Tehran-Qom Highway opened up in front of them, the surrounding land sparsely populated. The terrain, the atmosphere, and everything around was painted in dispiriting hues of beige. Pipes and funnels of a vast petrochemical complex dominated the landscape, and flames from the refinery burn-off defined the skyline to the east. Smoke and sand kicked up by a brisk northerly wind had vanquished the crisp, clear morning.

Agha Ryan

Mahdi

CHAPTER 2

The executive butler flashed gold-plated incisors in a smile of triumph after the silver breakfast tray he was carrying rested safely on the desk. Ayan nodded encouragingly. Amir Agha's hands were trembling more violently than usual, and one of these days, all that Caspian Sea caviar, lavash bread, and feta would end up on the floor. Amir Agha backed out of his office, his shoulders drooping obsequiously as he slipped past Colonel Heydar Hosseini, Iran Power's security chief.

Hosseini stood straight as always, stretching his five feet nine inches to the limit. His full head of hair, parted on the right and almost completely grey at forty-five, was neat. His dark blue suit highlighted his broad shoulders and slim hips—a good tailor had disguised a surprisingly undisciplined waistline.

Behind the distinguished look and avuncular potbelly was the SAVAK enforcer of Iran Power. Every major company in Iran had a man from the Shah's secret police in its ranks. Ayan tensed, the killing on Pahlavi Avenue replaying vividly in his mind as the Colonel sauntered into his office.

"A good holiday, Ayan Agha?" Hosseini said, his craggy features arranged in their usual sardonic expression. "I hear you're having fun, enjoying Iran."

"I just rest on weekends, Colonel," Ayan said casually, turning his attention to a file on his desk to diminish the man's air of authority. "This one was no different. I took a couple of extra days off so I could be here on this Monday, recharged and ready to be worked to death by Iran Power again."

"*Baleh, baleh,*" the Colonel said, smiling. He walked over to Ayan, invading his space with the honey and amber musk of too much Paco Rabanne.

Hosseini retrieved a handkerchief from his breast pocket and dusted the portrait of the Shah on the credenza behind Ayan's desk, fidgeting with the frame and the minia-ture Iranian flag placed next to it until the arrangement satisfied his eye. He patted Ayan's back patronizingly and then returned to neutral territory, sitting down in the chair opposite his desk.

Ayan knew what was coming next.

"Come, sing of wine and minstrels . . .'" Hosseini said, his manicured hands punctuating the quote from his legendary hometown poet, "'. . . seek less the secrets of life; none has solved—nor can—this enigma with the logic of mind . . .'"

The Colonel arched an eyebrow and waited, considering Ayan with melancholy brown eyes.

He started each morning by opening Hafez's *Diwan* and claimed that the lines his eyes fell on inspired his day. It was a Persian custom, the Colonel had said, a characteristic of a poetic people who returned to their literary and philosophic greats to knock the dust off their souls.

It was ironic that the SAVAK man used Hafez's wisdom for this purpose, thought Ayan cynically. At any rate, Hosseini reveled in poetic jousts, and Ayan had learnt to respond to him with a quote from Ghalib or Tagore. An ode to sentiment and intuition from the Bengali poet seemed an appropriate follow-up to the Hafez lines Hosseini had thrown at him.

"'A mind all logic is like a knife all blade . . .'" Ayan said mechanically, without the theatrical flourish he normally used to match Hosseini's grandiose presence, "'. . . it makes the hand bleed that uses it.'"

Hosseini brought his hand to his heart in a gesture of approval.

"*Kheili khoobe! Kheili khoobe!* Agha Ayan, I feel a great affection for you," he said. "You and I share much; we know that truth is sensed—that only mediocre people try to comprehend life through analysis, following straight lines to nowhere—and we both love beautiful women! Please convey my regards to your friend Gaby, the best-looking foreigner in Iran. With your permission, I would enjoy taking her to dinner."

He knew she was Ayan's girlfriend, but that meant nothing here. "Girlfriend" was just an invitation to join in the fun with a loose woman, get some for yourself—definitely if she was European.

"You have already tried your luck with Gaby," Ayan said, shaking his head and standing up. "Why keep getting insulted?"

He walked the Colonel to the door, savoring the three-inch height advantage he had over the man.

"Perhaps I have some reason for hope," Hosseini said slyly. "And I have important information for you that we can discuss later, perhaps during our management walk around the factory or after. For now, I leave you with some more of Hafez's wisdom: 'I make love in hopes this noble art will not disappoint me . . . For that beauteous face I pray for a beautiful disposition to keep our heart from any remorse or indisposition . . .'"

Hafez

The Colonel nodded and exited right, towards his office a couple of doors away.

Ayan exhaled slowly. The Colonel was just playing his usual games. Outside his window, Iran Power was awake and humming. Workers on forklifts stacked transformers in neat rows in front of the warehouse. Delivery trucks were lined up to take them across the country and all over the Middle East. He had the finances of a major public company under his care. How about concentrating on that?

Ayan drained the glass of chilled water and turned towards the stack of files on his desk. But it felt trivial, indecent almost, to work on banalities like inventories, cash flows, accounts, and Iran Power's stock price. Images of the morning's events—brutal, shocking, insistent, of dreams bleeding out onto the blacktop of Pahlavi Avenue—were all he could think about.

He felt depressed and anxious even as the presence of visitors from abroad forced him to refocus. Hauser, who had flown in from Germany, was at Ayan for hours to clear payment for the goods SA Stuttgart had delivered to Iran Power for its planned expansion in Qazvin, something that was not going to happen because the arrogant German executive from the affiliated company had not been convincing about the pricing. Ayan pretended to listen to Hauser. His limited concentration today was directed at the problem the banker Ben Arnold had created that afternoon by pulling out of the financing syndicate for Qazvin. First National's thin-lipped, perennially anxious regional boss had bizarrely suggested that Iran Power Qazvin could be providing the infrastructure for nuclear weapons that the Shah was surely planning to develop. "Not my view, of course, but Washington's, and we're a regulated entity," Ben had said. Ayan had recovered from his incredulity, given the banker assurances, customer lists, repeated the argument that Iran's growth required the additional 23,000 megawatts of power the Shah wanted to generate from nuclear plants because high-priced oil had to be preserved for export. The leading companies in Europe were fighting for the business; why not run on Iran Power's inside track?

He'd failed to move Arnold, but Nader wanted the American bank in the syndicate to keep the others from becoming too greedy. He couldn't give up, though he should have known better than to ask Nader to sign the guarantee letter Arnold had drafted. The boss had no problem making verbal promises. Written commitments were another matter. He knew that! Why had he sleepwalked into a humiliation? Nader had dismissed him with an irritated look and a comment about bankers being desperate for business of this size in a time of recession. "Make them compete," Nader had said, tossing the letter into the wastebasket. "Handle it. This is easy."

Ayan escaped Hauser when it was time for the weekly end-of-day senior management inspection of the factory with Nader. He sped up to catch the management posse that was approaching the warehouse, one of his responsibilities. Ayan glanced at the inventory status report as he walked, thinking about his next move with First National. There was one more play left: Mr. Ten Percent, the man with the cigarette-and-scotch-seasoned voice, Firouz Akhbari, entrepreneur and senior advisor to the Ministry of Energy, and part of the tribe of "connected to the Royal Family" aristocrats who made their living making introductions, facilitating imports and exports (lucrative 10 percent hand-in-the-till sort of stuff)—nothing so plebeian as doing real work. They ran things in Iran. Firouz was a big deal. A letter of assurance from him saying that Iran Power would remain a civilian enterprise should be enough for First National; and Firouz might do it. It reflected reality, and he liked Ayan.

This Iran Power job, even the fact that he was still living in Tehran, was because of a chance meeting with Firouz that had gone well. Firouz had placed him in this company. He was invested.

The stop at the warehouse was brief. Ayan had selected the right man to manage inventories: Bijan, trained in Germany and Japan, knew how to avoid bottlenecks as well as waste. The management team moved on to the fabrication and assembly building, and the head of manufacturing and Nader started a detailed discussion with the supervisors.

Ayan left the group and found a bench in the sun. The smell of oil, the flares of welding guns, and the rat-a-tat-tat of fabrication were hard on him. On some days, *Zen and the Art of Motorcycle Maintenance,* a present from Gaby, helped him feel less estranged from the world of these engineers. Gaby was an engineer too— she dealt with machines all day, loved the details of what she did. She said great engineers and great artists thought about vastly different things, but met on the common ground of Arete— they shared an obsession with excellence, with doing things perfectly; and that was how one side could understand the other, as *Zen* explained so brilliantly. Sometimes, this insight helped– made him more interested in the work of his technical colleagues. Today, it would be a forced crossing, an effort he was in no mood to make.

A whiff of cigarette smoke drifted over from workers leaning against the metallic walls of the enormous manufacturing hub. Gaby smoked occasionally; he never did. She'd once asked him to light a cigarette and pass it to her—and thanked him by kissing him with a mouth full of claret. The slow exchange of the wine, the cool menthol on her breath, and the taste of her tongue had driven him crazy with desire then; the memory of it made him frantic for her now.

Ayan started as the Colonel sat down next to him heavily.

"So," he said, "Ayan Agha, what are we going to do about Gaby Faber's exit permit?"

"Gaby?" Ayan asked with a frown. "Why are we talking about her again?"

"You don't care that Gaby is leaving Iran?"

"She's not leaving!" Ayan said angrily and stood. "She travels all the time. She probably needs the exit permit for work."

"Ayan Agha," Hosseini said, "Gaby Faber has just asked for an exit permit, not the usual exit and reentry visa. She's also given notice to Iran Air. You know that, my friend?"

Ayan looked down at Hosseini.

"Ayan Agha, I can see you're upset. Don't worry. I can delay her departure for a long time, you know," Hosseini said, placing his hand on his chest. "I'm at your service. Just ask, and I will block her application. It will give you time to persuade her to stay."

"Thank you, Colonel, but you don't need to involve yourself in this. Gaby is my concern—not yours."

"I'm only trying to help," Hosseini said.

But his triumphant smirk gave him away. The bastard was enjoying this.

"Don't. Mind your own business."

Hosseini got up. "No need to be rude, Ayan Agha," he said. "But you're not yourself. That's understandable. I won't take offence. Please remember I'm here for you, whenever needed."

The Colonel walked back into the manufacturing building.

Ayan slammed his fist on the door as it shut behind Hosseini.

The Colonel came back outside and looked at Ayan with raised eyebrows.

Ayan turned and walked away, his breathing fast and shallow. Walked straight to his office, called for Hamid, and left. Let Nader and the team wonder why he'd skipped the debriefing. He had nothing left. He was done for the day.

CHAPTER 3

Hamid had regained his composure. It would be a quiet trip to Shemiran, and for that, Ayan was grateful. Soon, he'd be home with Gaby. She would reassure him, tell him she had a routine reason for the visa, exit permit—whatever the hell it was. She wasn't going anywhere.

A sense of dislocation in Iran, of laughing together at the many absurdities of life in Tehran, may have brought them together. But something much more than an expatriate connection had developed between them. He was sure of that. "I love you, Ayan. Keep thinking I'm more than I am. I need this faith you have in me." Hadn't she'd said that last night?

He closed his eyes, sliding through memories from that flight to Tehran from Kuwait. There was the beautiful flight engineer greeting passengers and pausing to smile at him with more than professional interest, it seemed. What to say? Too slow! She turned towards the next passenger.

meeting Gabi 18

He heard himself describing her green-brown eyes and extravagant dimples to his friend in Iran Air and pleading for her phone number.

"That's Gaby Faber. She's booked by Captain Bahman. Number one girlfriend. She's in love with him, like all the women in Iran Air. No chance, buddy," his friend had said.

No problem, actually. He knew how the game worked in this town.

He was calling and talking to an answering machine, waiting, calling again, talking to that answering machine again . . .

Hamid yelled at a pedestrian he'd narrowly missed, dragging Ayan back to the present.

Ayan sat up, saw no harm was done, and leaned back into the back seat of the Paykan. He flexed his shoulders, trying to pull them down and back, and drifted back to the sound of a phone ringing on a gloomy Friday afternoon.

"You met me on a flight?" Gaby Faber was saying. "You're the one who flew to Kuwait and back with me on the same day?"

"Yes! I'm glad you remember!"

"Actually, I don't. I'm just repeating the message you left. How did you get my telephone number anyway?"

"I'm connected."

"I'll be angry if Iran Air gave it to you."

"Don't be. I'm harmless. I thought we could meet for a drink."

"Why?"

"Perhaps we could be friends. I would like that."

She laughed. "Yes, you would, wouldn't you! This happens quite a bit with us. Passengers try their luck. Sorry, I don't have time. Bye!"

She had hung up. He called back immediately.

"Don't be annoying," she said.

"Wait! How about tennis; do you like to play? Or we can go water skiing? Hiking?"

He had kept her talking—about sports, the pleasures of being outdoors in Shemiran, and the importance of the Imperial Country Club lifestyle that Tehran afforded its expatriates—until she agreed to meet for a game of tennis.

Club Veyssi, where they were to play, was his turf, an intimate private facility that the gregarious owner had developed into a social meeting ground for Shemiran residents. He had met his best friends in Tehran—Darioush, Hassan, and Nick—there and felt comfortable amongst the friendly staff in the pro shop and in the cozy bar and grill that looked down on the tennis courts.

His comfort and practiced nonchalance evaporated when she strode into the lobby, looking even more beautiful than he remembered.

"Hello," Gaby said, shaking his hand with a confident grip. "I suppose, again! What a charming club! All these terraced tennis courts, gorgeous flowers. I love the dark pink geraniums. It was such a surprise to turn down a lane in the middle of so many villas and see this oasis! And everybody's been very nice to me. You must be an important person here."

"I come often and tip well," Ayan said, trying not to stare at her long, toned legs. "It's my sanctuary from Tehran's madness."

"I can see why," Gaby said. "I should take time to do more things like this."

She wasn't a very good tennis player, but she was competitive and pushed herself to chase after every ball.

A perfectionist, Ayan thought. He'd happily fly any plane she piloted.

When they stopped for a water break, Gaby said, "You look very professional. I should have told you I'm a beginner. You must be bored."

"No," he said. "It's wonderful to see you again."

She shot him a look that made his heart leap.

After forty-five minutes of rallying, Gaby was done. She sat down on the courtside chair, and Ayan's attention was drawn to the adjoining court.

Shapour, one of the few unpleasant members of Club Veyssi, was berating Abbas, a ball boy who was filling in for the busy club pros. Ayan had taken a particular interest in Abbas. He'd first noticed the young fellow hitting a tennis ball against a wall using a wooden plank. His hand-eye coordination was superb; Ayan was moved to buy him a tennis racket. Now the talented kid was developing fast, but he was still a couple of years away from being able to deal with a bully like Shapour.

It was time to mediate.

"I'll be right back," Ayan told Gaby.

He gave Abbas 50 tomans, sent him off to the clubhouse, and calmed the irate Shapour by promising to play with him shortly.

"That was nice of you," Gaby said as they sat on the patio and refreshed themselves with melon juice.

"Perhaps too nice. That jerk Shapour is skulking about, waiting to collect."

Gaby took a last sip of her melon juice and stood up. "Well, I have to go now anyway. I have a taxi waiting. I have to work the Athens flight tonight. Thank you. I had a lovely time."

"As did I," Ayan said. "I know you called back, but here's my number again."

He wrote it on a cocktail napkin and handed it to her.

Gaby laughed and shook her head when she saw the heart he had sketched. She took the pen from his hand, crossed out the heart, and wrote, "Like you said . . . friends. That's all I want . . . "

She pushed the napkin back at him.

Chastened, he escorted her to the taxi and held out his hand. She surprised him by turning her face and kissing him on the lips. And then she said, "I lied, a little, you know, about not remembering you from the flight."

How could he sleep after that!

They played tennis a few times, and gradually, she let him pick her up from her apartment. Their idle chats in the car ranged easily across many shared interests—books, music, film, and travel. They started lingering for a cocktail after tennis, listening to the evening songs of *bolbols*, talking until the sun filtered to the intimate light of dusk. They confided in each other, sharing stories about family and home, life in Tehran.

As the days passed, her hand stayed in his longer, and her kisses came closer to the real thing.

And then, several weeks after the first tennis date, after what felt like a very long time, she changed their relationship.

"Do you have a music system?" she asked as they were chatting at Club Veyssi one evening.

"Yes, of course."

"I just picked up this Dylan tape. Let's go to your place and listen to it."

An hour later, they were sitting on his sofa, martinis in hand, and listening to *Blood on the Tracks*.

The soundtrack of that first time—"Tangled Up in Blue," "Simple Twist of Fate," "You're Gonna Make Me Lonesome When You Go"—reverberated in his head. He

Seven

shifted about in the car, reminded of the thrill he'd felt when she moved closer to him on the sofa, eyes closed, listening to the music.

She was ready when the alcohol gave him the courage to kiss her.

Her lips parted; she lay down and rested her head on his lap, allowed his hands to caress her breasts, breathing deeply as he moved down her stomach, tensing as he found her, responding to his touch, encouraging him.

He'd watched her take off her clothes and pull off his shirt, then made her wait and wait, savoring the sight and touch and taste of all her. ?

"Come on!" she urged, reaching for him, taking over, uninhibited, demanding, irresistible.

But she'd remained elusive, away on a flight out of town or busy with friends, even as he fell more and more in love with her. Then chance brought about another shift in their relationship. She had a fight with her roommate.

"I've got to clean my place before I leave on a flight tonight," Gaby said one day when he called to ask her out.

"Take a break. You've got to eat. Have dinner with me. You're like a ghost. You sure you live in Tehran?"

"I would like to see you, but I'm busy. Like I said."

"I'll come over and help."

"What, do my laundry?" Gaby laughed.

"I'm good at ironing and folding."

"OK, but I won't have much time, and you'll hate my roommate, Anna. She's a bitch."

The blonde woman who'd let him into Gaby's ground floor apartment in Zafaraniyeh later that night had a book in her hand. She frowned at him through large, round spectacles. Her hair was stacked in a messy bun on her head. Her beige slip, white dressing gown, bedroom slippers, and irritated expression let him know his visit was intrusive. Her face was well-formed, and her eyes were an intense blue, but her brusque manner detracted from her looks.

He liked the apartment. It was inviting and smelled of freshly baked bread. The large sofa and overstuffed chairs were upholstered in warm colors. His place looked Spartan in comparison. There was art on the walls here, warmer lighting, and markers of extensive travel in every corner: Persian handicrafts, Bavarian dolls, Masai bracelets, Sicilian pottery.

"She's in there—in her room," the reluctant host said, pointing towards a shut door.

So this was Anna.

Her German accent was strong. Gaby spoke English fluently, in a hybrid English-American accent, perhaps because of her years in a Swiss boarding school while her father travelled the world as a Schering sales manager. There was no mistaking where Anna was from.

He walked over to Gaby's shut door, knocked, and let himself in.

It was soon apparent that his domestic skills were not up to Gaby's exacting standards. So of course, the best way to spend the evening was to lie on her bed, drink beer, and watch her efficiently go about her chores.

After Gaby left for the airport, Ayan realized he'd left his car keys in her room.

Anna had ignored him whenever he came out for food and drink from the kitchen and snubbed his attempts at being civil. Would she even let him back into the apartment?

She didn't.

"Wait here," she said. "I'll get the keys for you."

As she handed him the keys, Anna said, "I know your voice from our answering machine."

gabi? communist?

"Really? I wondered if anybody ever picked up my messages off that device."

"I got it recently from New York, a PhoneMate. I'm sorry, but there was no way to avoid hearing your messages. You called a lot and used up most of my tape!"

"I called just twice."

"Four or five times!"

"No! Surely not! Anyway, I'm so sorry I bothered you."

"She's a communist, you know."

"What do you mean?" Ayan said, startled.

Cool blue eyes examined him through those glasses.

"She supports terrorists in Germany and communists in Iran, has people over here all the time, drinking and smoking and saying bad things about the Shah. I don't know what to do—she'll have us all thrown out of this country!"

"Gaby likes to discuss ideas. She likes politics and believes in helping people. She's no communist. Believe me, I know her."

"A lot of guys know her. You're not the only one."

She watched him with a hint of malicious satisfaction.

"Men are here all the time to see her . . ."

"All right! All right! That's enough!" Ayan said sharply, turning to leave. "I know—we are friends, that's all. Good night."

He'd thought Gaby probably had several admirers. It was not much fun to know that it was true. When he repeated Anna's words to Gaby, he had used a teasing tone, camouflaging his disquiet.

"She said what? That's just rubbish!" Gaby had said, glaring at him. "And you believed her?"

"I know about Captain Bahman. Who are my other rivals? Tell me. I'll find out, you know."

"None of your damn business! I find possessive men very unattractive."

"I'm not being possessive—just collecting information so I can kill all these men Anna says come to see you. Slowly and cruelly."

Gaby erased a smile and frowned at him.

"Stop! Enough already with this nonsense! Don't listen to that jealous, frustrated woman. I can't stand being around her! *Genug! Das ist genug!* I've got to find another place."

"Why don't you come and stay in my apartment," he'd responded offhandedly, not expecting a positive response. "There's plenty of room, and you like the view."

Gaby had looked at him for a while. "I'm not happy with you right now. Insecure man, listening to Anna's rubbish!"

She called the next day.

"Did you mean what you said—about me staying with you?" she said.

"Yes!" Ayan replied, heart racing. "Of course, I did!"

"Only for a short time. It's just that I confronted Anna. Things were said, and now I have to leave."

Gaby moved into his apartment that evening.

Khanom-eh Mohsen, watching with an approving smile, said, "Gaby *joon khelli ziba hast,* Ayan Agha! What are you waiting for? Marry her!"

That had been three months ago.

Now it was hard to imagine life without her.

CHAPTER 4

Ayan threw off his jacket and tie as he entered his apartment. He registered the large, suede fringed shoulder bag Gaby favored for travel and her overcoat draped on the raised handle of her pilot's rolling bag.

"You're leaving? I thought you had a few days of rest between flights," he said, embracing Gaby as she dressed in front of the mirror in the bedroom.

"They're short-staffed in Athens," Gaby said. "I have to deadhead there tonight." She looked at her watch. "But I may still have a couple of hours. I'm ready because you never know with these Iran Air drivers. There's some food in the kitchen. Have a beer. I'll join you in a minute."

She started running the lipstick over her mouth. Her short bob framed her oval face and accentuated her dimples; her chestnut hair had a hint of auburn in this light.

Thoughts of questioning her about what Hosseini had said left his mind.

He must have stared at her Hendrix T-shirt and tight flared jeans for too long.

Gaby looked down self-consciously before meeting his gaze in her mirror.

"Go!" she said, her eyes smiling.

Ayan took the lipstick out of her hand and placed it on her dressing table.

She turned from his kiss. "Go! Get yourself something to eat," she said, pushing him away. "We have salad, salami, cheese, *Bauernbrot . . .*"

Picking up her eyeliner brush, she returned to the mirror.

Ayan came behind her and kissed her neck.

"Stop! You know I have to leave. Soon!" she said, shivering as his lips moved over her skin. "Stop! You've had enough last night!"

He persisted.

She complained, said that her crew pick-up might come early, but he could feel her giving in as he eased her T-shirt out of her jeans.

She leaned back into him, her lips caressing his face as he embraced her. She turned to him and curled a leg around his hips. Her lips yielded, allowing his kisses to go deep. He guided her onto the bed and pulled off her jeans. She lifted her hips in anticipation as his mouth traced a path down her body. The aroma of her perfume and her desire filled his senses, intoxicating him.

"You know . . . you're not too bad-looking," Gaby said, rolling on top of him and pushing his hair off his forehead.

Her breasts pressed down on his chest; the softness of her skin against his felt sublime.

"I've said that before, haven't I? Don't get a big head," she said.

He put his arms around her.

"Don't fly out tonight. Say you're sick."

Gaby pushed away and slipped off him. "It doesn't work like that. Too many people are depending on me to show up. But I'll be back soon, and then you can have me all to yourself for a while."

She took a sip of the Lowenbrau he'd brought in from the kitchen.

"You seem a little down," she said. "What's wrong?"

He didn't say, *I'm worried that you're going away.*

He said, "I saw a teenager being beaten to death by SAVAK this morning—just for being part of a demonstration."

Gaby stood up as he described the murder.

"Bastards!" she said, pacing around the room angrily. "Fucking fascists are the same all over; I hate them all! How can they get away with it? We know the Shah's a dictator, SAVAK are thugs, but my god! Nobody did anything to help that boy?"

Why tell her about his instinct to surge forward and Hamid's restraining hand? It had been an effete half-measure. Futile.

"They had guns," Ayan said.

"These kinds of people usually do," Gaby said roughly. "And you just left? Went to work as if nothing had happened?"

"Come on Gaby! As opposed to what exactly?"

"Something! Anything except turning away! But then, I suppose I'm not much better, showing up for work, ferrying people around just after they murdered Baader and the others! Shot them like animals in Stammheim!"

"I'm sorry about Baader's death," Ayan said. "I know you're upset."

He got out of bed and massaged her shoulders.

"I'm worried about you, Gaby, worried about your involvement," he said. "Baader-Meinhof crossed a line by killing Schleyer. You know better than I do how aggressively the German government is going to react."

Gaby shrugged off his touch and moved away from him.

LOOK

"Don't worry about me! I'm not the one taking risks like the people who died in Stammheim—freedom fighters with the guts to do what was necessary! And don't mention Schleyer in the same breath as Baader, Raspe, Ennslin! He was a fucking SS *Untersturmfuher.* Good riddance to him and all those other fucking Nazis who found a way to creep back into power!"

"Even if all this killing is bringing Germany to its knees—the German Autumn I'm reading about everywhere?"

"There's no damn German Autumn! We're still in a Nazi winter, and we will keep fighting for the spring our country hasn't had for decades."

"Baader-Meinhof will keep fighting, you mean. What do you mean 'we'?"

"I'm going to keep fighting. And many people like me."

"Fighting yourself? Gaby, you're a pilot; your family's established; you're part of the system!"

"So? That doesn't mean I can't join the fight to free Germany from fascists, free women from *Kinder, Kuche, Kirche.* Fight for things you obviously don't understand!"

"Like death? Causing it? Being killed? Isn't that the reality of Baader-Meinhof?"

"That's such an ignorant statement! Sometimes, I wonder who you are!"

She looked at him as if he were a stranger.

"Gaby, where are you going with this?"

"The Ayan who joined the Naxalites and went underground would understand! That Ayan would understand me better."

She glared at him fiercely.

They were so far from the intimacy of minutes ago. So far from where he wanted to be.

"I was just eighteen then, Gaby—drunk on Che and Mao and the fight for the oppressed in the summer of '69—I was so full of it, the Naxalite guerillas thought I was one of

Naxalite commun

their own. And I signed up, as you know. But I saw what was ahead: the killing of civilians, being shot to death in fake police encounters, nothing really changing . . ."

"You turned back because you read *Darkness at Noon*, and that was enough to scare you and make you give up on your ideals," Gaby said, refusing to back down.

Her hard, Teutonic side—lecturing, self-righteous—that occasionally sent a shock of alienation through him was in full force now.

"Well, I'm not the kind of person who lets a couple of books and self-interest change me," she went on relentlessly. "Unlike you, I'm willing to go all in, go all the way for what is right!"

"Great! Keep going, Gaby, make things unpleasant," he shouted. How little he'd known about the world . . . and how long ago and irrelevant it all was. "I'll let you be the righteous, existentially 'authentic' one. I don't have your certainty. Sartre is not my god."

"Fuck you!" she said, gathering her clothes and slamming the bathroom door behind her.

Calm down, Ayan told himself. Gaby was quick to anger, but it never lasted.

The phone kept ringing in the background.

The bastard calling was not going to give up. Who the fuck was it?

It was the boss.

"Ayan, I was looking for you after the inspection," Nader said.

"I had to leave early today. Is there something you need?" Ayan said, worried but also annoyed. He put in long hours and wasn't some factory worker who needed to clock in and out.

"I just wanted to invite you to dinner this Friday. I'd like to catch up with you privately about the American bankers, about how you are doing. We need to talk freely without distractions. My house at 8:00 p.m. Come alone. Hope Gaby won't mind. Inga and I will see her another time soon."

Gaby wouldn't mind at all. She'd agreed to attend a few company dinner parties but considered it hardship duty. She didn't reciprocate Inga's affection for her, despised her countrywoman's mistreatment of her Iranian servants and her preoccupations: keeping a tidy house for her unfaithful husband Nader, playing hostess at extravagant parties, and spending as much time as possible in the German club with women like herself.

Gaby was being spared this time. Which was unusual. Nader had never asked him over for a private conversation. What was the devious son of a bitch up to now?

Whatever it was, he had other things to worry about at the moment.

"Why so angry with me, Gaby? Don't be," he said, stepping into the shower and embracing her.

Gaby sighed, turned into him, and rested her head on his shoulder.

"Baby, I'm sorry," she said, kissing him.

He pulled her in close.

"It's a difficult time," he said.

"Ayan, I'm fed up," Gaby said, pulling away. "I'm tired of the lies, the corruption, the killing of innocents. I'm tired of spending my time on meaningless things. I've had it with Tehran. You complain about it as much as I do. Why are you still here?"

"We've talked about that," Ayan said. "I'm from the 'Third World,' remember? And there is this recession, you know, stagflation . . . I have to go where the work is. For now, my work permit in Iran is my master."

"You know you could go back to India, despite all your weak excuses. There's so much to do there, so many people

to help. I'd have thought building a nation would be fulfilling
and exciting."

How do I explain it to you again, Gaby? INDIA

He was out of his depth in the Indian business culture,
couldn't see himself living the life of an academic or an
administrator, and there was nothing in between for him
in India—no place to make a decent living and keep his
spirit intact at the same time. And it wouldn't be much fun.
Life had to be fun. But Gaby was right. He was stalled and
knew he was coasting. People were succeeding in Iran just
by showing up in a country being remade by a ruler with
grandiose ambitions and an unlimited budget. Where was
the achievement in that? He should be challenging himself,
taking chances, trying different realities—before time and
expediency locked him into a pedestrian, compromised existence and permanently warped his sensibility. Tehran had
kept his options open after that bastard child of OPEC, the
disastrous recession, came out of nowhere and forced him
to leave London just as he was finding his feet. It was a way
station for him, just as it was for Gaby. He would return to
a city with more possibilities, reclaim a broader canvas. But
it was too soon to leave.

"I'm not ready for all that right now, Gaby. I'm in a
different stage in my life, feeling my way forward, finding
my path," he said, following Gaby out of the shower and
drying her back with his towel.

"So, for now, in whatever this stage is that you've
conveniently placed yourself in, following your so-called
dharma—basically being egocentric—is OK? Selfishness rules?
You sound like all the fucking Americans in this town: self-
indulgent, transient, irresponsible, doing whatever they feel
like doing!"

"I don't see it that way. It's about freedom to live the
way I want. And why should that just be an American
privilege?"

Gaby made an impatient sound and pulled on her jeans.

"I just need time to figure things out, Gaby. I'm wrong almost every time I'm sure of something. That makes me hesitant. And what's really on your mind? This is not you."

She shook off his hand on her shoulder.

"You want to know what's on my mind? I'll tell you. People have died: young people with ideals and courage and hopes that were wiped out in seconds. This makes me realize I'm wasting valuable time in Tehran. And so are you, Ayan! What about all that stuff you told me inspired you? You're not doing anything like that. Just crunching numbers."

"For fuck's sake, Gaby! I do a little more than that!"

She'd talked about flying, how she loved accelerating till gravity gave up and her aircraft soared, how preparation was everything and details took on life and death significance. "And you?" she'd asked. "What inspired you?"

He'd told her about the "master economist" imagined by Keynes and quoted bits of his favorite lines—one who can "study the present in light of the past for the purposes of the future . . . no part of man's nature or his institutions must lie entirely outside his regard . . ."—and said this catholic approach had suggested an exciting direction when he was casting about. He wasn't an academic—never wanted to be. But he had tried to think broadly while mastering the particular in his work, even in this Iran Power job.

And it *was* intellectually satisfying—easily as much as being a pilot! Yes, Iran Power was a stopgap. He would eventually be in a position to have more of an impact on people's lives. But the company was central to Iran's economic development and what he did every day was contributing to the employment of many. He was not just a fucking number cruncher! Not that Gaby understood or cared about any of this . . .

"I didn't realize you had such a low opinion of what I do—were so dismissive of my work," Ayan said.

Gaby's expression softened. She put her arms around him.

"Not dismissive, my love, just a little skeptical."

"You're giving me a hard time now, Gaby, but you'll see. I'll . . ."

"Someday, perhaps, you'll do what you really want," Gaby said. "But that boy you saw dying will not get to someday. Neither will the prisoners in Stammheim. You may decide that it's fine to compromise and justify it using your Hindu stages of life, postpone what you really want to do and should do. But I can't. Not anymore. Not after what happened last week. I have to go back home and help. I have to do more for my country. And be with my mother, who is not well."

"Is this about leaving? You're not thinking of that, are you?" Ayan said, his voice sounding distant, thin, unfamiliar . . .

"Yes, as a matter of fact, I am," she said. "I was wondering how to let you know, but here we are."

So it was true. He pushed away from Gaby and leaned against the wall to steady himself.

She put her arms around him again.

"Oh, Ayan! Don't look at me like that. Please understand. I feel I must do something—now!"

"What about me, us? How can you leave? Just like that? Without even talking about it!"

"For reasons that I just told you about! And we are talking about it!"

"I don't want you to go."

Gaby's eyes moved over his face.

"This is difficult for me too. I love you, love being with you."

"Then stay."

"I can't. Don't you see? We have to be part of something bigger than ourselves, bigger than what we're doing here. Now. Not someday."

"You've decided then. You've made up your mind. You're leaving me."

"I'm leaving Tehran. Not you. Please understand that! We're all going to leave Tehran at some point. My time's just come a little bit before yours."

You are leaving me, Gaby, Ayan thought. You're not going to take up arms against the Federal Republic of Germany! You're not insane. You couldn't possibly be going home because you want to throw your life away. It's not about your politics or your mother. You're just done with me. Letting me down easy. There's no other way to read this.

She hugged him and asked him to say he understood.

He said he did and went back into the shower.

It was so dry in Tehran.

He let the hot water rain down on him, breathing in the steam, breathing in life.

Gradually breathing in fight.

He had to persuade her to stay.

"Iran's difficult," he said, throwing on a shirt and jeans and sitting down on the sofa in the drawing room next to Gaby, who was ready and waiting for the imminent arrival of the Iran Air van. "But we are all here for a reason. You're not done racking up miles on the Boeings, are you? You need a lot more to land a pilot's job in Europe."

"That's not going to happen, I've realized," Gaby said. "European airlines will never hire a female pilot—not anytime soon. My future's in the cargo business, private jets and charters, things like that. I've logged enough flying miles for those kinds of jobs."

"How about me? Have you logged enough miles with me?"

She laughed.

"I don't know. Sometimes, I wonder if I'm just an adventure for you in this stage of your life. Am I?"

"Surely you know that's not true! Gaby, I love you! I want you with me in every stage of my life: now, tomorrow, always. Eternally."

She looked at him with suddenly serious eyes.

"You're not ready for eternity, Ayan," she said, pressing a finger on his lips. "And neither am I. You have to work through these stages of yours. I have to go back home and take care of things that are very important to me. Let's see what happens."

"What does that mean?"

"I don't know just now," Gaby said, looking at him uncertainly.

"So let's just see? Leave it to chance? And handicap things by throwing in thousands of miles of separation!"

"You'll find a way to make it work, Ayan, if we're meant for the long game. You'll make me believe."

"If this is a test, I'll fail," Ayan said, feeling despondent. "Long-distance relationships fade . . . Gaby, I don't want that to happen to us!"

"You won't escape from me that easily," Gaby said. "We'll meet often. Now promise me something."

"Anything."

"Be more like the Ayan you were in university: angry and fighting and involved in what's happening around you."

"Here? I just told you what happened to a protestor."

"I'm not saying be visible. Just do something. Start with Hamid. I talked to him quite a bit on that drive to the Caspian. His life revolves around you: He's at your service from first light till nightfall. His family shouldn't be worried about where their next meal is coming from. You make enough. Support him."

"Yes—but he's a proud man."

"Pay for his kids' education. Think of something."

"I will. He did put his neck on the line for me today."

She asked what he meant. He told her.

"All the more reason to do what I suggested," Gaby said, taking hold of his hand. "No one's fighting for people like Hamid. I'm going, Ayan. You're staying, so you have to do something to help."

"I don't disagree with you. I'll think about it."

"I hate the way you said that! You'll have to stop being so fucking ambivalent about everything!"

"I have things in my favor, too, you know. Positives in my column."

She smiled and kissed his cheek.

"I'm going to make you add a few more," she said.

The doorbell rang.

"That's my transport. I have to go," Gaby said.

She gathered her things and moved towards the door.

Ayan walked her to the Iran Air minibus with heavy steps.

Gaby handed her rolling bag and coat to the driver, told him she would just be a minute, and came back to Ayan.

"Baby, I'm not disappearing off the face of the earth," she said, rubbing his forehead, trying to erase his frown. "I'll just be a few hours away. And you still have me around for another month."

"That's hardly enough. Not even close."

"Ayan! Let me go! They're waiting."

Gaby looked towards the Iran Air van.

"I don't care."

Gaby fought to escape his embrace.

"Really?" she said. "This is my work!"

"I'm not letting you go till you kiss me again. And mean it."

Gaby looked at the van again. All eyes were on them.

"Oh! Fuck it!" Gaby said. She turned her back towards her crew, an irreverent smile bringing out her dimples. "You've already ruined my reputation."

"That's more like it," Ayan said as she put her arms around his neck and came in close.

She pressed her mouth to his and gave him a long kiss. Then she took out a lipstick from her shoulder bag and drew hearts and kisses on his face.

"There," she said. "You have my marks all over you. Don't wash them off. I want you to wake up with me tomorrow—my kisses to be the first thing you see in the morning—to remind you that I am with you always, even when I'm far away."

She was laughing as she hurried to the van, looking happy again.

He stood there waving till the van disappeared, not wanting to return to his empty apartment.

Her change of mood didn't change the situation. She was just going away for a few days tonight; soon, it would be forever.

Too soon.

And him? Time was passing. He should leave soon too. He should be more like the thousands of expatriates here who scurried about salting it away while the going was good.

He would be that way.

Act like the transient he really was.

CHAPTER 5

Ayan dragged himself through the next few days, working and worrying and swimming endless laps in Khanom-eh Mohsen's pool. The weekend was almost over when he set off to the north for the fifteen-minute drive to Nader's villa, still wondering why he'd been summoned for the private dinner. The boss had given him no hints since the phone call earlier in the week.

Nader's wife, Inga, greeted him with her usual warm smile. He'd liked her from the start. Pale and aging badly, Inga had her hands full if the rumors of her husband's affair with Shirin Madan, Iran Power's head of personnel, were true.

I hope you win this battle, Ayan thought as Inga took his overcoat and passed it on to her maid. But the odds were long. The Harvard-trained Shirin usually got what she wanted.

"Nader is waiting for you in his study," Inga said, patting his shoulder. "I'll send in some food soon."

Ayan followed the maid down the hall of the entrance foyer, his footsteps echoing in the unusually quiet house.

The CEO of Iran Power was standing by a bay window. Dressed casually in a denim shirt and beige corduroys, the man still exuded authority. *Like others of his type,* Ayan thought. *Men without obvious weaknesses, who give the appearance of a smooth sail through life.*

"Ah! Ayan! Please come in," Nader Ovessi said with a welcoming handshake. "What's your preference? Macallan, Laphroaig, or Talisker?"

Women got champagne as an aperitif in his house. Men got a single malt with a drop of water. Those were the rules.

"The Macallan, please," Ayan said.

The window behind Nader looked out onto a manicured green lawn—not easy to achieve in Tehran. Blue water shimmered in an elegant stone-lined pool.

Inside, floor-to-ceiling bookcases ran along the walls. A mahogany coffee table covered with books rested on an antique Kashan carpet. A sleek English Henry writing table with a leather top and fluted legs stood at one end of the study. Two comfortable leather chairs flanked the fireplace on the other side of the room. Dimmed wall lights and an antique chandelier added a warm glow to the wood paneling.

"Your study looks like a library in a Pall Mall club," Ayan said. "I would spend all my time here."

"I'm here whenever I'm alone," Nader said, looking around with satisfaction. "I know you like to read too. I wouldn't have hired you if you didn't. Everybody must read something every day; otherwise, how can you gain perspective? Come, let's sit by the fire."

They looked into the crackling flames, sipping their scotch in silence.

Ayan fought the need to start talking. Uncomfortable pauses were part of Nader's power play.

"So you want to make more money," Nader said finally, turning to Ayan.

Good. They were discussing this topic without Shirin's presence. Perhaps today, he could escape the frustrating "speak to her"/"speak to him" routine.

"Well, I was supposed to get a substantial increase when I was made CFO."

"Don't forget I gave you a big increase when I hired you," Nader said. "You're making much more than other Hadley Jones consultants. The reality is that employees make more money if they bring in more business, or lower costs, or make themselves valuable in some other way—or if they have another job offer. Do you have a job offer somewhere else? You are free to take it if you do."

"No," Ayan said, taken by surprise. "I mean, I could find something, but I enjoy working at Iran Power."

"Good," Nader said. He smiled and nodded. "So let's forget about that. Now you're a finance man, not in sales. So you are not in a position to grow our revenues. You can make us more efficient, yes—and complete that cost-allocation study so we can make better decisions; both are important, and I will pay you more once I see results. But you want to make more money now, much more, correct?"

"Yes."

"We all do, we all do. But for that, we have to go above and beyond. You follow me?"

"Yes. Absolutely."

Nader leaned forward.

"You've been thinking too small, Ayan—about employment contracts and a few dollars here, a few dollars there. Are you prepared to think bigger?"

"Yes, of course," Ayan said.

This guy was good, he thought. *I'm agreeing without knowing what it is he wants me to do.*

There was a knock on the door. Inga came in and supervised as the maid brought in chicken schnitzel, roast potatoes, and salad.

"Some Riesling with your dinner?" Inga asked Ayan. "Nader has some Pauillac in that cabinet, but I brought in this chilled Mosel. It goes better with this food."

"We'll have both," Nader said. "We'll start with the Riesling and have the Bordeaux later."

"Now here's the part that requires you to think big," Nader said when they had finished eating. "But before we go there, I need you to understand that the rest of this conversation never happened."

Ayan nodded hesitantly. Where was this leading?

"The Americans, despite their statements of support, want to keep us down. They don't really want us to develop our nuclear capability. You know that. You've had difficulties with First National and others. That man Brzezinski is handcuffing the research at the Atomic Energy Organization of Iran!" A frown creased Nader's deeply tanned face. "That's why the Shah has moved closer to France, Germany, South Africa—countries that recognize the sovereign right of Iran to develop as it sees fit, but even they don't want to publicly oppose Carter." Nader wagged his finger. "This is unacceptable! The Americans have no right to tell us that we can't be trusted with the full fuel cycle! Am I right?"

"Yes," Ayan said.

Nader sat back and sipped his Pauillac. He contemplated the glass in his hand.

"Let me ask you, how did you feel in 1974 when India tested a nuclear bomb—'Smiling Buddha'—what a wonderful name! Did you feel proud that your scientists were world-class, that your military could achieve this great feat and now defend India against anybody?

Why

"I have to say I was surprised by what happened at Pokhran," Ayan said.

"And proud? How did you feel about it personally?"

"Yes, very proud. I felt proud to be an Indian. Smiling Buddha said we were a capable nation."

"You didn't have any doubts? Many oppose nuclear weapons. After all, the whole world could be destroyed. I worry about that too."

Why do you care what I think? Ayan wondered. *Why these questions?*

"The genie is out of the bottle," Ayan said. "Many nations will have nuclear weapons in time. It seems to be an irreversible trend. No one likes war. But perhaps, nuclear capability evens the balance of power and forces negotiations. That's not a bad outcome. As long as the weapons are in safe hands." *Like / whos*

Nader nodded. "I have come to the same conclusion. We are an ancient civilization, wise and practical, that has existed as a country far longer than America. We are much safer hands than those trigger-happy cowboys who bombed Hiroshima and Nagasaki! How can America preach to us? Presume to set the rules after what they did!"

"They can't," Ayan said. He twirled his glass of wine and took a few measured sips. They were downing a lot of alcohol.

"Neither India nor Iran will risk being destroyed by using nuclear weapons first," Nader said. "That is so obvious."

"That makes sense," Ayan said.

"Of course, it does!" Nader said. He walked to the drinks trolley. "Some port or cognac?"

"No thanks, I'm enjoying this claret," Ayan said.

Nader refilled Ayan's glass and returned to his chair with a cognac.

"You know, Ayan," Nader said, looking at him assessingly. "India's project required complete secrecy, correct?"

"That's what they say. Only Indira Gandhi, the scientists involved, and a few military leaders knew."

"Indira Gandhi is a great leader. It's too bad she was humiliated this month—arrested by people far inferior to her. Anyway, she was able to maintain secrecy, and that is why India is a much more powerful nation today. We have to learn from her example."

What the hell does that mean? Ayan thought as he nodded mechanically.

"Look Ayan, the AEOI will keep working with Brzezinski and Carter and keep them happy; more nuclear reactors will be built by our friends in Germany; and the Shah will get his nuclear power stations. Everyone knows this. But there is another part which must remain secret."

Nader paused and looked into the fire contemplatively.

"The South Africans have large supplies of uranium yellowcake and are willing to sell it to AEOI without restrictions as long as no other country knows about it. AEOI is watched very closely. It needs help to make this transfer happen." He turned towards Ayan with a searching gaze. "Iran Power is a sister organization of AEOI," he continued. "We should help them."

Ayan sat up.

"AEOI employees are the highest paid people in this country," Nader continued. "If we do something to help AEOI—help them get nuclear materials without restrictions, without handcuffs, so their best scientists can do their work on the full fuel cycle—what do you think will happen?"

"Important people will be very happy with us," Ayan offered.

No wonder Nader had refused to sign the guarantee for First National!

"Exactly! I sensed your intelligence the first day I met you—not just ordinary book knowledge, but about how the world goes around. If we can use Iran Power to make confidential payments to the South Africans, AEOI will get their uranium, and they will be very happy with us. They will be inclined to show that happiness in the form you desire: substantially more money. Now. Am I right?"

He paused for a sip of his cognac.

"Probably," Ayan said hesitatingly.

Nader leaned in.

"Ayan, I've already told AEOI that you are the right person for this job. I took a chance, but I trust my judgment about you. I see big things ahead for you. Don't let me down. Now listen carefully. Here is the plan."

got yellow cake

He was to go to Germany with an Iran Power delegation, Ayan was told, but leave a week earlier for a holiday: first to London, where Chip de Groot, a South African purchasing agent known to the Energy Ministry, would connect with him; then to Geneva, where he would set up an account at Banque du Rhone and transfer funds to a corporation. Details would be provided. From Switzerland, he would fly to Stuttgart to join the Iran Power delegation and eventually return to Tehran from Germany.

Nader made it sound simple.

"Chip has been an agent for many Ministry of Energy enterprises," he said. "You can trust him completely. And my friend Luc Bossard at Banque du Rhone will have everything ready for you."

"But just to be clear," Ayan said, "the money being transferred will be going towards buying nuclear materials for AEOI and not goods or services for Iran Power?"

"We don't need to worry about things like that. Our work ends when the money moves."

"But what about our accounting staff, the auditors, our board?" Ayan said, dazed by the audacity of Nader's request. He was asking him to be the front man for acquiring yellowcake off the books, out of sight of international monitors—yellowcake that could be used to produce weapons-grade uranium, violating treaties that Iran had ratified. What the hell was going on?

"Don't worry about the board, Ayan. I will handle them. And as I've said, Chip is known; he's done several deals for many Iranian government organizations. The money we send to Chip from the Iran Power account in Switzerland will be documented as a transfer for consulting services provided by him for our Qazvin expansion. It will not seem out of the ordinary. A numbered account is also not unusual. I'll help you with the auditors. The head of the audit company is my good friend. It is more important to get things right with your internal accounting and treasury staff. I'll leave that up to you. Start the planning now. We don't have much time."

Nader stood and held out his hand.

Ayan got up and shook it without enthusiasm.

"What's the matter?"

"I'm a little worried about the lack of transparency . . ."

They were a public company. Nothing about Nader's proposal sounded right.

The friendly look in Nader's eyes vanished. "Have I made a mistake in bringing you into this opportunity?" he said in a tone that made Ayan ask himself: *What are you doing, you moron! Nader has shown his hand and will never accept a refusal. Buy some time to think about this!*

"I was just wondering if all this was feasible, could be kept confidential, for everybody's sake," Ayan said.

"Don't worry," Nader said, his hand on Ayan's shoulder. "We have thought through everything. And Ayan, it is time. It is time to reclaim our sovereignty. Do you know what Kermit Roosevelt and his CIA colleagues named their illegal overthrow of Mossagdeh? Operation Ajax. AEOI calls our plan 'Odysseus.' Odysseus is a very good name for this operation; Odysseus was clever and cunning, and that is why he won in the end. As will we. America should not be allowed to control and exploit Iran anymore. So can we toast to the success of Operation Odysseus?"

He raised his glass.

Ayan did the same.

"To Operation Odysseus," he said.

"Good!" Nader said. "And now this is going to make you happy. I will pay you a bonus of $50,000 when the account is opened and another $50,000 at the end of the year. That's an additional $100,000 that will be in your bank account in a very short time. And that's just a start. If we move forward without problems, I am confident that I can get the AEOI to pay you $100,000 every Nowruz as a bonus; probably several times that number. That is what thinking big leads to. Now enough business! Let's join Inga in the drawing room. Some neighbors are coming over. The kind of people you should know."

NOWRUZ

Ayan looked at his watch as he pulled out of Nader's driveway. It was not quite 11:00 p.m. Darioush would still be at the Key Club. That's where he would go. He needed his friend's level-headedness and that special Iranian gift he had, of making you feel like the most important person in the world.

Not that he could discuss any of this with him.

He mulled over what Nader had pretty much ordered him to do as he turned onto Fana Khosrow Street. If he refused, he was out of a job, and Nader would make sure no one else hired him. He would have to leave Iran immediately. Was he ready for that?

Odysseus was illicit. Gaby would be incensed if she learnt of his involvement, and his pacifist mother, about to descend on him soon, would be shocked. They both wanted

Darioush

nuclear weapons wiped off the face of the earth. But that was not going to happen. The world was what it was.

And Nader was right. If Iran had nuclear capabilities, there would be a fairer balance of power. Smiling Buddha had been a poke in the eye to Nixon and Kissinger after the Americans had tried to bully India, tried to stop Indira Gandhi from liberating Bangladesh by sending the Seventh Fleet into the Bay of Bengal. India was now a nuclear nation. Not to be messed with. Why shouldn't Iran be in the same position? The Americans and British might not like it, but why should that matter? The West would have to treat Iran with more respect. What was wrong with that? Why think like a colonial?

Nader had him trapped anyway. Why keep agonizing?

He should let things play out. See what room he had to maneuver.

That's what he would do.

CHAPTER 6

T he Key Club was on the corner of Darband and Fana Khosrow Streets, nestled behind cedar trees whose canopy camouflaged the hedonistic indulgence of Tehran's elite inside the classic European façade of the elegant two-story building.

Ayan parked on a side street and walked past the line of men and women vying for entrance. The doorman, Ali Agha, greeted him with a curt nod and opened the door. Ayan pressed 200 tomans into his hands as insurance for admittance next time. He was a regular, probably on some kind of list—friends of members or something like that. But why take a chance?

The steady drumbeat and syncopated bass lines of "Love to Love You Baby" hit him as he walked past the thick velvet curtain separating the entrance from the main dining area and the packed dance floor. The smell of cigarettes, perfume, and alcohol suffused the air in the split-level room.

He felt a hand on his elbow as he surveyed the scene of seduction and surrender. It was Nick Stasney, the Texan—part of his regular tennis foursome at Club Veyssi. Nick spoke fluent Farsi, travelled extensively, and did not seem to have any way of supporting his lifestyle besides translating *Time* and *Life* into Farsi. Everybody suspected he was CIA. Nobody cared.

Nick put his arm around Ayan's shoulder. "How are you, buddy?" he said.

Nick's fine blond hair was mostly gone. His glasses were thick, his face too narrow for his large frame; he seemed worried about something all the time—like an outsized kid. That could be why so many people, Ayan included, felt protective towards him.

"Staying alive," Ayan said. "Have you seen Darioush?"

"He left. But Hassan's still here. He has a couple of tables by the dance floor. Let's go join him."

Hassan Karimi was part of their tennis group too. Their hard-fought battles on the tennis court and frequent nights together at the Key Club had made Ayan feel they were close. Hassan had a competitive edge that Ayan was not ready for tonight, but he did not want to go home to his empty apartment.

Hassan's cousin, Fariba, jumped up as Ayan approached the table.

"Everybody's being very boring tonight," she said, taking his hand. "I want to dance. Come on!"

The free-spirited Smith graduate was the reason Ayan had joined Hassan's Friday hikes in Darband. Somewhere along the way, they'd begun to hold hands on these outings and kiss like teenagers. He'd thought about doing more. Fariba was a beautiful woman and seemed to be willing, but Hassan had noticed the growing chemistry between them and warned him off. Leave her alone, he'd said, unless you are ready to get married.

That's how it worked in these parts. It was the same in India. An extended look was a come-on; an invitation to go out alone was practically a lifetime commitment; any kind of sex basically meant game, set, match. So he'd reluctantly kept Fariba at a remove.

And then Gaby had appeared and run away with his heart and everything.

"Where have you been?" Fariba demanded as they danced. "What's happened, Ayan? Everybody's saying you've become so obsessed with one person that you've become a stranger to the rest of us. You've forgotten me."

"Not you, Fariba. You know you're unforgettable."

"Then show it!" Fariba said, pressing into him as the music slowed, making him sway in time with her.

She had downed a few screwdrivers, obviously.

Ayan glanced nervously towards Hassan. He was talking to a friend, paying no attention to them.

"Look at me!" Fariba demanded.

She brought her face up against his neck. Her mouth was angled towards his. She rose up and kissed him—and then opened her eyes in surprise as he pulled back.

"I'm sorry. It's late," he said. "I have to work tomorrow."

But she knew.

"It's not fair," Fariba said, eyes flashing. "I met you first!"

"Come on, Fariba. You know how much I care for you."

"See all these people here? Most of them care for me. I thought I meant more to you than that. Before that German woman—that glorified taxi driver threw herself at you!"

She moved away from him and began to walk back to Hassan's table.

He caught up with her.

"Go on then!" she said, waving him off. "Go home or wherever! Go back to your easy European girl. Go chase white flesh! Be like all the desperate Persian men here!"

Ayan retreated to a quiet table, out of sight of the Karimi clan.

Pegs

He asked the waiter to bring his bottle of Laphroaig. It still had a few pegs left in it.

He could see Fariba from where he was sitting. She hadn't dyed her hair or streaked it blonde, like other upper-class Iranian women. She was confident in who she was: an intelligent, educated Persian beauty. And why was he thinking about her when he should be concentrating on the fait accompli Nader had thrown at him!

But Fariba's intensity was distracting. He looked back at her. They had so much in common. She understood where he came from. And she was beautiful, the talk of Shemiran. They were kindred spirits in many ways: aspiring, independent, inspired by some idea of America, of Woodstock and the Vietnam resistance—citizens of a nation of the imagination.

Then why had he fallen in love with Gaby? Was Fariba right? Was he choosing Gaby over her because he was just another brown man enslaved by a base longing for a white woman?

No. He wasn't. Definitely not.

Fariba felt like an arranged marriage.

It was different with Gaby.

Perhaps it was a gesture, an expression that made him want her and nobody else; her layers and mysteries and moods; her touch and taste and smell; the way she challenged him, pushed through his defenses, and insisted on an intimacy that made everything else seem unimportant.

Whatever the reason, Gaby was his undeniable, irresistible passion.

He stayed awake a long time listening to Pink Floyd, letting sentiment and dreams and illusions and promises wash over him, trying not to think about Nader, thinking instead about love—about Rekha, never to be forgotten, his first serious affair; and of Jackie, the girl he'd loved so madly. He'd lost them; maybe he had been too young to realize how lucky he'd been; maybe the time had not been right.

He couldn't let that happen with Gaby. He couldn't lose something he would surely never find again.

—?
really

PART
TWO

CHAPTER 7

The phone rang seconds after he fell asleep, it seemed.

Ayan lifted the receiver wearily.

First, an operator connecting a call from India. Then: "Hello! Hello! *Beta*, can you hear me?"

"Yes, Ma! I can hear you . . ." he said, holding the phone away from his ear. Everybody felt the need to help their voices along on these long-distance calls.

"Isn't it time to get up? I waited till 7:00 a.m. to call you, as you told me to."

"I had a late night. What's happened? Is something wrong?"

"Listen! My flight gets in at 10:00 p.m. on Wednesday—that's the second—write down the flight number."

"I know you're coming on Wednesday. I know your flight number! See you soon! Bye!"

"Wait! Ayan, I hope you're organized. I want clean sheets and towels!"

"Ma, I just have one bedroom. I've booked you into the Tehran Hilton. You'll be more comfortable there."

"I can't afford any Hilton-Shilton!"

"On me—I can afford it."

"Not a good reason to waste money. Cancel the booking. I'll use your bedroom. You can sleep on your sofa; the whole idea is to spend time together. Now get up. You told me 7:00 a.m. is time to get ready for your office. Don't make your boss angry! And be on time to pick me up from the airport! Bye for now."

Ayan struggled out of bed. He could get by on five or six hours of sleep if he had to. Today was going to be tough. He'd been asleep for all of forty-five minutes.

He turned on the tap in his bathroom sink and waited for the water to become hot enough for his shave. The urgency that always surrounded his mother—the tension from having too many patients, never enough resources, not enough rest—had come through the phone line and made him feel he'd just seen her, though it had been a couple of years since his last trip to Delhi.

He associated her with slogging, study, homework; with the smell of antiseptic that came off her hands and clothes; with impossible-to-escape, long needles that delivered the annual Typhoid A and B and Cholera shots he dreaded; and with sounds of her impatient arrival: her Fiat skidding on their gravel driveway as she slammed the brakes, the front door giving way. Her return from work meant the end to an enjoyable game of cricket in the backyard with neighborhood friends and a race to his desk, where she expected to find him. The Christian Brothers at school had picked up on his inclination to be lackadaisical and set to beating it out of him during the day. His mother put the boot to him in the evening. There had been no place to hide growing up.

The exciting part of his life had started when he went off to London after college. He'd become competent there, transitioning to manhood messily but, thankfully, privately and away from Ma's appraising gaze. She still thought of him as a child. This life abroad, one that she only knew in outline, had been full of adventures and traumas one didn't share with a mother. It was his father he now felt closer to. Over the years, he'd deftly handled the progression from father to best friend, a transition Ma seemed to have no interest in attempting. His memories of time with his father centered around playing tennis, listening to Dicky Rutnagar and Vijay Merchant's cricket commentary coming in over the Sony transistor radio that was now on his desk— suffering together as Indian batsmen struggled on fast West Indian and Australian pitches. He remembered hiking in the Garhwal Himalayas with his father, sharing a bottle of Golden Eagle beer before lunch, and mocking corrupt politicians and hypocritical temple-goers over a scotch or two in the cocktail hour. He couldn't recall any such adult interactions with his mother.

He looked through his image in the mirror as he shaved, trying to bring up her face, expecting the person he'd always known: tall and overweight Ma, with features and figure rounded over the years from bearing three children. Instead, a younger version of her took shape in his mind, from a photograph he'd come across in his father's album: She was lounging by the sea, her feet caressing the sand, looking willful and beautiful and just like the person he'd heard she'd been: an irresistible force, who had become a physician when women just couldn't, and who had married for love, shocking everyone in a time of arranged marriages.

People remained much the same on the inside even as time dramatically alters their appearance. She was an irresistible force even now. And soon to be in this apartment! He should get ready for some inevitable drama. She always took charge of things.

When he left for London in 1971, she'd found a heavy military overcoat for him to take; quietly handed him her father's Jaeger-LeCoultre wristwatch that was coveted by every male in the family; persuaded him that an American flattop looked good, in addition to saving him money on haircuts for a while; and packed two suitcases full of clothes with an eye to function and economy.

He'd ditched the clothes a few weeks after arriving in London and grown his hair and sideburns. But he still woke to the alarm on the Jaeger, and its fading, browned dial still structured his days. The magnificent military overcoat had also endured. Double-breasted with embossed brass buttons, it smelled of cigars and a different era. He'd often thought of his mother when he turned its collar against the winter chill in London.

A surge of emotion raced through him as he thought about her now. He was lucky she'd always been by his side. She was the one who'd introduced him to Kafka and Turgenev and Flaubert; argued that his favorites—Hemingway, Conrad, Graham Greene, and Solzhenitsyn—were good but obvious, and there was more depth and nuance elsewhere; wrestled him off the tennis courts and cricket pitches and onto the academic track that got him into the economics program at St. Stephen's, the best damn college in the country . . .

Where would he be without all that unwelcome attention?

His mother looked older and frailer when he received her at Mehrabad Airport a few days later.

"You seem tired," Ayan said, settling her in his car. "We'll be home soon. Traffic is not bad at this time of night."

"Son, it's this unaccustomed travel, all the nonsense with passports and visas . . . no wonder your father refuses to leave India," she said.

She looked at his car admiringly.

"Is this your Mercedes?"

"A company car."

The Iran Power Paykan was history, replaced by a silver Mercedes that had been allocated to him the day after the private dinner with Nader.

"Someone's doing well in Iran, I can see!" she said, dropping into the passenger seat with an exhausted sigh. "I'm glad that my brothers taught you something about business. Your father and I know nothing about that world."

Uncle Ravi and Vikram had succeeded in life's game. One understood marketing and was adored by everybody who worked for him; the other was a financial genius with an eye for undervalued properties; both worked harder than anybody else. He was lucky they bothered with him, taking him to lunch whenever they were in Delhi. This was where he absorbed their casual observations about success in the business world: "Hire the best; lead by making people believe the direction you want to go is their idea; think strategically but act decisively; winners avoid overestimating the chance of success and underestimating the risk of ruin—never do that, my boy, never go down a path without an exit ramp . . ."

"The view from up here is beautiful," Ma said, perking up as they walked across Khanom-eh Mohsen's rooftop in the bracing evening air. "Good idea to build this *barsati*; everybody in Delhi's doing the same—adding a rooftop apartment and renting it out."

Ayan led her into the living room. It was just as well that Gaby was away. He'd packed her clothes and toiletries into a few suitcases. Why set Ma off with overt signs of their cohabitation?

But she was not to be fooled.

"Who decorated this living room?" she said. "It looks too nice to have been done by you."

Gaby had separated spaces in the large rectangular room to create a study, where he worked on his cherry roll top desk, and a niche with floor cushions on a rust Bokhara—a perfect retreat to read and listen to music.

"A friend who has an eye," Ayan said.

His mother smiled at him with an inquiring look.

"A woman's touch, I can see. Am I going to meet her?"

"She's travelling."

"It's nice that there are books everywhere. I think I'm going to like her," she said.

"Yes, I think you will. But you'll also like my other friends."

"How silly you are! It's time to become serious about somebody!"

"Anyway . . . this is where you're going to sleep. Settle in."

Revived after a shower, Ma came out and curled up on an armchair. She sipped her Baileys Irish Cream, giving him news about the family, asking questions, reestablishing a connection after their long separation.

He fell asleep before she did, drifting off on the sofa to the sound of her familiar and reassuring voice, finally getting a full night's rest.

"You don't look very comfortable on that sofa," Ma said in the morning, bringing him a breakfast of scrambled eggs, toast, and tea. "I thought I'd let you sleep. I took a walk.

I met your nice landlady. She wants us to come for lunch today."

"I have you booked up. You just have two days here. We can drop in to see Khanom-eh Mohsen at short notice. She never goes anywhere."

He took her through the itinerary he'd planned. They were going to the Bazaar, with Hamid as their guide, in the morning. An escorted tour of the museums was the afternoon plan. In the evening, she could catch up on her rest while he went to a business dinner with a friend of Uncle Vikram's, Firouz Akbari, a big shot in Iran and Uncle Vikram's largest customer. Firouz had agreed to help close a critical deal with First National's regional boss.

"God knows how Vikram managed to buy that tea garden," Ma said. "Where he got all that money."

He told her how Uncle Vikram borrowed from Calcutta banks and bought the estate from the British in a distress sale. People still talked about what a brilliant deal that was.

She looked skeptical. "I don't know about all that, but I hope you're prepared for the dinner. Such important people! Don't mess it up!"

She wasn't joking. She was actually concerned!

Tomorrow, he continued, they were having lunch with Darioush in the mountains, followed by a relaxing afternoon with another friend, Hassan, back in Tehran. Hassan had asked them to stay for their Friday night family dinner, a special invitation in her honor.

"But, son, that's too much fuss and bother!" Ma said. "I'm happy just staying here spending time together. I've no interest in fancy people and all that nonsense. You should know that."

He knew. She'd grown up during the Depression and lived through the horrors of Partition. Her life was long days and frequent nights in the maternity wards of Government Hospital in Delhi, where care was free. But she needed a break from the unremitting grind; it was fine to indulge in a little conspicuous consumption on this trip. There was nothing like India's aching poverty on the streets of Tehran, thanks to the billions of petrodollars flowing in; living luxuriously seemed less immoral here.

"Don't you want to meet my best friends? And see a slice of Persian life inaccessible to most foreigners? Come on, Ma! You'll enjoy the fresh air in Darioush's villa on the ski slope, and you'll get on with the Karimis. They control the chemicals industry of Iran but are civilized and charming. Old money people."

She mumbled and grumbled but provisionally agreed to the schedule and got ready for the imminent trip to the Bazaar.

Hamid had insisted on showing Ma around the Bazaar, his neighborhood, and had given up a weekend morning for that purpose.

Ayan was pleasantly surprised to see that Hamid's sons, Adil and Imran, had joined their father for a joyride in the new Benz.

"This is my mother, Padma Khanom," Ayan said to the boys.

"Salaam, Khanom," they each said in turn.

"Speak in English so Padma Khanom can understand," Hamid said. "They are learning English," he explained proudly to her.

"Hello, how are you?" Adil said, holding out his hand.

Ma shook it and ruffled the serious boy's hair.

Adil frowned, his green eyes unhappy, and meticulously patted it back into place.

He opened the door for Ma and sat down in the front seat next to his father.

"Hello, you're welcome," the younger one, Imran, said, scampering into the back seat without waiting for an answer.

"He swallowed his hamburger," Adil announced, turning and pointing at his brother as they began the drive. "And he created a fuss till we bought him a Coke."

"He'll learn—when his stomach hurts tonight," Hamid said.

"Would you like ice cream?" Imran asked Ayan, his expression purposeful.

"Yes," Ayan replied, suppressing a smile. He enjoyed the imp's antics.

"Vanilla or chocolate?"

"Chocolate, please."

Imran turned to the handle on the door and engaged in mysterious manipulations.

"Your ice cream," he said, holding out his hand to Ayan.

Ayan took a bite of the air and pretended to wipe his mouth.

Imran looked at Ma. "I'm sorry, Khanom, but now only vanilla left. You like vanilla? Have it—*kheyli khobe!*"

Ma cradled the boy's chin in her hand.

"First, tell me where you got these dimples!"

Imran smiled and shook his face free. "Here's your vanilla. Special cone."

"Now I want some pizza, please," Ayan interjected.

Imran seemed to be processing this for a moment, then busied himself transforming Ma's handbag into an oven.

After a couple of minutes, Ayan said, "That smells good. I'm getting hungry. Is the pizza ready?"

"Pizza not ready yet, Agha Ayan," Imran replied. "But soup ready." He cupped his hand and extended it.

Adil, who had been anxiously monitoring their reactions to Imran's imaginary kitchen, reached back and clipped his younger brother's head.

"Stop annoying them!" he said.

"It's fine, Adil," Ayan said with a smile. "We're really hungry."

Adil shook his head at him and turned away from the nonsense going on in the backseat.

Hamid pulled up at the entrance of a narrow lane near the Bazaar.

"Give my best regards to Sholeh Khanom," Ayan said as Hamid set off to leave his children at home before the excursion into the Bazaar. Hamid's wife had won a place in Ayan's affections with her concern and generosity when a bad attack of influenza felled him. She'd prepared elaborate meals for him: One day, it was *chelo kebab*; the next, *ghormeh sabzi*; then, *fesenjan*, a gesture even more meaningful because he knew how poor the family was.

Hamid placed his hand on his heart. "*Merci, Ghorboonet beram*. She will come to the Bazaar, *Inshallah*, to welcome Padma Khanom to Tehran."

The driver walked his sons down the alley to the entrance of a building at the end of a cul-de-sac.

The boys turned back and waved at them before disappearing inside. After a few seconds, Imran reemerged and waved again till Adil dragged him in by his collar. A large wooden door closed behind the children.

The principal structure of the Bazaar faced Mecca, angling away from the north-south tendency of Tehran.

The Sabzeh Meydan entrance on Khordad Street led to a skylit, arched, domed world of organized chaos. The entrance hall smelled of centuries past, wool and fabrics, leather and spices, and the press of humanity around them. Shoppers jostled past straining porters and makeshift stalls selling pirated cassettes and foreign magazines. Swivel-hipped tea boys rushed by, struggling to contain the steaming liquid they carried to merchants reluctant to miss a sale. The odd

motorcycle tried to make its way down vaulted lanes special-
izing in gold, carpets, clothes, electronics—and everything
else imaginable.

Ma was in her element. "Look at the details on that
dome!" she shouted over the steady hammering of craftsmen.
"The pattern on the arches!" She'd always enjoyed wandering
through markets in Delhi, haggling as she bought flowers,
fruit and vegetables, and eagerly followed Hamid towards an
alley where he said they would find the pistachios and other
dried fruit she was looking for.

Ayan fell in behind them. When he was young, he'd
hated going shopping with his mother: the crowds pushing
and shoving, the time wasted in browsing, the embarrass-
ment of arguing over a few rupees. He was now trapped in
something much worse: a Bazaar on steroids—huge, loud,
anachronistic.

"My mosque, the very famous Shah Mosque, is also here
in Bazaar," Hamid said as Ma stopped in front of a prodi-
gious display of pistachios, almonds, pine nuts, raisins, and
dates. "We can go there afterwards."

Of course, there was a mosque in the vicinity, Ayan thought.
*All around, people were doing what they could to fleece customers,
undercut competitors, screw employees, and stiff suppliers; no wonder
they needed a convenient place to pray for salvation.*

"We must make time to see the mosque!" Ma said, full
of enthusiasm. "This is the closest I'm going to get to the
world of the old Silk Route. I want to see everything!"

"OK," Ayan said, giving in.

"Here, let me pay for this," he added as Hamid helped
Ma negotiate the price of an assortment of nuts and dried
fruit.

"I can afford to pay for my own nuts. If my son wants to
be a big man, he can buy his mother a carpet," Ma said with
a smile, "A small one . . ."

"I'm going to buy you a carpet, and it doesn't have to be small," Ayan said, surprised but pleased. This was progress. She had never asked him for anything before and still insisted on giving him spending money when he went home.

They made their way to the carpet section and were captured by an indefatigable scout, who led them to a store halfway down an alley.

Hamid stayed by Ma's side as the owner and the scout laid out a range of Kashans.

Ayan, bored, heard heated voices from an adjacent shop and looked in to see what was going on.

A big American, probably in his fifties, was blustering over a seated merchant whose English was adequate for trade but not much else. The back and forth over the price of a carpet seemed unusually aggressive, and it was escalating.

Suddenly, the shopkeeper waved the American away. "The price is double for you now. Double! Twenty thousand toman. You can't afford! Go away!" he said contemptuously.

"Say what?" the American yelled. "Asshole—you've just been wasting my time! Fucking Arab!" He shoved his raised middle finger into the man's face and wheeled out of the stall, brushing past Ma, who had come to call Ayan back to see the carpet she liked.

Ma stumbled. Her head hit the doorpost.

Enraged, Ayan steadied her and set off to teach the bastard a lesson.

He saw the insulted merchant trip the American from behind and attack him with a shoe.

A group of young Westerners rushed forward to join the fight. One of them grabbed the Iranian and hurled him aside. The others formed a protective circle as the American rose unsteadily to his feet.

Ayan charged towards the American, but a kick caught him in the groin. He landed heavily on the ground and heard a thick brogue say, "Fuck off, you brown bastard! Get away from us!"

Ayan grabbed his abdomen and drew his knees to his chest. Feet raced by him. He looked around for the Irishman who'd kicked him. He was within striking distance, fending off one of the shopkeepers who had rushed forward to join the fight.

Ayan pushed himself up and swung wildly. But that kick to his groin had found its target, and he doubled over again. A surreal scene unfolded around him. Shopkeepers were pulling down shutters and hastening out of sight as the melee grew.

He looked around for Ma. The shop where he'd left her was closed. Where was she?

Somebody tapped him on the shoulder.

He spun around ready to attack.

It was the scout who had brought them to the store. "Come with me," he said. "Hamid has taken Khanom to the mosque."

Good man, Hamid, Ayan thought, relieved.

He stumbled after the scout through a labyrinth, stepping around hastily abandoned cups, plates, food, and merchandise.

"OK, no problem now, Shah Mosque is just there," the scout said, pointing towards the back of the restaurant they had arrived in. He caught his breath, adjusted his cap and clothes, and calmly greeted a few waiters who were cleaning up and preparing for the lunch crowd.

Ayan ran past him and into a narrow lane lined by two-storied buildings that led to the arched entrance of the mosque.

Ma was sitting on the side of a rectangular pool with fountains, sipping a Coke. Hamid and a woman in a chador stood next to her.

People chatted casually by the pool. Families strolled by laden with shopping bags. The chaos inside the Bazaar seemed some imagined, alternate reality.

"Are you all right?" Ayan said, putting his arm around his mother.

"Just a few minor scrapes," she said. "Where did you run off to? I was so worried! I didn't want to leave you in there, but Hamid insisted. He said you would find us."

"I told this boy to bring you to the mosque," Hamid said, taking some money from his wallet and slipping it into the pocket of the scout, who had joined them.

Ayan squeezed Hamid's shoulder in appreciation. He turned back to his mother.

"Ma, you're bleeding," he said. "Do you still carry around that first-aid kit?"

"Yes, it's in my purse. Put some iodine tincture on this and a Band-Aid; that should be enough."

Ayan opened the familiar black pouch that was almost part of Ma's person.

"I'm fine now," she said, pushing his hand away as he fussed over her. "What's that lump? You've hurt your head too?"

"Careful!" Ayan said as Ma ran her fingers over his bruise.

"Stay still," she said as Ayan winced. "Actually, this swelling is quite bad. It needs ice."

Hamid asked the woman hovering behind him to fetch some ice.

"My wife," he explained, smiling self-consciously.

Ayan had never seen Sholeh before. Hamid's wife had green eyes like Adil's and smiled shyly at him before looking down.

The scout, who'd hung around with an air of concern on his face, spoke up, taking advantage of a lull as they waited for Sholeh to return.

"What about the carpet, the small one you liked?" he said. "I will bring it for you, no problem. Six thousand toman."

"Don't bother about all that now," Ma said.

"We'll take it," Ayan said. It would salvage the morning.

"Go and bring the carpet—quickly," Hamid said. "Three thousand."

The scout made a show with his hands and his shoulders. "It's dangerous inside," he said, "I have to open the shop, it's a risk for me. Five thousand." He looked at Ma. "Khanom, it's a very beautiful carpet. Don't let it escape from your grasp."

"Four thousand. *Tamam shud*," Hamid said. "Go and get it. Pack it properly in plastic, tightly. It has to go in a plane."

The scout tried a couple more times before reluctantly agreeing to Hamid's price.

"I will bring it, *Inshallah*, but I could get killed, and my boss is sure to fire me."

"Go on, go on, don't waste any more of our time," Hamid said, waving him off.

The scout shuffled away, muttering under his breath.

A few minutes later, Sholeh returned, accompanied by a tall, bearded cleric and group of men.

Hamid, solicitous and uncharacteristically nervous, jumped up and greeted the cleric.

He wore a black gown over a high-collared cream robe, and his turban was black, signaling that he was a *Sayyid*, claiming descent from the Prophet. Half a dozen men flanked him in a protective ring.

The cleric smiled and looked at Ma with a concerned expression.

"Salaam Khanom. *Hale shoma khobe?*"

He turned to Ayan.

"I've been informed about what happened. It is very unfortunate that your mother had such a bad experience on her first day as a guest in our country."

"Thank you. It was a shock, but people were very helpful," Ayan said, liking the man. He had compassionate eyes.

"The *Baazaris* are in a bad mood," the cleric said. "They are religious people who are tense after the murder of a beloved person and marking the forty days of grieving for a martyr. In such times, a raging fire can start with a single spark."

Hamid looked earnestly at Ma and paraphrased the mullah's words in his halting English for her benefit. "American caused trouble," he added. "America very bad country. Israel also very bad, but India very good." He touched his hand to his chest and turned to the mullah for validation.

The cleric nodded. "America is the devil. Iranians are like Indians; we are both great cultures—old, very old." He looked at Ayan. "Ayatollah Khomeini's grandfather was born in India, in the kingdom of Awadh, where his ancestors preached. Tell that to your mother."

"Ayan was born there too," Ma said. "So we have a connection . . ."

The cleric smiled broadly.

"Indeed!" he said. "They say our ayatollah also writes religious poetry under the name Hindi. Agha, tell that to your mother. Tell her I admire your country and its history, like most Persians, and ask her if she wants a short tour of our mosque. It is surely one of the best in the world. Or perhaps, she should rest?"

"I'm really OK," Ma said after Ayan translated the cleric's words. "And I want to see this famous mosque."

The cleric turned to Hamid's wife. "Show the Khanom around the mosque and the area and find somebody who

Khube *(handwritten)*

Raga in mosque *(handwritten, left margin, vertical)*

speaks English to explain the architecture and history," he said. "*Khube.* Now I have to go. It is time for prayer . . ."

"Ayan Agha, please excuse me," Hamid said. "I will return after the prayer. Not long."

He walked off behind the cleric, arm in arm with a tall, wiry fellow who had been part of the mullah's group.

The area emptied as the call to prayer rang out.

Suddenly alone, Ayan found himself thinking about the Ayatollah who Hamid believed was the Mahdi, the person the imam of the mosque also clearly held in such high regard. What was it like to be in his presence? Did his sternness melt with friends and family to reveal the elegant manner of the Awadh Shias—the *nawabi* culture of Lucknow that his grandfather was familiar with? Perhaps. It was interesting that he was a poet, too, in addition to a brilliant religious scholar and this fearless opponent of the Shah . . .

Ayan meandered into the courtyard of the mosque. A few stragglers were walking towards the prayer hall. Why not join them? It would help to pass the time. He blended into the group, which was a good thing, he felt, in this time of inflamed feelings.

An odor of overused shoes and sweat, familiar from temples in India, came at him as he entered the crowded prayer hall after the ritual cleansing of the face, head, forearms, and top of the feet. He made his way to a nook in the wall and scanned the bright hues of the geometric patterns on the dome of the mosque. Rays of light and spirit and wisdom seemed to fan out over a growing sea of worshipers: standing, bowing, kneeling, prostrating.

But instead of contemplative calm and humility, Ayan sensed a collective rage.

The anger in the mosque gathered strength as the minutes rolled by, racing from body to body, ricocheting off the walls and columns, rushing out onto the twin minarets, sending a complaint to the heavens above.

The mood took Ayan back to that dreadful moment on Pahlavi Avenue: the shouts of the protestors, the boy's head split open by SAVAK, uncaring tires running through the stream of innocent blood.

Finally, it was over, and the crowd dispersed into the courtyard.

But Hamid and a small group of men remained behind, clustered around the imam.

The tall, wiry man, Hamid's friend, began speaking. "We have to avenge Mostafa's death!" he said. "We must let these SAVAK criminals know they have gone too far! *Allah hu Akbar!*"

"*Allah hu Akbar!*" the group responded.

The imam quieted the group and looked around.

Ayan stepped back into the nook.

"We must be wise and patient," the imam said in a low voice. "Our path is righteous. *Alhamdulillah.* Ayatollah Khomeini, in his greatness, has called the loss of his son a hidden favor of God. He says it is an *altaf-i khafiya.* He has asked us to show fortitude and hope. That is the right way."

The Imam paused to look into the eyes of each man. Then he spoke with a new urgency.

"It is approaching the fortieth day since the steadfast scholar of Qum, Haji Agha Sayed Mostafa Khomeini, beloved Morning Star of our resistance, was martyred in the holy city of Najaf by the SAVAK and the dog Saddam," he said. "You have shown your loyalty and bravery by demonstrating against this injustice. That is not enough. The future depends on you. My children, you must go out and get more people to join us. Our numbers have to become irresistible. Spread the word that we will hold a special gathering on Friday, December 2, to mourn Mostafa. We are in the hundreds now. *Inshallah*, we will be in the thousands soon, then in the millions! These infidels are drunk with corruption and power. But each time they martyr a true believer, each fortieth day of mourning, the flood will gather strength. It will become a wave of righteousness cresting ever higher and drown the illegitimate, evil Pahlavi regime and their backers: the Americans and the Israelis. In the name of Allah, The Most Beneficent, The Most Merciful: 'truly you do not call to one deaf or absent, but truly to one who hears and sees; and He is with you.'"

The imam punched both hands into the air, index fingers raised, and wheeled away dramatically.

His followers stared at the door that had closed behind him.

Hamid's friend raised a fist and called out "*Allah hu Akbar!*"

"*Allah hu Akbar!*" the others roared back at him.

Hamid stood on his toes, his clenched hand pounding the air.

"*Marg bar Shah!*" the tall, wiry man yelled, the veins in his neck bulging. "*Marg bar Amrika!*"

"*Marg bar Shah! Marg bar Amrika!*" the group echoed, driven to a frenzy.

Ayan slipped back into the courtyard and watched as the group walked out of the mosque a few minutes later, their chests puffed out with the momentary confidence of insignificant men made great by some common cause.

Hamid led the way back to the car. It was hard to square the polite, humble driver with the slogan-shouting, fist-pumping religious militant he'd been minutes ago.

Most of the shops had reopened. The press of commerce had closed over signs of the earlier turmoil. The scout walked alongside them, neatly packed carpet under his arm, continuing to argue his case for additional hardship compensation.

Despite the bizarre normalcy, it was impossible to ignore the tremors they had experienced.

I should get the hell out of here, too, like Gaby, Ayan told himself in the silence that accompanied the drive back to Shemiran. *But I have to leave on my terms. Play on the front foot.*

In the meanwhile, he should not be out looking for trouble like Hamid and Gaby.

Hamid knew the consequences of being part of the group he was in; he saw what SAVAK did to that boy. Gaby was chasing down the ghosts of Nazis past and would be finished, let's face it, if she was caught supporting Baader-Meinhof.

Both Hamid and Gaby were dancing on a razor's edge, but they were battling for the soul of their nations. There was some honor in that.

Gaby had said that he couldn't turn away if he was staying in Iran; he had to help the oppressed around him. He would lift the financial pressure on Hamid and do what he could for his family. But not get involved beyond that. Why should he look for false quarrels in a foreign land?

CHAPTER 8

Ma was exhausted. The scene in the Bazaar had brought back memories of traumatic Hindu-Muslim confrontations during Partition and triggered one of her famous migraines. The tour of the museums was cancelled, and she retired to the bedroom, craving darkness and silence.

Ayan lay down on the sofa and held a bag of ice against his forehead. By the evening, he'd recovered and was ready for the dinner in Firouz Akhbari's opulent villa near Niavaran Palace. He polished his shoes, dressed in a blazer and grey trousers, and added a flourish to the silk pocket square he'd selected for the occasion. His host was a stylish man who wore bespoke English suits and double buckle John Lobb shoes; Ayan's preferred attire of faded jeans and a well-worn black velvet jacket would not do tonight.

Ayan had met Mr. Ten Percent just over a year ago, on Uncle Vikram's last trip to Tehran, and they had hit it off immediately. He'd taken to the relaxed, charming Iranian, who was the main broker for the aromatic black tea that was the specialty of Uncle Vikram's estate in Darjeeling, and Firouz had quickly decided Ayan must be highly intelligent because he came from the same gene pool as the brilliant Vikram.

He'd lingered as Ayan and Uncle Vikram caught up, dismissed Ayan's musings about returning to Europe, said Iran needed talented professionals, and promised to find a big job for him in Tehran. And he'd delivered. Tea broking was just a sideline for Akhbari—advisor to the Ministry of Energy was his principal occupation, and Iran Power's CEO Nader was his friend. A week after the meeting, Ayan had received an offer to join Iran Power's senior management team.

Two hours into the evening in Firouz's villa, the relaxed smile on Arnold's face and the alcoholic twinkle in his eyes were good signs.

Firouz made his move after dinner was almost over and camaraderie had taken hold. "Will you accept my personal guarantee that not one dollar of First National's loan to Iran Power will be used for military purposes?" he said to Arnold. "It will be used exclusively for production of equipment to generate nuclear power for our civilians. My word is more meaningful than any piece of paper. Check around. And I speak on behalf of the Ministry of Energy and His Imperial Majesty."

Not long afterwards, after a string of weakening appeals for a written document, Arnold held out his hand.

"I will inform His Majesty," Firouz said, meeting Arnold's handshake. "He will not forget this. First National will get a lot of additional business by leading this transaction. And if the bank is stupid enough not to reward you properly, leave them and join us. The Shah needs senior bankers on his team."

"I might have to take you up on that," Arnold said. "This is a career breaker for me if something goes wrong. I'm just a simple banker supporting a family."

"We all know you are much more than that," Firouz said. "They call you the real prince of the Middle East for a reason. Nothing happens without you. Thank you for this. I will make sure you are taken care of."

"I appreciate that," Arnold said.

The two men embraced.

The deal was done.

The way most big deals went down in places like Tehran.

Ma recovered by the next morning. Or was a good sport and said that she had.

It was a steep drive up the Dizin Road to Darioush's place in Shemshak—not a journey to take lightly, even in the well-balanced Mercedes. Hairpin turns came every minute, it seemed, as they made their way through rock formations that had yielded to some extraordinarily competent civil engineering.

But traffic was light, and in less than an hour, they had climbed to 6,000 feet and were parking outside Cascades, Darioush's hotel and spa.

"What beautiful flowers!" Ma said as Darioush met them at the entrance. "Jasmine at this time of year! How wonderful!"

"I heard it's the flower you love, so I had to find some for you," Darioush said. "You're the mother of my brother, coming to visit me for the first time."

A broad smile lit up his ruddy face, glowing from a million hours spent outdoors on construction sites, ski slopes, and hiking trails. Darioush put his arms around Ma and kissed her thrice, alternating cheeks in the Persian fashion.

Ma blushed, amusing Ayan.

"I'm making lunch—something especially for you to make you forget the rough welcome you received in the Bazaar," Darioush said. "Come, sit by the pool. It's a nice day and one of the few weekends when the hotel is quiet. Ayan will get you a drink while I finish in the kitchen. It won't be long."

Ayan handed his mother a gin and tonic, and they settled into Adirondack chairs on the pool deck. An Iranian family talked excitedly on the other side of the pool. Some teenagers from the Tehran American School braved the cold water and splashed about.

The barren, brown slopes of Shemshak enveloped them. By December, they would be covered in snow, transformed into black diamond ski runs to the west and cross-country trails to the east. A mountain stream, tired from transporting the melt to Tehran all spring and summer, trickled below them. A light, fresh breeze carried the smell of lamb, onions, and herbs from Cascades' kitchen, where Darioush and his chef were cooking.

I am happy here, Ayan told himself as he sipped his vodka soda and chatted to his mother. *Happy to be in this place, happy that Ma is here.*

He told her about Darioush: how they met playing tennis at Club Veyssi, how they spent summer weekends in Darioush's hotel on the Caspian Sea, how they raced down the bracing mogul pistes of Shemshak in winter. He left out the parties in Darioush's cabins on the Karaj Lake and the decadent après-ski festivities that Cascades was famous for.

"My, what a feast!" Ma said when Darioush returned from the kitchen and joined them for lunch.

"It's nothing—a poor attempt," Darioush said, looking over the table with satisfaction and instructing the waiter to ensure Ma took generous helpings of everything: herbed rice with a golden disk of *tahdig* crust on top; *fesenjan*, pomegranate and walnut chicken stew; *ghormeh sabzi*, lamb cooked with herbs and kidney beans; *mast-o-khiar*, yogurt with cucumber; and *sabzi khordan*, herbs, feta cheese, radishes, scallions, and walnuts. And Ayan's favorite: *barbari* and *sangak* flatbread.

"Nonsense! Everything is absolutely delicious!" Ma said, dipping the *tahdig* into the *fesenjan* sauce on her plate. "This place is lovely. Ayan says that you do a lot of work here, care for it yourself; it shows."

"I try," Darioush said. "I love to be up here."

"I understand," Ma nodded. "My husband enjoys the outdoor life too. And Ayan takes after him. My other son and daughter are different. More like me."

"Really, Ma? I know you're not one for sports, but you and I—we are the intense ones . . ."

Ma laughed and patted Ayan's hand.

He thought about Shiv and Jaya. At seventeen, Jaya was the baby of the family. She was his mother's project, being groomed to be a doctor like her; she had the brains, but it was unclear if that's what she wanted to do. His older brother, Shiv, was the disciplined one. He'd married his college sweetheart, giving up his passion for journalism to run his wife's extensive farmlands. Shiv had succeeded by being the person he'd always been: competent, intelligent, and utterly reliable. Jaya seemed more interested in socializing and shopping. Ayan had tried to teach her tennis. Despite her beautiful strokes, it was a struggle. She negotiated how much time she had to put in, the number of rallies on each wing she had to complete, and as soon as the count had been reached, off she went to meet her friends at the pool. Perhaps Jaya would be all right—perhaps focus was for people without her extravagant talents.

"I want to know what you like to do," Darioush said, focusing his attention on Ma. "I hear you're going to make a speech in Scotland?"

"Nothing important! I'm just a substitute for another speaker," she replied.

"What's it about?"

"I don't want to bore you with doctor talk."

"You won't. I own a hospital."

"Really?" Ma said, straightening in her chair. "Why? I mean . . . is it a good business to be in here?"

"I don't do it for the money," Darioush said. "You see, there is a lot of anger against rich people—all that money controlled by just a few of us. The hospital looks after my hotel workers, all the staff here, and I subsidize most of the cost." He shrugged self-deprecatingly. "Out of self-interest, if nothing else."

"Well, then you may be interested in what I'll be talking about in Edinburgh," Ma said, trying but failing to dissuade the waiter from adding more rice and *ghormeh sabzi* to her plate. "I'm discussing the challenges of providing medical care to villages in India, making sure pregnant women and newborns get medicines, adequate nutrition, things like that. Women often fall into the hands of unscrupulous money lenders when they become pregnant and need money—often the start of lifelong poverty."

She looked around the vista and at the abundant table, fidgeted with her bangles, then met Darioush's eyes with a wry smile. "I'm talking about very different lives."

"I know those lives," Darioush said. "Most of our workers are very poor. Believe me, I'm doing what I can to help them too."

Ayan leaned back in his chair, listening to Darioush and Ma talk, learning things about his friend that he should have known. Darioush was concerned about the tension between the classes in Iran? The mood in Tehran University? The increase in unemployment from rising interest rates? He had all these charitable involvements?

This disclosure must be because Darioush was on a charm offensive. Information was a strategic asset in Iran, provided only when it was useful or necessary. These Persians give you a strand here, a hint there, unlike Indians who built friendships on impulsive torrents of self-revelation.

By the time dessert arrived—a perfectly balanced *faloodeh* sorbet served with pistachio and honey ice cream—Darioush had eagerly accepted Ma's offer to find nurses from Kerala to work in his hospital and insisted on contributing to Ma's passion: helping village women in India become independent by teaching them how to market their skills and handicrafts.

"What a nice man," Ma said as they drove back to Tehran. She'd placed a few of the jasmine flowers in her hair, as was her custom. "So hospitable and such a wonderful cook. Is this family property?"

"No—he's built everything on his own. His father is well known here, but they are not in contact," Ayan said.

"That's sad."

"It is, isn't it? Darioush is estranged from his diplomat father because he refused to follow in the family's service tradition. His grandfather was an ambassador, as was his father, and his uncles are high-ranking military officers. Darioush dropped out of college, went into real estate, and then made things worse by recruiting his younger brother. He's made a fortune by developing hotels in all the top resorts in Iran but remains unforgiven."

"Time usually helps with these situations, unless there is more to it. By the way, where was Darioush's wife? He didn't talk about her at all."

"Chantal? Oh, she's home in Bordeaux. Comes to Tehran now and then. They have a curious relationship."

"Well, she should watch out," Ma said, staring into the middle distance. "He's a very attractive man."

"And rich. That also helps. He's quite successful with women."

mom talking ?

"What about you, young man? Do you have a girlfriend? Perhaps the one who decorated your apartment?"

"No, not really."

"I've heard the opposite. Just remember, I know everything. I even knew about your Rekhas and your Jackies in London . . ."

She smiled.

Why had he assumed that his mother was in the dark about these things?

"You're like Colonel Hosseini," he said.

"Who?"

"SAVAK—secret police. He also asks a lot of questions and seems to know everything."

"So you might as well tell me about your girlfriend here. Is she an Iranian?"

"Nobody and nothing really to tell you about. Everything is transient here: just comings and goings," Ayan said.

"I suppose I'll just have to find out for myself," Ma said.

She ran her fingers along the back of his head.

"What?" Ayan said, aware of her steady gaze.

"You look different," Ma said.

"In what way?"

"I don't know—more foreign, I suppose. And you need a haircut."

She returned her hand to her lap.

He could see the veins through her thinning skin. Her knuckles and fingers were swollen with the arthritis that ran in her family. He squeezed her hand tenderly, reminded of wasted opportunities and racing time, of Gaby's imminent departure.

What ?!?

The Greek chorus of reprimands and warnings, which had existed inside him forever, resurfaced and made him feel low. It didn't help that they were descending rapidly, the euphoria of being in high country fading as the concerns of his life in Tehran came into focus.

They arrived at the Karimi estate to find Hassan dressed in his tennis clothes, eager to fit in a game before dinner.

Which was fine by Ayan. Tennis would restore his equilibrium; it always did.

He changed into the spare tennis outfit he kept in the trunk of his car as Hassan settled Ma on a chaise longue outside the guesthouse.

A breeze rustled through the mauve and amber leaves of the tall plane trees surrounding the tennis court. Slivers of clouds streaked the dark blue sky. Tennis's special alchemy lifted Ayan's mood as they warmed up. Countless hours and countless years of practice took over; muscle memory made the ball slice through the air—or arch high over the net—before touching down at the baseline for the briefest of moments, then rearing out of reach with snarling topspin. Ayan felt a rush with every purely hit backhand, with every stutter step that brought him to the right place on the court at precisely the right time.

When it was over, Hassan had won both sets, as he usually did. It might have been a different story on the fast grass courts of the Delhi Gymkhana Club, but it was hard to beat a counterpuncher on the slow clay of Tehran and harder still to suffer through Hassan's bragging afterwards.

Although today, he didn't have to. Ma had moved from the chaise longue to a chair with a view of the tennis court, and she walked down and joined them.

"Not bad," she said as Hassan sent the ball boy off for some tea and biscuits. "Ayan, you were a little erratic, and Hassan, you would have won earlier if you had been less defensive. But overall, not bad tennis."

"You're tough!" Hassan said, smiling at Ma as he poured a glass of fresh melon juice for her and toweled off.

"It comes from watching three generations of this family playing tennis," Ma said. "Usually in less pleasant conditions."

ASR prayf

From somewhere in the compound, they heard the lyrical, hypnotic call to the late afternoon *Asr* prayer.

"For my grandfather's benefit," Hassan said. "He prays five times a day."

"Go ahead and join him—don't worry about us," Ayan said.

Hassan grinned. "You're kidding, right? That's just for the old man and a few family servants. Not even my father's generation prays anymore. Let's go to the pool house."

He turned to Ma. "Do you play backgammon?"

"Scrabble's my game," she said.

"OK," Hassan said. "I'll have a quick shower, and we'll play Scrabble. I'm bored of beating Ayan at backgammon."

A couple of hours later, Ayan was sipping champagne by the French doors of the baroque drawing room in Karimi House. Refreshed after a nap in the guesthouse, Ma seemed comfortable talking to Hassan's parents and older relatives who had gathered for the weekly Friday dinner.

Overfull with furniture, paintings, and carpets, the place felt claustrophobic. The weather was still decent outside. Ayan walked out into the porch. He raised his champagne flute in appreciation as the trio providing background music raised their volume to herald his arrival. Some of the faces gathered by the corner bar seemed familiar, probably from the Key Club. Fariba was there, too, but she refused to meet his eyes.

Ayan drained the champagne, asked the bartender for a Macallan, and tried to join the conversation. Hassan would expect him to. But his forays drew only a few polite responses, followed by turned backs. He was nobody here.

Ayan stepped down to the garden, embarrassed and lonely, an outsider looking in. It was not unfamiliar—this sense of estrangement that came with being a foreigner—but it was dispiriting after the camaraderie he'd just shared with Hassan on the court. He missed Darioush and Nick Stasney, his only other close friends in Iran. Darioush was probably not invited. The Karimis, led by a still-engaged patriarch, were from the establishment, spinning connections and Ivy League educations into gold: two of the sons were in the military, and a daughter worked in the Empress's office; Hassan was being groomed to take over the pharmaceuticals business; Fariba ran ballet and opera programming for Roudaki Hall. Darioush had descended into property development, become an owner of questionable establishments in Karimi eyes. But Nick was always everywhere, and Hassan liked him. Hopefully, he would arrive soon.

NICK STASNEY

After a few minutes, a hand slipped into Ayan's.

He knew the feel of the skin and the perfume.

It was Fariba.

"Pay more attention to me," Fariba said. "Why don't you?"

Ayan raised his eyebrows and laughed. "You have the nerve to say that? After icing me just now?"

"You blame me? After ditching me in the Key Club?"

He put an arm around her shoulder and hugged her.

"That was friendly," Fariba said.

Hassan's cousin

"Yes, we're friends, and I really, really need your friendship!" Ayan said.

"See those men," Fariba said, pointing towards the group on the porch. "I'm friends with all of them. I can see myself in twenty years with any one of these men up there and know exactly what my days will be like. I don't want to be that person. So please understand, dear Ayan, I don't need more friends."

She looked to check if anybody was looking at them and then kissed him on the mouth.

"Ayan, I really like you," she said, her honey-brown eyes intense and searching. "I want to be hopeful and brave and free and crazy, taking chances, seeing what happens—with somebody as unmoored and untethered as I am, and I've chosen you, so be flattered!" She squeezed his hand.

He didn't need this right now.

"I really like you too," Ayan said, "but . . . I'm with Gaby."

"She's not worth it, Ayan! I am! You know that."

She kissed him again before pushing back suddenly.

"It's Nick. He's coming towards us," she said. "I'll see you inside. Just remember. You're mine. I'm not letting her steal you from me."

"I saw that," Nick said with a wink. He had a can of beer in his hand. "You fucked her yet?"

"None of your business! And no—she's Hassan's cousin, as you know."

"Don't let that stop you," Nick said. "These Persian chicks are as hot as firecrackers and great in the sack."

"I guess I should believe you," Ayan said, "You're married to one."

"Whoa! Careful now! Leave my wife out of this. I was speaking in generalities."

"OK—we'll put your wife on a pedestal. It would be easier if I had met her, you know."

"Soon, brother, soon. I'll ask the missus—just you, though. You're a foreign-working stiff like me, although you make much more. Fucking translating jobs don't pay much. I live on the chump change *Time*, *Life*, and a few other publishers throw at me. My place is pretty basic, not for the likes of Hassan Karimi and Darioush."

"That's a lame excuse. They don't care about that stuff. They know they're richer than everyone else in Tehran. You're just a cheap bastard."

"You're a cheap bastard, you're a cheap bastard," Nick said, shaking his head from side to side, exaggeratedly mimicking an Indian accent. "Don't worry, don't worry— you will meet my good wife very soon! Very soon indeed!"

At dinner, Ma and Ayan were seated with Hassan, his parents, an important Karimi brothers customer who was visiting town, and—why should he be surprised—Nick Stasney.

The American had placed himself between the senior Karimi and the customer and was engaging them in fluent Farsi.

People changed tables and circulated as the entrée plates were cleared. Hassan took Ayan to meet a friend interested in joining their tennis game. He returned to find his mother sitting with Fariba to her right, Nick to her left, and no place left for him. There was nothing to do but find a seat at an adjoining table, make distracted conversation, and watch warily as Ma turned her back on Nick and focused on Fariba.

Later that night, back in his apartment, Ayan made tea for his mother as she relaxed in her dressing gown.

"I don't mind if you marry a Persian girl, like that lovely Fariba," Ma announced.

"OK, but I'm not really planning to," Ayan said.

"A mother can tell when somebody is in love with her son. Though, being a Muslim, things will not be easy for her in India. Your father just got transferred from the peace and quiet of the mountains of Pithoragarh to manage Hindu-Muslim tensions during the elections in the plains. You can imagine how difficult that is."

"That's too bad. Dad will hate it," Ayan said, seizing on this information to deflect the conversation. "I just received a letter from him posted in Munsiyari."

Every expatriate had a survival toolkit, Ayan thought. His was work: throwing himself in and letting routine propel the initial days in a new place. Friendships that developed quickly in tennis clubs and liaisons with other lonely foreign colleagues helped, too, but what really pulled him through were these letters from his father. They came regularly, whether he replied or not, bringing news from home, full of unconditional faith in him and his future; they had sustained Ayan through his days as a stranger in London and in Tehran.

"Your father loves hearing from you. Write more often. Ring up sometimes too," Ma said. "He's one of the few officials tough enough for this election management job. You are right: He will hate the politics and the ugliness. But it's his duty. Anyway, leaving aside the Muslim thing, Fariba would settle into India really well. She's educated, intelligent, from a cultured family—and so beautiful!"

"I'm not interested in marrying Fariba, or anyone else for that matter," Ayan said, escaping to the kitchen to retrieve a box of the Godiva chocolates Ma loved.

"I'm barely able to take care of myself," he called out. "So can we please talk about something else?"

"You'll grow old alone if you think like that!" Ma yelled back to him.

When he returned, she said, "*Beta*, I think you should come back to India."

"There's nothing for me there. I'm not interested in settling down, signing on to an organization, and waiting my turn to move up the ladder. The idea is suffocating. I want to expand my horizons, have adventures, not become a *boxwallah*."

He sounded vague and petulant, even to his own ears. But it was true.

"I love you all, Ma, but I don't want to stagnate."

"You'll grow and learn by settling down with somebody brilliant and focused—and by helping the less fortunate. Not by being selfish and thinking only about yourself! If you don't want to join a company, come back and start a charity, like Anu Sinha. Bunty and Manmeet are both doctors and are working in a government clinic in Bihar. They were your friends in college. Wonderful young women! Do you know how many lives they are changing? Or be like Bunker who is making a huge difference in India. I'll help you if you do something like that."

"Yes—maybe someday. Not now."

There was a knock on the door. Ayan looked at his watch. It was 11:30 p.m. He squinted through the peephole.

It was Gaby! Good god!

Ayan looked at his mother as he unlatched the safety lock. What the fuck was he going to do?

Gaby breezed past, swinging around to kiss him.

She was in her uniform.

"I'm back early. Schedule change," she said, throwing down her bags and putting her arm around Ayan's neck.

She gave him a long kiss.

Padma meets Gaby

"What's the matter, aren't you happy to see me?" she said as Ayan looked over his shoulder.

Gaby followed his eyes and pulled back with surprise when she saw Ma sitting on the sofa.

"Sorry! Ayan, I didn't know you had company! Hello!" she said to Ma, recovering.

She walked over to the sofa and held out her hand.

"I'm Gaby," she said.

Ma looked at Ayan, surprised. She fussed with her nightclothes and hair and stood up to greet Gaby.

"Hello, Gaby, I'm Padma, Ayan's mother. So nice to meet you!"

Gaby looked at Ayan with raised eyebrows.

"Your mother! Wow!"

"Yes, a surprise visit—to catch up with my son," Ma said, smiling at Ayan with her eyebrows raised.

"It's late, I'm disturbing you. I should go—somewhere else . . ." Gaby said, looking inquiringly at Ayan.

"Have a cup of tea at least," Ma said.

She took Gaby by the wrist and made her sit down with her.

"What would you like? We have some nice Darjeeling, chamomile, or perhaps something stronger? Brandy?"

"I'll just have regular tea. The Darjeeling."

"Good! It's from my brother's tea garden. Ayan, brew it for exactly five minutes."

"Yes, yes, I have made tea before, you know."

Gaby gave him a knowing smile.

Ayan beckoned her towards the kitchen.

"So what's the plan?" Gaby said after Ayan explained the situation to her.

"Let's just tell her that you live here. She'll get over it."

"My mother wouldn't. Not that easily," Gaby said. "And she's European."

"I'm not having you go off and sleep somewhere else."

"It's just for tonight, after all," she stroked his cheek. "Anyway, there's no chance of me sleeping on a sofa after this last flight! I need to rest. I'll stay at the Hilton. Book me a room while I talk to your mother."

Ayan strained to hear their conversation as he made arrangements for Gaby.

"That's an airline uniform," Ma said.

"Yes, I'm a pilot with Iran Air," Gaby said.

No, Gaby explained, she didn't fly the jets, though she was perfectly qualified to do so. She was still a flight engineer. Yes, she was based in Tehran; yes, she was German, from Bavaria, though she felt more like a Berliner and spent as much time as she could in West Berlin; yes, she had a place there; no, it wasn't hers. It belonged to her father; he'd bought it when he worked there for Schering; yes, she flew back regularly to visit her parents and her younger brother Mathias; yes, she was Catholic, though lapsed; yes, she could visit a priest and confess and make things right, but she had no plans to do that anytime soon.

"Never mind," Ma said, "Your parents must be so proud of their daughter, achieving what very few women have. Becoming a pilot and everything! But don't they worry about you living alone? Especially in this country. You're such a pretty young thing!"

Gaby laughed. *Really.*

Ayan stuck his head out of the kitchen and saw her looking at her hands. It was time to rescue her. The tea had been brewing for four minutes. That was enough.

Eventually, his mother retired for the night.

He embraced Gaby the minute the door to the bedroom shut.

"You're crazy! She'll hear us! What if she comes out?" Gaby said, even as she lifted her hips to allow him to slip off her trousers.

She gasped as he began to make love to her, craning her head to make sure the bedroom door remained shut. Then everything else seemed to stop mattering. Her hands slowed him, guiding him into the rhythms and patterns she wanted. She opened her legs wide and tightened them around his back, biting into his hand as he tried to muffle her moans.

Fuck my

"I've missed you," he said, bringing her a cognac. "All I've been thinking about is how little time I have left with you."

She patted the sofa and kissed him as he snuggled next to her. "That makes me happy. It means you'll come to see me. Often. You'll love West Berlin."

"How can you be so casual?"

"What do you mean?"

"It ain't me, babe. . ." he sang tunelessly.

"Oh, Ayan! It's not like that at all! And can we not discuss this right now? Please? I've just worked hours and hours across multiple time zones, and I'm really tired. Pass me my clothes. I don't want your mother walking in and finding me standing here naked."

On the way to the Hilton, she said, "Why don't I take your mother to the airport? We'll have a chance to talk some more. I'll make sure she's treated like a VIP at Mehrabad."

This was a bad idea. There was sure to be some drama.

"That's nice of you, Gaby, but she'll expect me to see her off. My mother can be difficult."

"I can handle her. Wait till you meet my mother. Yours is so normal compared to her."

"What's the matter with your mother?"

last night

"You'll see," she said, "when you come to Starnberger. And don't be silly. Go to work. I'm taking your mother to the airport. I really want to. I'm good with mothers."

Ma called him from the airport the next day.

"I'm sitting in the first-class lounge having a drink; they're bringing me lunch!"

"Good! Have a safe flight and call me when you reach London."

"Talk a little, *beta*. Gaby rushed me through everything, and now I have a lot of time to kill, sitting here all by myself. My son has become quite the charmer, I can see. Gaby's also quite interested in you, and—no need to pretend—it's obvious that you're mad for her."

"Ma, I'm preparing for a meeting. I really can't talk right now."

"You can talk to your mother for a minute! Who knows when I'm going to see you again, and there's too much time pressure on long-distance calls."

"We talked just this morning!"

"Not about this. I want to know about you and Gaby. Where's all this going?"

"She's a friend," Ayan said, leaning back in his chair. "Nothing's changed since I told you that a couple of hours ago."

"Girlfriend. She said she was your girlfriend. Please be careful. Take precautions. I told Gaby to change the birth control pills she's taking."

"No! You didn't!"

"Her pills aren't good for her. I've seen bad outcomes; she'll want children someday. There's a chance they're going to be my grandchildren. I have to think about their welfare. Be responsible; take care of Gaby. And yourself."

"How did Gaby react to your lecture?"

Beta – Nick Name

"She laughed and tried to change the subject."

"Naturally. I can't believe you embarrassed her like that."

"Never mind. I made her write down the name of the pills I recommended. And she was not that embarrassed. She even talked about how good-looking your children would be if the two of you ever decided to have them. That may be true, but . . ."

"OK, Ma. You've done your bit. I'll go into my meeting now, and you enjoy your lunch."

"No! Wait and listen to me! You've had your fun. I want you to come back and start living like a serious man. Meet a nice Indian girl. Settle down."

"I can't tell you how boring that sounds!" he snapped.

"Son, we Indians can only be truly at home in India."

"Working in India is not for me."

"You're just infatuated with Gaby. I can understand that."

"That's not it. That's unrelated to our discussion."

"She's beautiful, exciting, and everything," Ma continued.

"Bye!"

"*Beta*, she's a handful—more than a handful. Very different from us."

There was no stopping her.

"You were like her, weren't you? Independent. No shortage of admirers. You did everything your way. You were more than a handful yourself!"

"There was a difference. Your father and I were from the same culture and had a commitment to each other. That helped us pull through. Gaby and you are friends, just playing; that's what you are saying, isn't it?"

"Leave it, Ma! Don't worry! It may be hard to believe, but I know what I'm doing."

"Do you? Let me tell you, young man, men and women can't casually play these types of games without somebody's heart getting broken. And don't tell me times have changed."

young man?

CHAPTER 9

Gaby left Iran sooner than she had planned.

It was probably his fault.

It was hard to be a bystander while she set up a life that didn't include him, hearing her talk to friends in Germany about her return, watching her pack. The distance between them seemed to grow greater with each day.

They became short with each other. Then came the evening in Tehran University that escalated the tension beyond repair.

He'd come home from work to find her about to leave for a talk with some Iran Air people. It sounded interesting; he wanted to go, too, and persuaded her to wait for him.

Gaby had started walking down the stairs by the time he came out of the shower. He threw on his clothes and hurried after her, shaking the moisture out of his hair with one hand and downing his vodka soda with the other. He placed the empty glass in the niche at the base of the stairs where Khanom-eh Mohsen left his mail and jumped into the Mercedes.

"I should have gone with my Iran Air friends as I was planning to," Gaby said, knocking his hand off her knee. "Move! We're going to miss the fucking lecture."

It was just fifteen minutes since he'd come home from work. But that was apparently too long.

"I'm sorry! Your pals couldn't be too far ahead," Ayan said, weaving through the still-heavy evening traffic.

She gripped her seat but didn't tell him to slow down.

"I've been talking about this Ali Shariati lecture for the last ten days. I really wish you'd told me earlier you wanted to come. I've made plans . . ."

"That I don't fit into?"

"Well, you've forced yourself in now . . ."

"All right—screw this! The hell with it!"

Gaby said something in German. It didn't sound friendly.

"No need to curse. I'll just drop you and go back home," Ayan said.

Gaby breathed out slowly. She looked at him coldly. "You might as well come and listen to the talk," she said. "It's only about the most important thinker in this country—the person who was the most important thinker. He's just been murdered, like everybody else."

"Even I know that Shariati had a heart attack," Ayan said, feeling feisty after her rough treatment. "You can find conspiracies where there are none if you're determined."

You and Hamid both, he thought but didn't say.

Gaby shot him another look.

"Jail, torture, and exile have nothing to do with heart attacks, I suppose! I was going to tell you more about Shariati to prevent you sounding stupid tonight. You're on your own now."

He felt tired after a long day at work. Pedestrians wandered across the road, forcing him to brake just when traffic started moving. He would drop Gaby and go home.

"I've looked through that book you've been reading, you know," he said, pointing to the heavily underlined treatise on Shariarti resting on Gaby's lap. "And am less impressed than you. Certainly not a believer in the New Man concept Shariarti has lifted from Frantz Fanon. Hopefully, he offers a transformation to his New Man that doesn't result in the Iranian version of Pol Pot's Killing Fields."

"Ayan!" Gaby warned with a frown.

"Pol Pot was influenced by Sartre and Fanon too. You know that."

"OK, I'm done," Gaby said, turning to look out of the window.

"No marks for class participation?" Ayan said.

"Don't joke!"

"Wasn't exactly joking."

"This is Shariarti's idealized Persian," she said, opening the Shariarti book to a marked page and reading out loud, "'steadfast in the defense of truth and justice—holds the sword of Caesar in his hand—has the heart of Jesus in his breast—thinks with the brain of Socrates and loves god with the heart of Hallaj.' How the fuck can you link anything about Shariarti to that savage in Cambodia!"

"Things have a way of descending from high-mindedness to brutality when you try to take power from people who have it. That's all I'm saying."

She glared at him angrily.

They were crawling. It seemed silly to sit in the car and sulk.

"It's odd that mullahs still hate Shariarti after he called for Islam to be the force that liberates Iran," Ayan said, taking the initiative to break the silence, even though she was being so damn condescending. He had inserted himself into her evening.

Gaby looked straight ahead.

"Come on—let's not fight over something like this," Ayan said.

"You're being really irritating tonight," Gaby said. "Watch it."

"OK, OK. I will."

"Because," she said after a while, still not looking at him, "Shariarti warns the mullahs would be the most tyrannical of all if they come to power. They think they have a direct line to God and cannot be questioned. They must be checked."

"Rile people up with religion and, at the same time, control the power of the mullahs? How do you do that?"

"I don't know," Gaby said, finally turning to him. "Perhaps we'll learn about that today—understand why Sartre said he had no religion, but if he did, it would be Shariarti's; why Fanon the psychiatrist encouraged Shariarti to use Islam to inspire the Persian freedom movement . . ."

"Look, we've caught up with your friends," Ayan said, flashing his lights at the white Chevy Iran in front of them that was pulling up outside the modernist gates of Tehran University.

The car honked back a greeting.

Gaby jumped out of the Mercedes. She started towards her friends, then came back and looked at Ayan through the passenger side window of the car. "Ayan, please . . . Shariarti is Marx, Engels, Lenin, and Mao combined to my friends; they revere him. We're listening to a legendary professor who is part of the Iranian Resistance. Promise you'll watch what you say tonight?"

"I'll see you later," Ayan said. "I'm going home."

"OK. Do whatever you want," Gaby said, running to catch up with her group.

Ayan started towards home. But a car pulled out of a parking spot right in front of him. How often does that happen in this town? He might as well go in and hear the talk.

uH. oH

His mood had lightened by the time he edged his way into room 201 on the second floor of the Literature and Humanities Building. The neatly trimmed hedges and tall sycamores of the campus had brought back memories of college days; they had been the best of times.

The lecture was still in progress. Ayan leaned against the back wall, catching his breath. People were sitting in the aisles and everywhere he looked. The students around him looked cool and sophisticated, but it felt good to be him and not them. He'd hurdled the obstacles and anxieties that awaited them. The last few years, despite the slips and disappointments, had led somewhere.

Gaby was in the front row. She waved for him to join her, pointing to an empty seat next to her, but it would be too disruptive to reach it.

A tall, slim man stood by a lectern on the podium, speaking without notes. He had a prominent nose, a strong jawline, and a thick mane of greying hair brushed back and running untidily below the shawl collar of a white Irish cardigan. He wore slightly flared, black corduroy jeans and black ankle boots that would need to be polished soon.

The professor paused, his appraising eyes lingering on Ayan. He frowned and looked away, took a few puffs on his cigarette, and ground the stub into an ashtray on his lectern. He scratched the top of his head and eased some strands of hair back into place.

He needs sleep, Ayan thought, *and fewer cigarettes, and a better diet.*

"Successful anti-colonial revolutions tap into national authenticity, an understanding of the people's essence," the professor continued. "Shariarti's philosophy does the same. He believes a resistance movement in Iran must be centered around Islam's teachings and traditions because religion nourishes all us. Let me quote him. 'Islam influences and reveals the Iranian's soul in its fullest, from his instinct to be a warrior and embrace martyrdom for righteousness and justice in the spirit of Imam Ali and Imam Hussain, to his need for the understanding and intoxication with love for Allah, for the divine, that results from an inward pilgrimage of solitude, reflection, and purification.'"

The professor decided it was time for another cigarette. He pulled out a new packet, tapped it several times, turned it over, tapped it again, and slowly extracted a cigarette. Somebody in the front row rushed up, struck a lighter, and offered it to him.

"Shariati's success in Parisian intellectual circles, at the Sorbonne, in the trenches of the Algerian freedom struggle, and his logical words appeal to your educated minds," the professor said, nodding at his benefactor and inhaling deeply. "But Shariarti also speaks to the heart of the common man through his faith in Islam. He says *Intizar* is not passive, waiting for the return of the Mahdi, but demands action to bring about the emergence of a classless society, a society freed from tyranny, injustice, where the people are being led by the progressives—not by a dictatorial clergy; true Islam belongs to the oppressed. Shariarti wants to rouse Iranians from stupor and acceptance of injustice brought about by the Safavid Shiism that only protect the interests of monarchs, the clergy, and Western colonial exploiters."

The professor looked around the room, compelling an engagement with individual students.

Gaby was straight up in her chair. This professor was a smart guy. It would be fun to discuss his ideas with her tonight.

Half an hour later, the professor concluded, "I will leave you with Shariarti's words aimed at people like you. 'Shed the *gharbzadegi*, the *Westoxification* that the Shah's modernization program has brought about. You must reinvent yourselves by reclaiming the energy and passion for justice for the common man of the Prophet Mohammad. Shake off lethargic acceptance of oppression. Assume the mantle of true patriotism with muscular determination. Be a fearless warrior for Islam like Imam Ali and Imam Hussain.'"

Several hands rose as the professor ended the lecture. He shook his head and stepped down from the podium.

Ayan made his way to the front, eager to meet the man who had illuminated the thread connecting these Tehran University students and religious people like Hamid and his militant friends in the mosque.

He tried to organize the thoughts that were racing through his mind—ideas that the professor had triggered and that he wanted to discuss with him: the similarities between Gandhi's approach and Shariarti's, Nirad Chaudhuri's explanation that the Mahatma had harnessed the essence of the Indian soul, its mysticism and proclivity to asceticism and non-violence into a nationwide opposition to British rule, and wasn't that analogous to Shariarti's call to deploy Islam to force change in Iran?

A mob surrounded the professor. Gaby and her Iran Air pals stood to the side, talking animatedly. Ayan pushed forward till he was in the inner circle.

"Ah! The latecomer!" the professor said as Ayan put his hand forward and introduced himself. "Normally, I wouldn't have allowed you to enter, but it was too crowded to make a fuss tonight. You sound Indian. Who are you? What do you do in Iran?"

"He's a businessman, Professor Mehran, head of finance at Iran Power," Gaby said, joining them with a worried look on her face.

"I thought so. He looks like he's in the money-making game," the professor said. He turned towards Gaby's Iran Air friends who had also gathered around. "We treat foreigners so well and our own people so badly. All the big jobs are given to foreigners."

The Iran Air staff nodded their heads in agreement.

Gaby looked at Ayan nervously.

"Professor, no one in the Bazaar is talking about Shariarti," Ayan said, thrown off his game and suddenly feeling defensive. "They talk about Ayatollah Khomeini. They believe he is the Mahdi."

It was not what he'd wanted to say. But he felt forced to assert himself and challenge this arrogant man.

The professor raised his eyebrows.

"I didn't mention his name for the same reason I didn't take questions," he said. "And why I didn't discuss Shariarti's imprisonment, exile, and martyrdom: because SAVAK is here. But then, you obviously don't understand our country." He drew a long puff on his cigarette. The smoke blew out of his mouth, his nose, his entire head, it seemed. "I can try to enlighten you. I can tell you how cleverly the Ayatollah is taking on the mantle of our prophesied savior from Qom and also refuses to criticize Shariarti—instead incorporates his thoughts and language into his tapes and becomes the leader of these students as well as the Bazaar and the *ulama*. I can educate you, but I need to fill my stomach before I talk anymore. Are you coming to dinner?"

"No—he's not coming," Gaby interjected. "It's going to be a late night, and he has to get up early for work."

[handwritten: why would he be invited]

"Well, on then to Captain Bahman's house! Journalists and professors never say no to a free meal!"

"I'd like to come," Ayan said. "I can do without sleep, as you know."

When did Captain Bahman come back into the picture? Or had he never left?

The professor turned to Gaby with a smile. "Let him join us; we need somebody rich to pay for the taxi!"

"Reza here has a car, professor," Gaby said, directing Mehran towards her Iran Air coterie.

She took Ayan by the arm and pulled him aside. "Bahman just wants people he knows well, so everybody can speak freely. And you won't enjoy it anyway. The professor looks like he wants to make a game of you, and you'll create a scene—I know you!"

"Only because you introduced me as some dumb businessman!" Ayan said fiercely.

"What! You're crazy! I built you up! I don't need this! Ayan, I don't want to ruin Bahman's dinner with you arguing with the professor. I won't do that to him. I'll see you at home later."

She kissed him on the cheek and was off.

Leaving Ayan to go back alone, fuming, feeling humiliated.

[handwritten: Bahman pilot]

Gaby came back at 4 a.m.

No dinner lasts that long.

He was waiting with reprimands and accusations of infidelity.

She threw books and things and fists and kicks at him till she had exhausted her rage.

"We're good alone together but not in each other's worlds," she said when calm descended, almost at daybreak. "I hate that you make me go to boring office parties. I hate hearing business talk, and I know that you'll hate the people and things that have meaning for me."

"So don't go to any more of my company events. Give me a chance to live in your world. Don't shut me out like you did last night," Ayan said.

He held her in his arms until she fell asleep.

But the make-up trip to the Hyatt Regency on the Caspian coast the next weekend was a disaster. They made love just once—on the first night, when she was not really in the mood—and then she refused to let him come near her again.

It was as if she was trying to change their relationship, make it easier for her to live without him.

That's how he felt, he told her when they returned to Tehran.

"Then I should go now," she responded. "That's best."

She wanted to take a taxi to the airport. He insisted on driving her there. In the hours before she left, he helped with the mundane preparations for her departure, feeling more diminished and desolate with every step completed. In the end, as time ran out, there was nothing to do but let himself get caught up in her efficiency—and hurry: hurry to lock her suitcases, hurry to load the car, hurry to the airport, to check in her luggage, to wave goodbye.

They were so polite to each other that last day—so formal—it was devastating.

A month after she left, he received a letter from her apartment in Carmerstrasse 10, in West Berlin. He looked it up on the map. It was off Savignyplatz, in Charlottenberg, West Berlin.

She'd found a job, with a regional airline, starting in six weeks. She'd be flying mostly holiday charters to Spain,

East vs West Berlin

Greece, and Italy, but that was OK. It gave her time to resettle after all these years abroad. Spend time with her family. She'd bought a used BMW 2002, a really fast car, so Starnberger, Bavaria wasn't as far as it sounded. She actually looked forward to the trips back and forth despite the permits and checks required to transit via East Germany. West Berlin was exciting, she said, and that he would love it: People lived for the moment; art galleries were everywhere; cafes were full, and the clubs never closed. But the East Germans and the Soviets had made it impossible to use as a base to fly in and out of. She'd have to move to Munich but would never give up this Berlin apartment.

She signed off with words that surprised him. "My dearest Ayan, I am back home and taking care of what I have to. I am happier, not like the person I was in those last days in Tehran. You become what you spend your time doing. I wasn't doing what I wanted. Every day in that city was alienating me from myself. Can you understand that? I find myself thinking about you and missing you. More than you can imagine. Why haven't you written? Send me news. Your Gaby."

He didn't reply.

She had left him feeling empty, feeling worthless. Easy to toss aside.

He'd said all the things he had planned to say to her, pledged himself, and opened up in ways that had been terrifying; she had just kept on packing.

Then another letter from her arrived, with names of some new friends and a photograph from a holiday in Lisbon. "I've been waiting to hear from you. I am so disappointed," she wrote. "Do you have the right address for me? Remember to add c/o Andreas Faber—the apartment is in my father's name. The code is essential: 10623 West Berlin. With much love, Gaby."

He sat down and wrote to her after the second letter. But the drafts never felt right. There was too much anger in them. And hurt. The tone didn't match hers at all. Then too much time had passed, and there was no point in thinking about how he should respond.

What was the point of the lecture?

PART
THREE

CHAPTER 10

Nick + Football

"Nick, let's get this over with; where do you want to start?" Ayan said, starting down crowded Pahlavi Avenue and dodging weekend shoppers.

Nick was going back to Texas on vacation and wanted help selecting gifts. Darioush and Hassan had good excuses handy after they'd played their usual Saturday morning tennis match. Ayan hadn't, so here he was.

Ayan stopped and looked back when there was no response.

Nick was still in the taxi arguing with their driver, a big surly man who'd been muttering and scowling at them in the rearview mirror.

Finally, Nick slammed the door of the taxi and came up to Ayan.

"The bastard wanted to charge me twice the amount on the meter," he said.

"And?" Ayan said, following Nick towards a handicrafts store.

"I paid him what the meter said and gave him the finger!"

Not a good idea.

A few seconds later, Nick lay on the ground, his head bleeding from hitting the pavement. Their muscular taxi driver had abandoned his car in the middle of traffic and slammed into him.

Ayan recovered from his shock and pulled the driver off the dazed Nick.

The Iranian elbowed Ayan and began throwing punches at him.

It was lucky that his moves were wild and well-telegraphed. Ayan staggered from the force of his blows but was able to block them with his forearms.

He tried to get the crazed fool to calm down, but there was no reasoning with him, the punches kept coming.

Fuck this, Ayan thought, dodging an exaggerated roundhouse swing and catching him in the chin with an uppercut.

The taxi driver reeled.

This brought him face-to-face with a recovering Nick, who had picked himself off the ground.

The taxi driver shook his head and spat at Nick.

"Fuck you, asshole!" Nick yelled and hammered a right fist into the middle of his face.

The taxi driver sank to his knees.

Nick grabbed his hair, lifted his head, and punched him again.

The taxi driver was done for.

By this time, an angry mob had formed around them.

They began to shout, "*Marg bar Amrika!*"

Two men from the mob jumped into the fray.

Nick, bleeding but apparently ready for action, pushed Ayan behind him protectively. He sidestepped the first man, swept him off his feet, and then launched himself forward to deliver a brutal headbutt to the second man's jaw.

The first man was regaining his footing.

Nick pivoted, kicked him in the groin, and followed up with a left boot to his head.

Three Iranians now lay on the ground. They were not going to move any time soon.

The mob surged towards them

"Let's get out of here, Ayan! Now!" Nick said, grabbing him by the arm.

Half a dozen men gave chase as they sprinted north, towards the more cosmopolitan stretch of Pahlavi.

Nick stumbled, fell, rolled back onto his feet, and began to run again in one continuous movement.

The guy is a warrior and a gymnast, Ayan thought, slowing down till Nick caught up with him.

"Sorry, fucking astigmatism's gotten worse," Nick said after they had put some distance between them and their pursuers. "I've no depth perception without my glasses; they're gone."

"Yeah—I saw them come off as you fell."

"Expensive as hell to replace. Fucking asshole son-of-a-bitch cabby!"

"You're bleeding pretty badly," Ayan said.

Nick stopped and looked back.

The chase party had dwindled to a few young toughs. They pulled up and looked hesitantly at each other.

Nick put his head down and ran towards them with a madman's yell.

The Iranians bolted.

It was over.

Nick touched his forehead. "Let's go in here," he said. "I need some tissues."

They walked through the doors of a stylish café and entered a different world. It could have been a Saturday morning in Paris or London. As Nick cleaned up in the bathroom,

Ayan ordered cappuccinos and croissants and listened to the excited conversation of people enjoying a morning of leisure and acquisition.

"That was some impressive commando stuff," he said when Nick returned. "Where'd you learn to fight like that?"

"Vietnam," Nick said, waving away the coffee and croissant Ayan pushed in his direction. "Come on, man, let's get out of here. This bleeding is a son of a bitch! I have stuff at home that will stop it."

"I think you should go to the hospital and get that cut on your forehead stitched," Ayan said, keeping an eye on Jones, Nick's black-mouthed cur.

The dog had jumped up next to him on the sofa in Nick's basement and was looking at him belligerently.

"What are you, a fucking doctor?" Nick said. "I'm fine."

Who was this guy? Gone was the nervous, worried look, the persona everybody felt protective towards.

"Where did this rash, brash Nick Stasney come from?" Ayan said.

"This did the trick," Nick said, waving an empty bottle of Shiner Bock.

"Good beer," Ayan said. The Shiner had a rich, malty flavor. "Takes care of business."

"It's hard to find outside Texas. You'll have your fill of Shiner if you leave Shemiran once in a while and slum it with us in downtown Tehran. Good action here too. Plenty of hot Iranian women looking for rich foreigners like you. In fact, my wife, Shenaz, has a couple of friends you'd like. You should ask her about them. She's out visiting her parents but should be home soon."

"Not rich, not in the market, not interested."

Nick laughed his belly laugh, and for a moment, he was familiar Nick again.

"You're only saying that because you have Fariba. She has all the Karimi money you can spend, and more. I've been watching the two of you sneaking off together, real cozy after that mad bitch Gaby dumped you. Good riddance, by the way!"

"Wrong, wrong, and wrong," Ayan said.

"Right, right—I'm right. Particularly about Gaby. She cut your balls clean off, man! We were all worried about you. Stay the course with Fariba. She's for real."

She was. Fariba had saved him. They had tried to be discreet because of Hassan, but it was getting difficult pretending Fariba's constant presence around him was just innocent friendship.

"Things are going well between you, I hope?" Nick said.

"I'm not sure of what's ahead for the two of us—not sure of much really," Ayan said, taking a long swill of his beer.

"Listen, buddy. Be sure of one thing. Hassan knows Fariba's sleeping with you. And he's cool with it because he's assuming you two are going to get hitched. I think you're going to make it. Fariba and you are good together. Gaby was bad news, man. So stuck-up. I knew she'd fuck you up."

"Nick! Give it a rest!"

"I'm sorry. I shouldn't have said that. You still care for Gaby?"

After a long silence, Nick said, "I take it that's a yes; I can see it in your face. You masochistic bastard! So what you going to do now? You can't dump Fariba. You know that, right?"

He had no plans to dump Fariba. He was happy with her, but it was a day-to-day kind of thing. For a while, that last month with Gaby, he'd been ready to do anything, even get married, to keep her, but he'd regained his sanity. He was not going to think about settling down with anyone when everything about him was so unmade.

"You're bleeding again," Ayan said, changing the subject.

"Fuck that! I've washed the cuts with Dettol and put antiseptic cream everywhere," Nick said. He rose from his chair and moved towards his stereo. "Let's cheer things up!"

"Country music and Texas beer do wonders for a man!" Nick said as guitar licks and Waylon Jennings' baritone filled the room. "Won't help those poor bastards I leveled on Pahlavi, though."

He looked up at Ayan, and grinned.

"I think you may have killed that taxi driver," Ayan said.

"Nah! He'll wake up eventually, spend a few days in the hospital. Probably more than a few days. He's never going to look the same again, though, not after the number I did on his face: busted his jaw and nose, probably wrecked his smile for good. That'll teach him not to pick a fight with an American again!"

"You've had some kind of special training, haven't you?" Ayan said.

"The Draft, man. I told you. We all learnt to fight. You were not so bad yourself, Ayan. Who'd have thought you were such a scrappy bastard! Happy to have you in my foxhole anytime, pal."

"Same," Ayan said.

"Love you, man, but I still don't understand why all these beautiful women fall for you," Nick said. "I don't get it. You're not handsome. In fact, you're an ugly fuck, no offence."

"Nor am I charming. And you know I'm not rich," Ayan said, smiling. "Perhaps it's something else? Persistence? Perhaps they give in out of exhaustion with my begging?"

"Whatever. You've no business getting all these women."

"Fuck you too, Nick, you horse-faced bastard! But you can fight. I'll give you that."

"I work out in a boxing club near here, hike carrying my entire family's load—and they don't believe in travelling light, run with the Hash House Harriers—that sort of stuff. Stay fit is all. Comes in handy sometimes. Like today. And what's with you Indians and questions anyway? I was at the Karun River crossing last week and met this engineer from Bombay. Within five minutes, he wanted to know if I was married, how many children I had, how much rent I was paying, how much I had saved. I mean, fuck!"

"That'll be a good Indian," Ayan said, laughing. "I'm a good Indian, too, and very curious about what you were you doing in that part of the Karun River."

"Writing an article for a newspaper back home, trying to make a few extra bucks, nothing exciting," Nick said. He pulled his dog off the sofa and swatted it on the head as it growled in protest.

"Spot! Now!" Nick said firmly, sitting down next to Ayan, where his dog had been.

The dog retreated to a towel next to his water bowl and laid his head down, still keeping his eyes fixed on Ayan.

Nick smiled. "Don't look so scared, Ayan," he said. "Jonesy won't attack—not unless I give him the command. Just don't make any sudden moves, and you'll be all right."

"That's reassuring. So tell me, what really took you to the Karun River? There's a big power plant here. It's an energy center and not much else."

"Fuck off with your questions, man!" Nick said. "Enough! OK?"

"OK!" Ayan said. "No need to sound so defensive. I should be off anyway."

"No—stay," Nick said. "Want some popcorn? I just got this VCR—coolest thing; I have a tape of the Super Bowl. Let's watch the Dallas Cowboys thrash the Broncos."

"Does Shenaz ever get to see how you spend your life down here?" Ayan said as Nick returned with two plastic tubs of popcorn.

"She has her own space. Love Shenaz and everything, but down here is the US of A. I have a pantry, fridge, music, TV, office, bathroom . . . everything! Now watch!" He pointed to his TV. "See those big guys warming up? That's what I call athletes. See how light on their feet they are, despite their size? Iran's all excited about the soccer World Cup. They don't know what real sportsmen look like; their soccer team is full of thin, little softies whom these guys will chomp on as appetizers. Now here's the deal with the game you're about to watch."

Ayan's mind wandered as Nick went into great details about various strategies and the key offensive and defensive players in the Cowboys and Broncos lineup. It was hard to feign enthusiasm for an unfamiliar sport.

"This place looks nice," Ayan said, picking up a book with photographs of lakes, forests, and snow-capped mountains.

"That's Oregon, my home state," Nick said, keeping his eyes on the TV. "I was born in Eugene and grew up there."

"You're supposed to be from Texas," Ayan said.

"I moved to Houston after my wife divorced me. That's where I met Shenaz. Her father was with the Iranian Oil Company. He'd been transferred to Houston. The oil business was booming. I escaped from a real bitch and found the love of my life. So it worked out, I guess. But a big part of me is still in Oregon."

"Must have been hard to start over."

"I had to leave Eugene," Nick said.

He stopped watching the game and stared at the wall opposite.

"My wife was having an affair with my best friend. She got the house, took half of everything, and married that bastard!"

Ayan leaned back in the sofa, shook his head and said, "That is one sad story."

"The worst part was when my son called me six months later," Nick said. "He told me he wanted to change his name. He wanted to call himself Roberts, not Stasney, because he felt closer to his stepfather."

"I wouldn't be able to handle what you went through," Ayan said.

"I don't know how I got through that year," Nick said.

They both looked at the TV for a while.

The announcers were discussing a possession that gave the Cowboys a 13-0 lead.

"Think you can put on some rock?" Ayan said. "Love Waylon but need some lift. Bad Company? Seems that'll be appropriate."

Nick laughed. "I have Springsteen." *was it invented*

He jumped up and played air guitar.

"Drifters like us, Ayan, we were 'Born to Run,'" he sang, strutting towards his stereo.

Ayan laughed, drumming along on the coffee table.

"Drifters like us, we were surely 'Born to Run,'" he echoed.

"I left town to get by, to survive," Nick said after he'd refilled their tubs of popcorn and brought over more beer. "Heard there were plenty of jobs in Houston, so that's where I went. At first, it only made things worse: didn't know anybody; the place looked dry and awful; it was summer; the heat and humidity made me want to turn around and go right back to Oregon. But you know how these relocations play out:

you find work, you join a tennis club, you make a couple of friends, and you begin to live a little."

"Here's to tennis," Ayan said, raising a bottle of Shiner, "and friends."

"Amen to that," Nick replied, holding up his beer in acknowledgement. "I met Shenaz on our local tennis courts."

"Nice!"

"Show a red-blooded American male a woman with big breasts and slim hips, and everything will be all right," Nick said.

"I take it that Shenaz has big breasts and slim hips," Ayan said.

"You bet!"

They heard the crowd roar and turned to watch the screen. Roger Staubach had thrown a forty-five-yard pass to wide receiver Butch Johnson for a spectacular touchdown and a Cowboys lead of 20-3.

Johnson's diving catch matched anything Ayan had seen on the cricket pitch, or anywhere. Perhaps he could get into this sport.

"I think I'm going to become a Dallas Cowboys fan," he said.

"Fucking A!" Nick said. "Even if you'll only ever be a fair-weather supporter."

After Nick had replayed the touchdown a couple of times, he turned to Ayan and said, "You believe in the Lord?"

"The Lord?" Ayan said, surprised.

"I came back home to him in Houston. More than anything, my faith is what kept me going. Keeps me going."

"Really?" Ayan said. "I'm sorry, didn't mean it that way, but . . ."

"Gaby didn't try to convert you? She's Catholic, isn't she? Showed she wasn't serious about you. Shenaz converted."

"I'm not much for organized religion. Neither is Gaby. And please stop talking about her!"

"OK. Relax," Nick said. "You Hindus have a complex system—all those deities, all those arms!"

"Not that complex. Your personal moral code. The Bhagavad Gita. Not much else matters. At least not for me."

"Leaves room for ambiguity. Convenient," Nick said.

"We're not doing this now, are we? Comparing religions?"

"Don't have to—look, the Cowboys' lead has narrowed to 20-10; the Broncos think they've caught up, but the Cowboys are about to shut them down."

"Hey, Nick—on another topic, something's bothering me."

"Shoot," Nick said.

"I told you about the incident in the Bazaar a little while ago, when Hamid helped my mother escape from a riot? An Iranian and an American getting into a fight caused it. Kind of like today. I heard a mullah in the Bazaar whip up frenzy and talk about Khomeini. And I attended a lecture at Tehran University where a professor riled up students with that guy Shariati's Islamic path to revolution. A hundred people were shot at a protest in Qom last month. You're attacked in the middle of Pahlavi Avenue . . . what's going on?"

"Fifteen people died in the protests on January 9—not a hundred," Nick said. "An article said a few bad things about Khomeini, and that set people off. Perhaps the Shah's people planted it. He hates Khomeini's guts, and the feeling's mutual, but Khomeini's opinions don't really matter. The Shah's so in charge here, it's not even funny. Khomeini's sitting in Iraq and is watched 24/7; Ali Shariarti's dead. What does that tell you? Anyway, all this doesn't concern me, a poor man who's trying to get by on the pittance that *Time* and *Life* pay me to translate their stuff. And neither should it concern you."

"You're not a fucking translator, Nick. Definitely not just a translator."

"Keep being bloody-minded, and you'll find the trouble you're looking for," Nick said.

"You're supposed to be my friend. How can you be—if I know you're lying?"

Nick snapped his fingers.

His dog sprang at Ayan, snarling.

"What the fuck!" Ayan said.

"Down, boy!" Nick said, laughing.

The dog ignored him, baring his fangs.

"Down, I said!" Nick yelled, pulling the dog off Ayan and pointing to the towel on the floor.

The dog retreated, still growling.

"See what happens when you call me a liar? Annoy me?" Nick said. "And relax, it was meant as a prank. Jonesy and I were just messing with you. A different signal, a different tone, and he would have you by the throat."

"Fuck you, and fuck your uncivilized hound," Ayan said.

Nick laughed.

"Ayan, take it easy," he said. "Don't worry about a few protests and bullshit like today; things are under control in Iran. We got this."

"What does that mean?"

"Like I said. Leave the local politics to SAVAK. We do. Keeping track of Russia up north is more important."

"Why is a *Time* and *Life* translator sitting in Iran and keeping track of Russia?"

"What you don't know can't hurt you. Good motto to live by, you nosy bastard," Nick said.

"I had been wondering why it was so urgent that I come back early from work and join that game with you and the Soviet ambassador," Ayan said.

"Playing tennis with him was the best thing you could have done for Iran Power's business that day," Nick said. "I was doing you a favor."

"No, you weren't! But that's OK. It's kind of cool having a friend in the CIA. I've heard stories about Americans like you hanging around the Tollygunge Club in Calcutta during the Second World War, attending parties, trying to find out what was going on—keeping an eye on people like my grandfather."

"Why would anybody be keeping an eye on your grandfather?"

"He was helping your countrymen on the Eastern Front get supplies to Chiang Kai-shek: finding alternatives to the China Road destroyed by the Japanese, getting the trains across the Brahmaputra, being clever and dogged in the face of obstacles that stymied their British colleagues. And they returned the favor, pressured the Brits to make him the boss of the Indian railways."

You act like a sad sack, Ayan thought as he waited to see how Nick would respond, *but you know everybody in town, and probably everything, just like the Yanks in Calcutta.*

"Good story, but by 'we,' I meant the United States," Nick said casually. "Now let's watch the final plays again. You talked too much. Distracted me."

"OK—I can concentrate better now. I feel a lot safer now that you got this," Ayan said with a smile. "I'll forget that Iranians hate Americans for overthrowing Mossadegh and stealing their oil, the mullahs blame Kennedy for the cultural changes after the '63 White Revolution, and now the Shah and SAVAK are pissed off with Carter for his human rights lectures. Everything's fine."

Nick threw a punch towards Ayan.

"Wise guy. You're living large, aren't you? Stop talking to the crazies and grab another beer."

"You know America put the screws on Churchill when he dragged his feet on Indian independence. That America might eventually show up here. Force the Shah to be more democratic."

Nick pointed to the action being replayed on the screen. "Cheer for your new favorite football team."

The welfare of heathens and Muslims didn't naturally find a place in the hearts and minds of the West. Why should Nick pay much attention to the situation on the ground in Iran? Care about people like Hamid? Their suffering was just collateral damage of larger aims. He had no real answers anyway. He was just a cog in a shifting US strategy now obsessed with fencing in communism.

Ayan tried to picture the balding, nondescript man next to him making sorties across the Caspian into Russia, sending coded dispatches to Langley, meeting clandestinely with Iranian informers. It didn't seem so far-fetched.

Operation Odysseus had wrapped its tentacles around him immediately after the dinner at Nader's house. He had been pushed onto some secret track, running in a relay with faceless teammates, the baton in his grip, his boss spurring him forward with a stopwatch in his hand.

Should he worry about how open he should be with Nick?

Not yet. There was not much that he knew himself.

Nick
Balding

CHAPTER 11

London, United Kingdom, February 1978

R ain streaked across the window as the Pan Am 747 descended into Heathrow. The flagman guiding the jet to its parking stop fought to hold his ground in the whipping wind. It was a dreadful start to the European leg of Odysseus.

But it didn't matter to Ayan. He was back in his favorite city, and the real business for Nader was a week away, in Geneva.

The taxi slogged through heavy traffic on the approach to London, but the wildly racing meter held none of its normal menace. Nader was paying.

"Enjoy London," Nader had said.

He would.

"To the Stafford in St. James's, please," Ayan had said to the taxi driver, and he'd liked saying it.

The A4 into central London, usually so banal and depressing, felt comforting today—like an old friend. He missed London's sense of possibility. It had been so liberating to arrive in this city as a twenty-one-year-old with a college degree and not much else because everything imagined could be made real in exciting, cosmopolitan London.

Even the solitariness of life here suited him, Ayan thought, looking at the billboards as they crossed the Hammersmith flyover. He would make time in the week he had here for long walks alone and impromptu visits to galleries and museums. London made him want to do things like that. Its atmosphere nourished an interior life. *And romance,* Ayan thought with a smile, recollecting love affairs that had periodically swept him into another's world. It was that kind of place, a bracing hint of a chance ever-present, his natural habitat.

He indulged in some flirtatious banter with the pretty receptionist at the Stafford Hotel who escorted him to a small but elegant room. The bed looked inviting after his long journey. Ayan stretched out on the Irish linen sheets and goose feather duvet, luxuriating in the perfection of small details. A knock on the door awoke him an hour later. It was the maid arriving for the evening turndown service. Ayan ordered dinner and unpacked as she went about her business.

The meal was excellent. The 1970 Grand-Puy-Lacoste he'd ordered was better. He'd come a long way from student lodging and living on luncheon vouchers.

Ayan tried to sleep after dinner, but the extended nap had aggravated his jet lag.

What to do?

He drank some more.

And became disturbingly aware of the voice that had been tormenting him since the lecture in Tehran University. He shouldn't have listened to Shariati's tapes; he had enough commentary and scolding running on repeat in his head, his personal, incessant Greek chorus.

"Beware of this *Gharbzadeghi*! This *Euromania*! This *Westoxification*! . . ." Shariati's voice now admonished. "Think of your own Asian culture! Think of serious things!"

Ayan reached for the bottle of wine and thought of love instead, of the women who had changed his life here in London.

He closed his eyes and was twenty-one again: back in Regent's Park on a sunny July day, finding himself alone with Rekha Roy, wondering how to console the vivacious beauty from Calcutta whose heart had just been shattered by Ayan's friend and tennis partner, a flute-playing charmer.

"Look after her," the Charmer said to Ayan as Rekha ran towards the boathouse after slapping her betrayer a thousand times. "I didn't want her to be alone when I told her I'd decided to marry an old girlfriend from college. That's why I asked you along on this walk. I know Rekha likes you."

He had no idea what to do after the Charmer left to welcome his fiancée at Heathrow Airport. But he must have found a way to be distracting and amusing, because eventually Rekha had stopped crying and accepted his offer of a boat ride around the lake.

A few days and a movie and a play removed from that brief encounter in Regent's Park, they had returned there. It was cold, and Rekha had snuggled up against him when they sat on a bench under a weeping willow. He put his arms around her, and they had kissed and laughed, then kissed some more and stopped laughing. She'd come back to his room at International House and become more than a friend, become his girlfriend from the Dark Side of the Moon, forever associated with the heartbeats on that album.

He'd slept with a few women before, but the sex had been full of impatience. Rekha was the one who had made him take his time, taught him more about a woman's body, guided his hands and lips, and showed him what she desired. He smiled as he recalled how on one particularly adventurous occasion, she had poured wine on herself—who knew that cheap Mateus Rose wine could taste so good!

Where had a nice Indian girl learnt all this? Who cared! They made love everywhere for six months: in bed-and-breakfasts in Ross-on-Wye and Edinburgh, in Southampton and the Isle of Wight. They had such fun together.

Then Rekha went home on holiday and met a rich businessman. He found out she was married when her aunt in Calcutta answered the telephone and said Rekha was in Kashmir on her honeymoon.

Rekha hadn't even hinted about being ready for marriage. She'd been determined to get a PhD from the LSE. How could she have thrown that dream away for an arranged marriage to a stranger? And blithely erase what had happened between them?

He'd tried to rationalize her decision—that he was a student, inexperienced, and frankly, poor, not what she needed, not what any woman with half a brain needed.

It didn't help. Nor did the drunken call she made to him in the middle of the night weeks later, saying she was sorry, there'd been pressure from her family.

The pain lasted for months.

He got up and began to unpack. It was still pouring outside. He would have to buy a raincoat tomorrow.

An hour later, he'd called friends and filled up his week with lunches and dinners.

He flicked through his address book, stopping always at Jackie's phone number.

Jackie

Was it even safe to think about his mad love for the woman who, like Rekha, entered his life as a friend?

How excited he'd been whenever Jackie came by to see his French roommate! She was lucky Bertrand's girlfriend, a foreign correspondent with a first from Cambridge. How could anyone resist her perfect features that required no makeup and that hip-swaying walk which made him want to give up whatever he was doing and chase after her?

He'd tried to remain calm the times she paid attention to him, summoning all his intelligence as she articulated her thoughts in elegant sentences and paragraphs brimming with opinions and indignation and wit. Her silver bracelets, tight jeans, and knee-length boots were Kings Road, but she delighted in kneecapping idiots with scathing irony.

Jackie started an affair with him the night a group of them went ice-skating to get into the Christmas spirit. She'd dumped Bertrand and was now with Owen Ashton, a strutting, landed Welshman surely destined for a political career. It was Ayan's first time on the ice, he remembered, and Jackie, who had come without Owen, guided him around the rink a few times. She'd slipped her hand into his in the bar afterwards, jokingly telling their group that her hold was the only thing between an upright Ayan on ice skates and disaster.

He'd kept his grip loose, not reading too much into her friendly gesture. But Jackie kept her fingers intertwined in his, and her continued touch became impossibly arousing; more so when she returned after a few expertly executed rounds of the rink and put her hand back in his.

She'd held onto him on the way home, holding on tight as the crowded tube banked and swerved.

He had to kiss her then.

The first time on her forehead: a test.

She had looked up at him and smiled.

So he braved a kiss on her lips. She kissed him back.

He kissed her all the way home.

But she had refused to go up to his room when they returned.

"I like you, Ayan, but I don't like you that much!" she'd said, smiling and going off to her room on the women's floor.

Or perhaps, to Owen's room.

Which had been OK. He'd been lucky she'd flirted with him.

Perhaps she would sleep with him, too, someday.

It was all good; it was the times.

Ayan poured himself another glass of wine. He would regret it in the morning, but he needed to keep this mood going; it was bringing back those exhilarating days when Jackie ratcheted up the sexual tension between them.

They saw each other often: in the International Students House dining room, the library, and the pub. He learnt to let Jackie come over and say hello; she was perennially on a deadline for some assignment and could be testy when disturbed. Eventually, she trusted him enough to come up to his room. She never brought up her relationship with Owen. Neither did he. Mostly they talked, and there was so much to discuss: the fall of Saigon, the Khmer Rouge genocide in Cambodia, the Watergate convictions and sentences, and the IRA attacks in London. It was a momentous year. Jackie published a couple of articles on the Emergency Indira Gandhi had imposed in India and another on the flickering revival of the Naxalite movement. He thought he read some of his ideas in them. When the conversation petered out, they listened to James Brown and Joan Baez and drank whatever was around. Sometimes, he kissed her, and if the lyrics and the alcohol and something else combined in the right proportions, she kissed him back. And sometimes, she let him take off her bra and kiss her breasts.

Really.

But that was where she had always drawn the line, pushing gently but firmly away.

She would say, "That's not who I am."

He was prepared to wait, just go with the flow.

Then, on that New Year's Eve, Jackie called him from the Cotswolds, where she was spending Christmas with her family, and asked him what his plans were.

She had come up and stayed with him, because her room had been let out for the holidays. When "Auld Lang Syne" had been sung, and several glasses of champagne had been downed in the ISH discotheque, they had gone back up to his room. She had undressed slowly, standing by his sink for a long time, washing her face and taking off her jewelry, looking at herself in the mirror and at him. Then she slipped under the covers and turned into him, pressing her body against his.

He'd kissed every inch of her, Ayan remembered, lingered over her beauty, and hesitatingly guided her nervous hand to his thighs, expecting her to stop him. But she gripped him and moaned, and then he was inside her, and he could hardly believe her exquisiteness.

She had been asleep on top of him when he woke.

Their parting had been full of tenderness, but after that, whenever he saw Jackie, she was always with Owen and averted her eyes.

He waited and hoped that she would come to see him again.

But she didn't.

Bewildered and distraught, he'd knocked on her door.

She hadn't let him in. "Owen has found out about us," she said.

"So what? I don't care," he replied.

"I do. He's furious and jealous, and he'll kill me if he sees me talking to you."

"The hell with Owen!"

"Ayan, I'm probably going to marry him."

"You're not going to marry him. You can't! What about us?"

"Us? That night—I shouldn't have . . . It was a mistake."

"No, it wasn't! I'm mad about you."

"Ayan, I'm confused. I need to be left alone. Please! Give me time to think."

Owen had arrived as he was desperately making his case. There had been yelling and a few blows. Doors around them had opened. Then an embarrassed and furious Jackie had come between them, pulled Owen into her room, and told Ayan to leave.

The Welshman had come to his room a few hours later, apologized for hitting him, and asked Ayan for his word— "gentleman to gentleman"—that he would stay away from Jackie, his love and bride-to-be.

Ayan had found himself meeting Owen's extended hand.

Soon after, Ayan's world was upended again. He got the "good news and bad news" phone call from Hadley Jones personnel: He was one of the few recent graduates the firm had decided to keep on, amidst the layoffs forced by the great recession—that was the good news. He was being transferred to Iran, the only place they were still expanding and had a vacancy—that was the bad news.

Soon after, he was on a plane to Tehran.

He'd stayed away from Jackie and thrown himself into preparations for Iran.

It was a sort of chivalrous act, he'd told himself. But time and reflection had revealed it for what it was—a disgraceful surrender.

Why hadn't he been more forceful about getting what he wanted? Why hadn't he thrown everything into keeping Jackie like Owen had done? Why had he shaken Owen's hand?

Why, dammit, why?

He turned the pages of his London address book. There it was again. Jackie's address and phone number. What did he have to lose?

Jackie picked up after the first ring.

"Hello, Jackie," he said, his pulse racing. "It's been a long time. How are you?"

"Oh! It's you . . ." she said. Then, after a pause, "Hello, Ayan. Yes, it has been a long time. Are you back in London?"

"Just for a short visit."

"Are you still living in Iran?"

"Yes—how did you know I was there?"

"You left a note for me. You told me you were going. Remember?"

"Did I? My departure from London was such madness."

"Well, I got it. How are things under the King of Kings?"

"I'll tell you over a drink."

"Ayan, no! There's no point. Owen and I are getting married this June."

"Please—just to talk? I've become quite interesting."

Jackie laughed. "How so?"

"I live in Tehran; I've had adventures."

"Ayan, it's late, and I have to get this story out tonight. It was lovely hearing your voice. I hope you have a wonderful time in London."

"Wait! You're a journalist, aren't you? Still freelancing it?"

"Yes. Nothing's changed."

"Then you must do your job and interview me about my experiences in a faraway, dangerous place. I'll give you material for an article that will make you famous: *Time Magazine* will come chasing after you."

"Tehran's a comfortable, rich place—as far from danger as parts of London are. If you were living in Beirut, that would be a different matter."

"You're wrong! Tehran is simmering! Protestors are taking to the streets; the University is aflame with Shariarti's revolutionary rhetoric; the Bazaar in an uproar because of Khomeini's tapes."

"Fibber."

"It's true!"

He talked fast, about the incidents, the lecture in Tehran University, Hamid's group in the mosque, the assault on Pahlavi Avenue.

She didn't hang up.

"Tell me more about this man, Hamid," she said and finally agreed to meet him the next evening for a drink at her neighborhood pub in St. John's Wood. Owen would kill her if he knew she was meeting him. He mustn't. Ever. And this number was out of bounds for Ayan. Owen usually spent the nights at her place and often answered the phone.

He arrived in St. John's Wood early, with enough time to buy some newspapers from a corner shop to inform his conversation with Jackie and settle into a quiet table at the Duke of York, which was right off the High Street.

He would be confident and charming when he saw her, he decided.

But he failed.

He stood up quickly, almost upending his pint of beer when Jackie arrived, all silver bangles and Rive Gauche, her presence still shockingly familiar after so long.

Her beautiful face was pale from the London winter. He was tanned from the bright Tehran sunshine and skiing in the Alborz. The contrast as their hands met in greeting was startling.

"Hello, Ayan," Jackie said, kissing him lightly on both cheeks. "Tehran seems to be suiting you." She ruffled his sideburns with the palm of a hand, still cold from the London chill, and ran her fingertips over the shoulder of his black velvet jacket. "You look trendy, quite the man."

"And you look—amazing! As always," Ayan said, drowning out the voice telling him not to read too much into this familiarity. Jackie was always touching people.

But she was really happy to see him. He could see it in her eyes.

He took her coat and scarf, laid them over a spare seat back, and pulled out a chair for her, not sure of what he was going to say, still not sure what this meeting was about despite thinking about it all day.

Jackie placed her large, stuffed handbag on the floor next to her and turned to face him as she sat down.

"So! Tell me about the awful Shah, SAVAK, the mullahs . . . What's going to happen?"

Her breezy manner and cheerful expression suggested a direction out of the awkwardness, a repositioning of their relationship towards friendship.

He took it.

"Have a drink first. Relax a bit. What can I get you?"

Jackie sighed deeply. "I'll have a Glenmorangie with a dash of water, please," she said, lighting up a cigarette.

"That's new," Ayan said. "When did you start?"

Jackie looked at her cigarette.

"What, this?" she said. "Ages ago."

Ayan brought over her scotch and settled down in his seat. "Foreign correspondent, war zones—booze and cigarettes go with the territory, I suppose," he said.

Jackie smiled. "I have to be careful. Some of the places I go, men see an English girl smoke and drink, and they get ideas. They think she's probably—you know—available."

"That's understandable. Men hoping you're available."

Jackie stared at Ayan with eyebrows raised.

"Well, they mustn't!" she said. "And stop looking at me like that, Ayan! I'm absolutely not!"

They laughed together. Then there was a silence.

They looked at their drinks.

"I'm so happy to be back in London, even if it's only for a week," Ayan offered.

"Why? Things are awful here," Jackie said. "No jobs. Inflation. You're lucky to be in Iran, making pots of money inside OPEC instead of being on the receiving end of Arab extortion."

"There is that silver lining; at least, I've avoided the fate of a friend: a Rugby and Cambridge man who's been forced into the retail trade on Jermyn Street. I bought an extra pair of ridiculously expensive shoes from him this morning out of guilt."

His arms had felt heavy carrying indulgences from a couple of hours of spending freely on luxuries: Dunhill and Montblanc cufflinks, a Bally briefcase, a dozen cotton shirts with French cuffs from Turnbull & Asser, a pair of suede shoes from Firouz Akhbari's favorite, John Lobb, a couple of monk straps from Foster & Son.

Peter Compton, a former colleague from Hadley Jones in London, had been his unlikely salesman in the shoe store. "The recession you know—there's good money in this business," Peter explained, obviously embarrassed. "I'm helping the family position itself for the future; everybody chips in with customers; we have an exclusive client list, you know, royals and all that." It was sad.

"Financier in Tehran does sound a whole lot better than a shoe salesman on Jermyn Street," Jackie said.

"I suppose so. But that shoe salesman can pop into the RA after work and see the Miro exhibition, or visit the Courtauld, go to the theater—do things like that as often as he likes."

"Tehran must have culture too."

"We have some ballet and classical music in the Roudaki Hall—courtesy of Empress Farah Diba—so if you're craving the arts and want to make the effort, there's that. But it's episodic—not part of the fabric of normal existence like it is here, at least not for foreigners. I have more of a sporting life: tennis, hiking, skiing in winter, trips to the Caspian shore in summer."

"Now you're bragging . . ."

Ayan laughed. "I enjoy all that but miss the mood I have in London, the inclination for the intellectual life. I fall into a different mindset in Tehran. Do you know what I mean?"

"Yes. I'm sure I'd hate Tehran. I certainly wouldn't get on with the Persians. They act like awful philistines when they're over here."

"Actually, the people are the best part of being in Iran. This *taarof* of theirs—endless courtesies and deceptions, telling people what they want to hear, playing games and not being straightforward—takes some getting used to, but I've become very close to a few Persians. I love their hospitality, their warmth. It's just that I know another culture, another way of life that's better for me."

He smiled and took a long sip of his lager.

"Lord Macaulay succeeded terribly well in your case."

"Come on!"

"Why deny the obvious? Macaulay's education system produced an English sensibility thousands of miles away, and well done, sir, I say! I love travelling, but I'm always relieved to be back in England."

"I wouldn't mention Macaulay around Indians now."

"I can see that his influence is fading. Sorry if I'm being rude, but these days, your countrymen in London are just as annoying as the Persians and Arabs. Particularly the younger ones who are awfully aggressive."

"Jackie, the brown man has submitted to you Brits for long enough; an over-correction is part of adjusting to a new equilibrium. It's a different India now, more muscular. Get used to it."

Jackie looked skeptical as he went on about the evolution of this modern Indian.

"We're now more inspired by the ideas of America than of Britain. Sorry."

He paused and smiled.

"How dreadful that sounds!" she said. "Your loss. Wrong direction."

This conservative side of Jackie must be that bastard Owen's influence. He was always telling off foreign students in International House, bristling with British upper-class condescension as he picked on the French, the Africans, the Asians.

Jackie had changed; where was the idealistic liberal he'd fallen for?

Ayan didn't get a chance to challenge Jackie's views again.

An Englishman, who had been sitting quietly with his friend and downing pints of lager on the next table, suddenly barked, "Fucking wogs! Go home!"

Ayan tensed and turned.

The Englishman was directing his taunts at a group of Indians standing by the bar.

The Indians looked and sounded like they were from East Africa—probably Ugandans expelled by Idi Amin.

Ayan let's radicalize

Ayan felt a rush of outrage.

"No! Ayan, he's a stupid drunk!" Jackie said as he stood up. "He's not bothering you." She placed a hand on his arm and made him sit down again.

Then the drunken man yelled again at the group of Indians.

They averted their eyes and crouched around their drinks, grinning sheepishly.

"Go on then, get out! Fuck off!" he said, waving dismissively towards the door.

If he touches any one of them, I'm going for him, Ayan decided.

Jackie strengthened her grip on Ayan's arm.

The second Englishman trained his eyes on Ayan. "You're right, Henry. Here's another one. We've got too many damn wogs stinking up the place. Filthy bastards."

Ayan got up and said, "You fucking sons of bitches, shut your mouths, or I'll shut them for you!"

"Ayan! Ignore these drunken swine," Jackie said, also standing up.

The single waitress covering their area was in the kitchen. The bartender seemed overwhelmed by punters trying to get his attention. No one else seemed to notice them or care. It was just another altercation in a London pub.

Ayan sensed the louts evaluating him, calibrating their chances if they attacked.

They had no chance. He was in the best shape of his life. It would be no contest if these reedy drunks came at him.

The Englishman who had abused Ayan reached the same conclusion.

He put a hand on his companion's shoulder and said, "Come on, mate, let's get out of this shithole."

The two men shuffled off.

A couple of the Indians in the group nodded at Ayan. One of them gave him a thumbs-up.

Ayan looked around the pub, surreally detached from the scene, still in fight mode.

"Ayan, I'm so sorry," Jackie said, taking his arm. "Come on, let's go somewhere else."

He helped Jackie with her overcoat and told himself to calm down. There were assholes everywhere. Ignore what they said to you. Any country he chose to live in, including this one, was lucky to have him. He had more education and talent than most, and soon, he would have enough money to insulate himself from scum like these men.

"How about Richoux? We can get a coffee there," Jackie suggested.

"Come to the Stafford instead. It's quieter, much nicer," Ayan said. "The American Bar has nice cocktails."

Jackie looked at her watch. "Owen is working late tonight. I've got a couple of hours. Why not?"

They got into a taxi and made their way down Baker Street.

She sat close to him. The situation in the pub had breached the slightly formal remove she'd maintained.

Stimulated by residual adrenaline, Ayan asked the question he had been waiting two years to ask.

"Jackie, what did I do wrong? We were having such a wonderful time; I was so in love with you, and then the curtain came down."

"Ayan! Please don't ruin things," Jackie said, shifting away.

"I missed you terribly."

"Stop it! I knew you were going to ambush me. I should never have come."

She turned her face away and looked out of the window of the taxi.

They were stuck on Baker Street. The traffic was now at a standstill, and the weather was turning foul. Umbrellas had come out. A woman pulled her scarf snug as she walked by, shoulders drawn in against the blustery chill.

Jackie could easily get out of the taxi and leave.

It looked like she might.

He should have waited till later in the evening, when they both had more alcohol in them. If she left now, he would never see her again.

"OK, forget it," he said. "That's history. I won't bring it up again—I promise!"

She didn't reply and kept staring out of the taxi window, avoiding his eyes.

He willed the traffic gridlock to ease, so she couldn't jump out and just walk away.

"I'm sorry," he said.

The taxi started moving again.

"You should be," she said finally, "coming up with stories about Iran just to trap me."

"What I said about Iran is true. You'll see—you'll be happy that you came to see me after I've told you what's been happening."

He felt her turn to look at him.

"Ayan, you know what happened between us was lovely and beautiful. You must know that! I will never forget it. But we made our decisions. Let's move on."

"You're right," he said slowly, and to his surprise, he believed it.

He had moved on. Jackie was a different person now. So was he.

He had felt a greater love for somebody else.

Now was the time to build a bridge to something less personal, follow Jackie's lead, and move to a terrain where they could meet in the future.

"You're right," he said again. "Let's move on."

"Owen proposed the next day," she volunteered after a silence. "He found out that I was with you on New Year's Eve. His friend Jason saw us and told him that we had spent the night together. Owen was waiting for me when I got back home the next afternoon. He had driven several hours from Wales and made an awful scene. And then he got on his knees, in front of my parents, and said that he would not leave until I agreed to marry him."

"Lady Ashton sounds nice," Ayan said. "A beautiful manor, a large estate, a man who will be a lord or marquis someday. Who could say no?"

"It's not like that! Owen was very insistent, and I was— am—in love with him. And I'm keeping my name. We've agreed that it'll be Ashton Smith."

"That has a nice ring to it. And I understand," Ayan said. "He's a good catch. Far better prospects than me."

"Ayan—don't! I was very taken with you, otherwise I never would have . . ." She looked down, and for a second, it looked she might cry. "I had to make a choice, and Owen persuaded me that he loved me more than you ever could." Then her chin was up, and she said, "Anyway, enough of the past. I'm very happy with Owen. And you, Ayan? Do you have someone? I'm sure you do, and I'm sure she's wonderful!"

"Yes, I have a girlfriend," he said.

"Who is she?"

"Fariba. She works in the programming department of Roudaki Hall, the concert venue I mentioned."

"Do you love her?"

"Perhaps. Yes, probably."

"We are in the company of irritating ambivalence."

"Excuse me?"

"It's not an attractive quality, Ayan; women pick up on it, and it makes us nervous."

"Somebody else said that to me; she used a word starting with 'f' before ambivalence."

"Yes. You're still fucking ambivalent! I'm sure Fariba's very clever and beautiful and has choices. You better get off the fence."

The fence was not unappealing. He was between *ashramas*, but Gaby had dismissed his talk about Hindu stages of life. Jackie would be at least as scornful.

And she would be justified.

Let's face it. He was just drifting—and fucking ambivalent. He would just have to hide it better.

Looking out of the rain-streaked window of the taxi and considering his situation, it all became very clear. He was never going to be ready to get off the fence with Fariba. It was not her he'd felt the greater love for.

He was still in love with Gaby. And always would be.

He would have to break it off with Fariba. Stop wasting her time. He was never going to marry her.

How would he even bring it up? She would be devastated. And he would be alone again.

He felt sad for her, and suddenly very lonely.

"OK, it's my turn to request a change of subject," he said.

"Of course! I'm sorry. I have no right to lecture you."

"We'll be arriving soon. They make a great cocktail at the Stafford. It's called 'French 75,' after the field gun. The French Resistance used to hang out at the American Bar in the Stafford. The bartenders have to be French; it's tradition. It's also filled with all sorts of American stuff that guests have gifted to the place. It's a little crowded, but I think you'll like it."

"Surrounded by bloody Frenchmen and ugly American things—sounds wonderful!" Jackie laughed.

The greeter at the American Bar tried to seat them in the first alcove.

"Too many ridiculous model airplanes hanging down from the ceiling," Jackie said, sweeping past the man and walking towards the back of the main room.

"This will do," she said, pulling Ayan down by her side as she settled on a couch to the right of the bar, facing a bank of equestrian paintings.

Against the wall and at right angles to them, below a display of autographed photographs of Aston Martin racing, and of pilots and sporting heroes, a well-dressed young Englishman with an Oxbridge accent stared into the eyes of a sexy Scandinavian girl. There was no chance either of them would pay the slightest attention to Ayan and Jackie. All the other tables around them were unoccupied. Excellent!

"I'll have a vodka martini. Dry, dirty, very cold," Jackie told the protesting waiter who was pointing to the reserved sign on the table. "And you, Ayan?" she said, picking up the reserved sign and handing it to the waiter. "You're not going to have the dreadful French 75 or whatever it's called, are you?"

"A Manhattan, please," Ayan said.

"Bring us some hors d'oeuvres too," Jackie said, waving off the defeated man. "And quickly, please. We're in a bit of a hurry."

She extracted a weathered black leather folder from her handbag, maneuvered her hair into an untidy bun, and said, "I've been thinking about an interesting connection: the unrest in Iran you mentioned and the German urban guerillas. I've just written about the Red Army Faction, and the magazine that's commissioned me wants more."

"You've written about the RAF? Really?"

"Terrorism is pretty much a front-and-center issue in Europe."

"I know that. It's just a friend of mine is very involved with what's going on in Germany. She's a supporter of Baader-Meinhof."

"She has a lot of company in Germany if she is on RAF's side—I'm assuming she's German?"

"Yes."

Jackie pulled out a newspaper from her oversized handbag. "Take a look at this headline," she said, pointing to the bottom left of the front page.

"RAF member Christiane Kuby arrested following a shoot-out. 'Commando Benno Ohnesorg' bombs Supreme Court in Bern, promises further attacks if 2JM members extradited."

"Benno Ohnesorg was killed in 1967, on the second of June," Jackie said. "Hence, 2JM—it's a movement inspired by his story. Ohnesorg was twenty-six years old, a student with a pregnant wife, who was shot in the back of the head when he joined the protest against the visit of the Shah and the Empress Farah to West Berlin."

Jackie paused, looking at Ayan. "That's the random, or maybe not so random coincidence I may want to do a piece on: The Shah comes to Germany and the protests against him—protests you say are picking up steam in Tehran—give birth to the 2 June Movement and, by extension, Baader-Meinhof. Here, read this."

Jackie pointed to an underlined paragraph in the newspaper that read: "The image of a young woman cradling the fatally wounded Benno is thought to have forever separated young Germans from the generation of Auschwitz. Almost 20 percent of Germans under thirty supported the Baader-Meinhof Group and 2JM. There were thousands of Commando Benno Ohnesborgs now, ready to die for their armed struggle against the reactionary forces of establishment Europe."

"My friend, Gaby, is part of this 20 percent," Ayan said. "I wouldn't take the other side of any fight she's in."

"It's dangerous for her. I interviewed some RAF commandos. It's a tough life, darting from safe house to safe house at night, throwing bombs and dodging bullets in the day."

"I don't think she's in the trenches. She was an Iran Air pilot and still has a job flying planes in Germany, as far as I know."

"You don't have to be a gunman. Baader-Meinhof needs an infrastructure: logistics, cover, training camps in Jordan. She could be doing any number of things. She sounds fascinating. I'd have loved to interview her. Schmidt and his cronies are cracking down on the terrorists in Germany. But they are fighting a movement, an awakening against residual fascism, and that's what I focused my report on. If there's enough in the Iranian resistance to the fascist Shah, that could be an interesting companion piece—a bookend to that 1967 visit."

"There is plenty of unrest in Iran for you to report on, Jackie," Ayan said. "Farms destroyed by wheat from America, rice from India, beef from Argentina, eggs from Rumania; urban migrants, young men mostly, living with their families in poverty, suffocated by inflation, resentful of the easy lives of foreigners and the Iranian elite; reactionary fundamentalists in the Bazaar, convinced that the country is going in the wrong direction under an infidel Shah. And to add some urgency to it all—the mullahs have found a rallying point with the death of Ayatollah Khomeini's son and are inciting large numbers to protest. Hamid, my driver, was part of one earlier this year—on January 9th—against what he called 'the shameful lies' the Shah published in the newspaper. Hundreds, perhaps thousands, were killed during the protest, Hamid said, but it was worth it, because people lost their fear of the army and SAVAK on that day."

ARBaeen

They talked about the situation for the next half hour or so. Jackie took notes and asked for names of potential sources. Then she said she really had to leave.

"I think we have to watch this forty-day mourning cycle, the *Arbaeen*," Jackie said as Ayan asked for the bill. "I'll think about the two themes, the bookends. I can see my article—'the Shah's arrival in Germany leading circu-itously to the German Autumn, just as his troubles crash onto his shores on waves of *Arbaeen*, change riding in on ever more powerful surges of mourning every forty days after demonstrators are gunned down.' I'll try to sell that—get a commission and come to Iran to do some research. You'll help me set up interviews?"

"Yes, of course. When do you think you'll make it over?"

"Not too soon, I'm afraid. But I'm working on a piece about Sadat and Begin and will be back in Egypt and Israel at some point. I could add Tehran to the trip. Let's see. It will be a tough sell. Nobody here believes the Shah's in any trouble. He's made Iran into a modern, rich nation, knocking on the doors of first-world status. But here's my work number. We'll stay in touch."

Really

"Yes, I want to. Very much."

"We're going to be great friends, Ayan, aren't we?" Jackie said, hooking her arm in his as they walked out towards a waiting taxi.

"Yes! Don't let Owen cut me out of your life again."

"Just give him time. He'll be fine with you once we're married. He's really awfully sweet; you'll see."

She kissed him lightly on the lips and got into the taxi.

"Stay madly in love with me, Ayan—always!" she said breezily, rolling down the window. "And don't give up on

Gaby as easily as you did me. I can see that she's not a friend but something much more. I'm almost jealous!"

The taxi pulled away. Jackie turned to wave at him through the rear window, till she was out of sight.

Ayan was nervous and inarticulate when Gaby answered the telephone.

She was surprised and distant.

If work brought him to West Berlin, where she was probably going to be—she'd have to check—it would be nice to see him, was her non-committal response.

He shouldn't have expected more but did and felt the echo of a barely forgotten disappointment.

He fought it with a new resolve.

The impulses that had compelled him to pick up the telephone and call Jackie were really the embers from another, more incandescent flame.

He was going to West Berlin.

CHAPTER 12

"**M**r. de Groot is expecting you," the receptionist at the entrance to the Royal Automobile Club said. He pointed Ayan towards a flight of stairs. "He's in the cocktail bar, one floor up, to the left."

A man sitting in a booth stood up to greet him as Ayan walked into an intimate room fronting Pall Mall.

"Hello, Ayan, I'm Chip," the man said, extending his arm. "I recognize you from the photograph Nader sent over. Do sit down."

The freckle-faced man in his forties, with curly red hair and a gap-toothed smile, was very different from the sinister character Ayan had visualized.

"What can I get you?" Chip said. "Gin's the specialty here."

"A Tanqueray and tonic," Ayan said to the waiter who was standing by.

"Some olives and nuts too," Chip added.

He turned to Ayan with an intrusive look.

"Nader tells me you're a good tennis player," Chip said. "How long are you here for?"

"Another couple of days."

"Do you want to play? I can get us a court at Hurlingham."

"That could be fun," Ayan said. "You play often?"

"Not really—squash is my game—but I can give most tennis players a run for their money."

"How about I take you on in squash instead?" Ayan said.

He got in enough tennis in Tehran, good tennis. Squash at the RAC, walking distance from the Stafford, was a much more efficient use of his time in London.

"Fine. I have to warn you though—I'm an Oxford Blue."

"I'll try to give you some exercise," Ayan said, "together with the joy of inevitable victory." He would be the one getting the exercise, he knew. Good squash players positioned themselves strategically. He would have to run around like a frantic border collie, which was exactly what he needed after all the lunches and dinners with friends in London.

"First thing tomorrow?" Chip said. "7:00 a.m.? I have a full day."

"Yes. You're on," Ayan said.

He would have to be careful, or he wouldn't have many secrets left after a night out with Chip followed by morning squash and breakfast at the RAC. This character knew what he was doing.

Well, two could play the game.

"Is London home now?" Ayan asked. "Or South Africa?"

"I live on aircrafts—the sky is my home."

"That's got to be difficult."

"You get used to it. I belong to clubs in the major stops, use reciprocal clubs in other places. Always find a decent spot to rest my head and get in some exercise."

"You do spend a lot of time in Switzerland, though . . ."

"Yes."

"We could have met in Geneva."

"London was more convenient for me this time."

"Your company, Alpine Global, is not a name I've come across before," Ayan said, taking a sip of his cocktail that had just the right amount of Tanqueray and tonic from a freshly opened bottle. "You haven't done business with us recently, right?"

"Not since I took over. My father was a purchasing agent for Iran Power years ago, when the factory was first set up. I've been concentrating on petrochemicals and defense. Can't spread yourself too thin if you want to deliver the service our clients expect."

"How did you connect with Nader?"

"He's been a star in the energy business for some time. We make it a point to know people like him. You've hitched your wagon to the right guy. Now how about some business before dinner?"

Chip took out an index card and handed it to Ayan.

"This gives you wiring instructions for two accounts," he said. "It has swift codes and account numbers. When you have Iran Power's Banque du Rhone account open, wire 15 percent to the first account and 85 percent to the second account. Same procedure on every payment after that."

Ayan scanned the room. The bar was full, but their booth gave them adequate privacy. He examined the index card. Somebody picking it up would just see a series of letters and figures. Nader had told him to follow Chip's instructions. But he couldn't possibly transfer millions, probably hundreds of millions of dollars, to numbers scribbled on an index card.

"Do you have something on Alpine Global's letterhead?" he said. "I'll need that as well as corporate documents verifying that both accounts are official transaction accounts. I'll also need invoices from your company before I can move any cash."

Chip sat back and smiled.

"I've done billions of dollars of business in Iran. Nader can confirm the accounts are legitimate. I like to keep paperwork to a minimum in situations like these, for obvious reasons. Luc Bossard, your company's banker in Geneva, will store all the documents, including our invoices. Swiss secrecy laws will protect them."

"I don't know if that arrangement works," Ayan said. "I doubt it. I'll call Nader and talk it over with him, but you should expect to send bills and receipts directly to me in Tehran."

"You do that—go ahead and call Nader," Chip said. "Come on then, time for dinner. I've booked us a table next door in Brooklands at eight, but we can get in earlier, have a quick bite, and head off to Annabel's—look at some beautiful women, maybe get lucky. What do you say?"

"How did you get into this situation?" Chip asked after they'd ordered.

"What do you mean?" Ayan said.

"You're obviously unfamiliar with this type of transaction."

"Well, there's nothing normal about what we are trying to do."

"On the contrary, it's pretty standard. Just another deal, only this one is bigger than usual."

"Do you specialize in this kind of procurement then? Arms?"

"We cover the spectrum: technical know-how, manpower, international JVs."

"You must have a big team."

"No, just a few people. That's our advantage. Senior people do everything. We focus on situations where access to people who are very difficult to reach is required and where speed and confidentiality are essential."

"A price insensitive segment," Ayan said. "Good strategy."

"If cost is an issue, it's the wrong deal for us," Chip said. "It's easy to get onto our blacklist, and trying to negotiate our commission is the fastest way."

He looked at Ayan.

"Getting your knickers in a twist about bureaucracy and paperwork is a close second. We don't deal with bean counters. Not normally. Perhaps I'll make an exception for you."

"Start over," Ayan said. He was representing a big customer, wasn't he? "Perhaps try to be reasonable. Our auditors will want original invoices, approved by the right people, in our files in Tehran. I can't move the kind of money we're talking about without evidence of value provided and authorization."

He took another lingering sip of the 1961 Haut-Brion.

"Good man," Chip said, refilling Ayan's glass. "I see you appreciate the wine. I thought your Indian palates were destroyed by curry. I was concerned I was wasting the vintage of the century on you."

"Thanks for this brilliant claret," Ayan said, "but I'm still going to be difficult. You're not the one whose head could be on the line for making fraudulent payments to some shady consultant in Switzerland."

Chip's expression hardened.

"Nothing leaves Switzerland," he said. "I want everything covered by the Swiss laws restricting disclosure. You do realize the kind of deal this is, don't you?"

"Yes, of course—but . . ."

"No! Spend as much time eyeballing the fucking invoices and any other papers you need in Luc's office; send in your auditors. We'll drown them with all the paperwork they need. We will have detailed documentation but nothing outside Switzerland. You hear me? Let's get things straight:

Your job is to open the accounts in Switzerland, transfer in the money, and then leave it to Nader, Luc, and me—to professionals. You think you can manage that?"

"Go fuck yourself, man!" Ayan said, leaning forward. "I work for Iran Power, not you. And understand this: I'm not committing to anything until I'm satisfied that the paper trail is acceptable."

Chip put up his hands.

The gap-toothed smile reappeared.

"No offence, mate," he said. "You get to survive in this game by being careful, keep everything on a need-to-know basis, operate on handshakes, and keep the bloody paper-work to an absolute minimum. Do you know the Kapoor family in Tehran?"

"Heard of them. Don't know them. Why?"

"They should be doing this deal. They're professionals. The Kapoors have been in Iran for a long time—very successful trading house; they know everybody. We work with them on some politically sensitive deals. I don't know why Nader got you involved in Odysseus. You don't seem like the right guy."

"Probably because I'm good at my job, somebody people like you can't manipulate."

"Think again. You've got it backwards. Nader probably wants to maintain control over Odysseus, so he's picked a lackey; the Kapoors would grab all the glory. That's their style. You're a hired gun who can be managed. That's the reason you're here. And I don't appreciate the risk I'm being exposed to: being forced to deal with a puffed-up amateur. Again, no offence, just facts."

They talked and parried through the rest of dinner, not learning too much more about each other.

"You know, it's late. I should get to bed if we're still on for squash at 7:00 a.m.," Ayan said finally.

"We're definitely on for squash. It will be fun to thrash a self-important Little Lord Fauntleroy like you!" Chip said.

"Fuck you too," Ayan said.

Chip laughed. "You know, I actually like you; you're in over your bloody head and don't know it. But I like your fight. Come on, I need some company: Let's go to Annabel's and pick up some classy blondes. Fuck their brains out."

"I'll come along for a nightcap," Ayan said. "Then you work your blondes. I've been out every night. I need to catch up on my sleep."

They walked to 44 Berkeley Square and into the basement world of Annabel's, surely the inspiration for the Key Club in Tehran. The deference shown to the doorman and maître d'hôtel, the décor and dance floor, and the exclusive atmosphere reminded Ayan of his Tehran watering hole.

Drink on, man, he thought as Chip downed two cognacs, then a third. *Soon, you'll be telling me more about your connections with the South African government, more about the shipments of material to the Atomic Energy Organization of Iran.*

Ayan nursed his port through the evening. An hour later, he decided his host was sufficiently inebriated, and he went in with a few pointed questions.

Chip just smiled enigmatically and told him to fuck off.

"You're all right," Chip said, sticking out his hand as Ayan gave up and rose to leave. "You don't have a clue, but you'll learn. I'll take care of you. Now bugger off. I'm off to steal that beauty from the old codger."

Chip sat down next to an interested-looking woman and her bemused companion.

Ayan retrieved his overcoat and stepped into the cold of Berkeley Square, feeling that he'd not been at his best tonight. He'd been a blunt instrument with Chip, not a master of *taarof*. He should have just listened to him, jollied him along, and been difficult later—when he was in Geneva. Luc was a banker with a big, bureaucratic institution; he would understand Ayan's position better. He would make amends tomorrow, Ayan decided. When they played squash. He would persuade Chip that he was the kind of person who could play the game on a stage like this. Do some damage control before Nader fired him.

He knew what he had to do with Chip, but not so much with Fariba. She was calling him from Tehran every day. She was the last person he wanted to hurt. It would be hard on him too; he would miss her terribly, but he had to tell her about Gaby. He couldn't lead her on anymore.

CHAPTER 13

Geneva, Switzerland, February 1978

The lobby of the Cigogne in Geneva was bustling at 8:00 a.m. Luc Bossard had chosen a convenient, classy place for Ayan's stay, but like so many European hotels, the Cigogne was not geared towards discreet entrances and exits.

Ayan, feeling conspicuous in his tracksuit and running shoes, eased past breakfasting businessmen and, escorted by the concierge, walked through a narrow corridor towards the door on Place Longemalle. He had time for a relaxing run before his 11:00 a.m. appointment with Luc at the Banque du Rhone branch on Quai du General-Guisan, which was just a short walk away from his hotel.

The concierge, taking the job of finding a suitable trail for Ayan very seriously, conferred with the doorman. "D'accord," he said, returning his attention to Ayan. He pointed towards the Jardin Anglais and Lac Leman. "You can start your gymnastics there. The Prom du Lac is on the right and has good views. Please be careful of the ice on the road."

Geneva felt brighter than London. The cold air drove the sleep from Ayan's eyes as he waited for the traffic light to change on chic Rue du Rhone. He walked towards the Jardin Anglais, appreciating the panorama of the Jura to the east, the Alps to the north and west, and Lac Leman and its Jet d'Eau in front of him. The fresh air and exercise would help to clear his mind. He'd made his peace with Nader's project and the dangers and compromises it entailed, but now that he was about to pull the trigger, move from planning to initiation, he was again agitated.

The footing improved as he reached the Prom du Lac, and he began to run, focusing his thoughts on Operation Odysseus: where things stood, next steps. Behrouz and Parviz—his treasurer and chief accountant—were standing by for his phone call, ready to wire money to Switzerland after his due diligence was completed and the account was operational. Both men were discreet and meticulous, and he trusted them. Nader had advised him to elevate Behrouz and Parviz above his three other department heads and through several pay grades. They could now afford European vacations, live in decent apartments, and drive good cars. They had agency and respect. They would be loyal and keep their mouths shut. Iranians were driven by sentiment and personal relationships. That's what Nader had told him, and of course, he'd been right.

Fifty million dollars from the Ministry of Energy had been received and documented by Behrouz and Parviz as an interest-free advance for discounted access to the output from the Qazvin expansion. The terms were open-ended. The bookkeeping plan was bulletproof. If somebody questioned the growing size of the advance, he could point to the Shah's ambitions for nuclear energy to be a major source of power for the national electric grid. Nader, acting under his board-sanctioned authority, had made Chip's company, Alpine Global, an official Iran Power purchasing agent and technical advisor and given it a broad mandate for the Qazvin expansion; that cleared the way for him to transfer money to Chip's company for invoiced and approved services rendered.

It would be difficult for an auditor to challenge the payments to Alpine; accountants couldn't credibly take on Nader when it came to engineering and manufacturing requirements—and certainly not on what was needed for nuclear power generation and distribution. The Jamieson McClintock audit partner in charge of Iran Power was a friend of Nader's anyway. As long as the paperwork followed their internal control process, there was nothing to be concerned about.

He had to have invoices from Alpine Global in the Tehran files—and get Nader to approve them before payment. Preferably, Ali Fard should sign off as well—assuming the head of engineering was in on the plan. He would be given a black mark via an internal control deficiency letter to the board if he only got Nader's signature, but he could survive that as long as Nader backed him up. And of course, he would. But a paper trail was essential. While the squash game with Chip had gone well, and they had parted with a "let's get this done" handshake, he wouldn't push the secretive wheeler-dealer any further. He would get what he needed from the banker, Luc Bossard.

Ayan was in the lobby of the Banque du Rhone office on General-Guisan early.

At precisely 11:00 a.m., one of the two uniformed guards staffing the reception desk came over and escorted him to the seventh floor. The elevator was cramped, and he could smell processed meat, cheese, and coffee on the man's breath.

Once they got out of the elevator, the guard led him towards the right. They passed a series of offices. All the doors were shut, and it was impossible to gauge the level of activity that morning.

Luc Bossard was waiting for him in the corner conference room. He was in his early sixties and looked exactly like a senior banker should: grey hair swept back, prosperous face tanned, presumably from weekends spent on the ski slopes in Verbier, white shirt, Hermès tie, and a dark blue suit with a crisp white pocket square.

The banker politely asked if Ayan was comfortable at the Le Cigogne. After coffee and some polite conversation about skiing, he pointed to five neat stacks of paper on the side of the table facing the lake.

"These are the account opening documents," Luc said. "They have been finalized and just require your signature. If you would go left to right, please, we can complete the formalities and walk over to Le Chat-Botté, a very nice restaurant. I've made a 12:30 p.m. reservation."

"I don't know," Ayan said, sitting down in front of the first stack. "There's a lot here, and I read everything."

A brief frown appeared on the suave face.

"Please go ahead," he said, picking up the phone. "I'll ask for more coffee."

"I can't sign this," Ayan said, pushing his chair back from the table after forty-five minutes. "I shouldn't be taking sole responsibility for opening the account; give myself the ability to transfer $50 million; give you, Luc, or your successor the power to transfer $10 million; or give some unnamed 'client representative' carte blanche!"

It was bad enough that he was colluding with his boss to violate international treaties Iran had signed; these documents also had him initiating an account from which millions of dollars could be stolen!

"Nader has reviewed the particulars," Luc said, sounding surprised. He pulled out a handkerchief and dabbed his eyes, dealing with a sudden allergy or irritation. "Everything is as he wants. He has confirmed to us that you have the authority to open the account as documented and has identified the client representative."

He tapped his Breguet. "Don't forget our lunch reservation."

Name Org

"I'm sorry. This is going to take as long as it's going to take. Can you show me Nader's instructions?"

"They are confidential. Believe me, the bank has the paperwork we need. We are careful. We have to be."

"I'm uncomfortable with this situation," Ayan said. "I need to speak to Nader."

"Really? Perhaps I can answer any questions. It's a very sensibly set up account. Better than most."

"Please get him on the line, thank you," Ayan insisted.

Luc looked displeased, but he complied.

"How are things going?" Nader said after Luc handed the phone to Ayan and made to leave the room.

Ayan paused till the door closed behind Luc.

"Nader, we need more time to correct the documents," he said. "To begin with, I'm the only person listed by name in the documents. That can't be right."

He heard an exasperated sigh.

"You know how confidential this is," Nader said. "The fewer names the better; less is more. You make sense because you are a foreigner; no one is tracking you."

"I'm authorizing people I don't know, including Luc and an unnamed client representative, to transfer out assets. Without restrictions."

"Luc is a highly respected banker. Trusted by all of us here. The client representative will be somebody from the Ministry of Energy, which also makes sense, given the source of the funds."

"Our auditors are not going to like this," Ayan said, feeling trapped. "There's too much scope for money to go missing."

"Why? I'm the one designating people who have the ability to make transfers, and I'm authorized by the board to do that, so what's the problem?"

"We need to be in a more defensible position; at a minimum, we have to eliminate two leakage points: the $10 million Luc can transfer on his own and my ability to transfer $50 million without your signature."

"Ayan—let me be very clear," Nader said, his voice suddenly aggressive. "Set up the accounts exactly as documented. I have gone over the provisions with Luc and given him detailed instructions. He can't act independently. I will approve all transfers out. I have told Luc that you are authorized to transfer the $50 million to Alpine Global. Just open the account, fund the account with the $50 million we received, give the transfer details you received from Chip de Groot to Luc, and leave the rest to him. Now I have to go into a meeting. Next time I hear from you or Luc, I want to be told that it's done."

Ayan leaned back in his chair, cornered, deflated, but not completely defeated—at least not yet.

He would work the man in front of him.

"Everything all right?" Luc asked, back in the conference room, a smile plastered on his face.

"Luc, let's go to that lunch. I need time to clear my head."

"Better to sign the documents first. It won't take more than fifteen minutes. Then we can relax."

Nader and Luc had him on the clock. Perhaps hoping urgency would camouflage the reality that they had him setting sail alone in dangerous waters: the sole signatory on a rogue bank account. Meanwhile, Nader's involvement was veiled behind Swiss banking secrecy protocols.

He was caught in a tunnel. There was light at one end, where Nader stood, beckoning him with a reassuring smile and promise of financial independence. The other end led to unemployment and dislocation and a desperate flailing to find another footing in another land.

He had to keep going, even if the risk was greater than he had thought. He would just have to slow things down and create the strongest paper trail possible to protect himself.

"No, Luc. I need to talk to you before we do that. I need your help."

They walked over to the Beau Rivage, ten minutes away on the Quai du Mont-Blanc, and were escorted to a table in a quiet corner of the hotel's Le Chat-Botté restaurant.

"Luc," Ayan said after he'd complimented his host's choice of the Chasselas. "Bankers like you have to know their customers, fill out paperwork. Well, I'm in the same position: I have an obligation to do my due diligence and maintain records. Our company policies and professional standards demand that."

The Swiss banker raised his eyebrows.

"No doubt you took care of these matters prior to this long-planned visit," he said.

"There are gaps. Unexpected issues have appeared, and they must be dealt with. For example, I was not told that I would be granting you power of attorney to withdraw $10 million at your discretion. That will raise questions."

"The power of attorney is Nader's idea. You'll have to take that up with him."

"I have."

"Then there's nothing more to discuss. It's routine in these situations—clients trust me with many times that number!"

"Yes, but they know you and have known you for a long time. I don't, and I'm the one opening the account. I'm uncomfortable giving you the power of attorney as structured. I mean no disrespect. Nader tells me that you have a superb reputation in Tehran, earned over many years."

"Thank you. I know that. I've worked hard on it," Luc said, looking at Ayan warily.

"If you can get me a copy of your bank's policies with respect to power of attorney withdrawals from client accounts, that might help. And I must see Nader's instructions to you." Ayan sat back with an air of finality.

Luc threw up his hands.

"But this is extraordinary! I've never heard of doing such a thing—giving outsiders internal documents and sharing confidential materials! And these are not the kinds of questions that should be raised when we're at the final stage and on a deadline! I have the account opening staff ready. Nader wants the transfers to happen by tomorrow."

"We can still open the account today. You don't have to give me your documents. Just let me read them, and I can make a note that I've done that for my files."

Luc looked at his watch. "It's 1:00 p.m. The bank's cutoff is 3:30 p.m. There is no time for that."

"I'm a fast reader. And I know what I'm looking for."

"You're serious about this? Banks are slow. Who knows how long it will take me to get you to see what you need, if at all. Are you willing to tell Nader that we failed to sign the papers on time? Because I'm not; you'll have to call him."

"I don't want to, but if it comes to that, if I can't see evidence of satisfactory checks and balances—I will. It won't be a disaster if the account is opened tomorrow."

"No!" Luc said. "We must do it today!"

He stopped the morsel of fish that was on its way to his mouth and returned it to his plate.

"I have an idea," he said, the helpful banker expression reappearing. "Excuse me for a minute, I need to make a phone call."

"I've solved our problem," Luc said upon his return. He sampled his entrée to make sure it was still edible. "I've arranged an interview with our chief internal auditor at 2:00 p.m. You can ask him what you need to ask him. He can also confirm the account is appropriately authorized. We can still finish the paperwork before the cutoff."

"That's perfect! It is very good of you to set up the meeting with internal audit, which I'm sure will answer all my questions. At the risk of pushing my luck, may I also ask if you have contacts at Alpine Global whom you can connect me to?"

"I know Hermann Gerber well. He's Mr. de Groot's office manager. We did our military service together. I can introduce you to him, but I suggest you clear it with Mr. de Groot first."

"I have no way of contacting Chip. He said that I could reach him through you or Nader. I obviously don't want to bother Nader."

"What do you want to discuss with Hermann?"

"This does not relate to account opening, so don't worry. I need to verify the legitimacy of the account numbers Chip wants the transfers to go into and review the invoicing and receipt protocol, and I should really visit their offices in Zug."

Luc stared at Ayan for a long moment, as if examining an extraterrestrial.

"Nader informed me you were just here to sign and fund the account. Why didn't you speak to Mr. de Groot about this in London?"

"He has no patience with these matters. Luc, you know high-level executives like Chip and Nader agree to a deal and leave it to people like us to fill in the blanks. I'm sure your friend Hermann can quickly address the two routine issues on my list."

"I'll see what I can do, but first, let's open the account and tell Nader that everything is on track. I presume that the money can be wired immediately after the account is operational?"

"Yes, the money is ready," Ayan said.

It wouldn't be transferred until he'd visited Alpine Global. But there was no need to bring that up now.

— Peg —

Ayan strolled back to the Cigogne, looking forward to decompressing over a peg or two of Laphroig. The account had been opened. He had driven Luc crazy by delaying the funding, but Nader was off his back for now.

He looked over his shoulder as he returned to Place Longemalle and laughed at his insecurity. Nobody was following him. Those who should be concerned about what he was doing were in the dark. Everybody in a position of authority in Iran was on his side. Hopefully. Surely.

It was going to be fine. His briefcase had extensive notes from the meeting with Alfred Krieger, Banque du Rhone's director of internal audit for the EMEA accounts. They recorded his assurances that the Iran Power account would be run strictly according to Nader's specific instructions. Would the notes be enough to satisfy the Institute of Chartered Accountants in England and Wales? Probably not, but they showed that Ayan had asked the right person the right questions and got the right answers: Luc Bossard

EMEA —

could only move money out of the Iran Power accounts with Nader's approval or the approval of a client representative appointed by Nader. Who could expect him to do more in this situation?

Signed?

"You're a pain in the ass," Chip said, his phone call pulling Ayan out of the Cigogne bar.

"An effective one," Ayan said. "The account is open. On time. Everything is on schedule."

"So what's this about wanting to go to our offices and bothering Hermann?"

"A few loose ends to tie up," Ayan said. "Straightforward checklist type of things. I didn't want to waste your time with them. Once I've talked to your staff and completed my due diligence, I can transfer the $50 million. I have Nader's approval and my people in Tehran are on standby. All I have to do is call them."

"Here's what I'll let you have, you annoying bugger," Chip said. "Two hours with Hermann. That's it. Then I want the money transferred. I'll see you in Zug tomorrow afternoon."

"You don't need to bother coming," Ayan said. "This is just a process thing. I'm sure everything will be in order after I meet Hermann. You'll get the money the day after."

"I'm coming. You're a sneaky bastard. I'm going to watch you—also show you how things get done. You have to build relationships, not files. So here's what we're going to do: You talk to Hermann, look at all the paperwork you need. Then I'll drive you to Luc's chalet in Haute-Nendaz, a couple of hours from Geneva. Ski in, ski out, very private. Spend the night. Nader has—several times. Luc's raclette is great and so is his wine cellar. Hopefully, your skiing is better than your squash. I've told Luc. He's going to meet us there tomorrow

Really — Name caller *NO*

night. The three of us are going to become friends. Find a train from Geneva that gets you to Zug by 2:00 p.m."

The Alpine Global office was small and sparsely furnished. But Hermann Gerber seemed competent enough. Alpine Global was a registered entity in good standing in the canton of Zug. Chip was the chief executive officer. The board of directors included Luc Bossard as well as a partner of a major Swiss law firm. The auditors were just below the top international tier. The transfer details and account number where 85 percent of the payments would go was confirmed, via bank statements, to be Alpine Global's principal transaction account—all good news.

As Ayan had suspected, the account where 15 percent of the payments were to be sent was a secret numbered account.

"It's controlled by Mr. de Groot," Hermann said, looking hesitatingly at Chip, who was watching the proceedings.

"To make the world go around, turn a no into a yes, change later into now . . . the usual business," Chip added.

Some of this 15 percent would probably find its way back to people in Iran, Ayan thought. The rest could be for South African officials, procurers, and consultants. Who knew? People were going to make a fortune on this deal, obviously. How much would Nader pocket? Millions probably. Ayan's six-figure payoff was loose change—serious money for him— but a rounding error in this plan.

"Fifteen percent of payments will be sent to an undocumented account," Ayan wrote in his note to file. "Against my recommendation, and on the approval of the CEO of Iran Power, Mr. Nader—on --/--/----."

Then there was a resumption of hostilities with Chip on documentation for the value received by Iran Power and subsequent payments.

It was slow going, but Ayan persevered through his questions and reviews, extracting concessions, taking careful notes, checking and recording the architecture of a smoke-screen over the mocking taunts of Chip.

CHAPTER 14

West Berlin, February 1978

The early dusk of the Northern European winter had brought out the lights of West Berlin, though it was not quite 5:00 p.m.

Ayan was feeling good and feeling rich. Fifty thousand dollars had made its way into his bank account soon after Alpine Global confirmed receipt of the first transfer. This thing was for real. Skiing with Luc and Chip and staying overnight in the banker's chalet after an extended alcoholic evening together had reduced some of his misgivings. There was a human being behind Luc's professional façade, and Ayan sensed a kind of gallows camaraderie developing with Chip.

He ate another of the chocolates Gaby had left for him at the reception of the Kempinski Hotel and downed the last of a surprisingly good cup of Darjeeling tea.

He still had two hours to kill before he would finally be with her.

The damn time had slipped into slow motion.

He set out towards Gaby's apartment, still an hour early, lingered at the shops recommended by the Kempinski concierge, bought flowers and champagne, and left the crowded boulevard to explore the side streets of Charlottenburg.

Berlin nightlife was awakening in the bars and restaurants he strolled past. Large windows opened to tableaux of sophisticates in art galleries, who were mingling and browsing with glasses of wine in their hands. A couple brushed past him arm in arm. Their indifference to his existence did not make him lonesome; nothing would on this hopeful evening.

He continued in the westerly direction of Savignyplatz, past the linden trees Gaby said she missed, beginning to understand her affection for communist-surrounded West Berlin; feeling the edgy, devil-may-care zeitgeist of the city of intrigue and revelry build on his venturesome mood; and finding himself hoping Gaby would be as happy to see him as she'd sounded when he confirmed his visit.

The Greek chorus was out in force, warning of the Gaby who'd left him, reminding him they hadn't communicated for months and that he had no idea of her current reality.

No matter.

He would win her over if she kept him at a remove. Tonight was for bold thinking. He wasn't going to play Heathcliff to her Cathy. He'd be like Michael Corleone returning to Kay in *The Godfather* and refuse to take no for an answer. Perhaps not him, perhaps not Michael Corleone, but more like that Welsh bastard Owen with Jackie—commit totally, convince Gaby that no one could love her like he did.

After all, he was the one she'd chosen out of all the men who'd pursued her in Tehran; he would take heart from that.

He reached Savignyplatz, walked onto Carmerstrasse, and was soon in front of number ten, Gaby's apartment building. Flowers were painted around its entrance. A mural of a hungry crocodile looked down on him. Moorish arches on the first floor gave way to Doric columns on the second floor, then more arches on the third, and a synthesis on the fourth. He looked into the wood-paneled entrance hall. Crests and crimson drapes on the walls merged into a blue roof decorated with twinkling stars. It was playful, but also of a piece, and such a contrast to the drab architecture of Tehran.

Ayan waited till it was 7:00 p.m. and rang the bell against the name "A. Faber" on the brass plate listing the building's occupants. Seconds later, he was face-to-face with Gaby.

"Ayan! I can't believe you're actually here!" Gaby said, presenting her cheeks to be kissed.

"I'm so happy to see you again!" he managed to stammer out. "You look, well, *wonderful* . . . I brought you some flowers."

"Thank you! Roses—and champagne! That's so sweet! Come in and take off your coat. Hang it in that closet. I'll put the roses in a vase."

Gaby disappeared down a corridor.

"Open the champagne," Gaby said from within. "It seems cold enough. The glasses are in the cabinet—and turn on the cassette player. I'll be right back. I just want to cut the stems on these before I put them in water."

The apartment was bright and modern: white walls, a large, colorful Kandinsky print, minimalist furniture, and polished hardwood floors. It was chic and functional—but cold. Where were all of Gaby's things?

He opened a door. It led to a small bedroom, also neat and sparsely furnished. A worn backpack lay on the floor next to a pair of Adidas sneakers. A half-empty jug of water and a glass sat on the bedside table. The bathroom door was open. Bras, panties, jeans, and some socks were hanging on the curtain rod of the shower. The room felt like the camp of a transient; it made him uneasy.

Ayan retreated to the living room and pressed the play button on her cassette deck.

Coltrane. Perfect.

"Smells delicious," he said when Gaby returned with a cut-glass vase containing the roses.

"Bavarian chicken," Gaby said, placing the vase on a table and smiling at him as he handed her a glass of the Veuve Cliquot he'd brought. "Wine, some herbs. As usual, my mother's recipe. We're going to have it with spätzle and salad, then cinnamon apple strudel and cake—I know you'll love that! Ayan! I still can't believe you're here! Come, sit."

Gaby kicked off her slippers and pulled her legs up on her beige sofa. "Tell me all about yourself. What have you been doing? How's the gang—Darioush, Hassan, Nick—still playing tennis, hanging out in the usual places?"

"Same old. The usual scene." Ayan said, sitting down next to her.

She was happy being back in Europe, Gaby said. Happy being near her family, more involved with what was going on, had a better job—just charters and cargo, but at least she was in charge of her aircraft and not some junior flight engineer on a big jet.

She knew about the violence in Iran, knew more than him, it seemed; was not surprised Nick was attacked, knew he was CIA, dismissed Ayan's defense of his good qualities, wondered why he spent so much time with a jerk; and asked him to talk about Hamid instead.

Hamid was continuing his anti-Shah tirades, joining protests, looking for trouble and would surely find it, Ayan told her. Then he said he was now helping Hamid, giving him 1,000 tomans a month for food and his sons' education.

He should have told her that earlier, because she leaned over and gave him a kiss. Never mind that it was a quick, friendly kiss.

The scent of citrus and summer he remembered so well returned when Gaby sat down on the sofa again after checking on dinner.

Her feet were inches from his hands.

He exhaled and took a long sip of the champagne.

"Tired?" Gaby said. "They had you working hard in West Berlin today?"

"Gaby, I didn't come here on work. I came to see you."

"You're such a liar," Gaby said, a skeptical smile on her face. "You didn't even bother replying to my letters."

"I'm sorry. I'd nothing left in me."

He touched her feet. She tensed.

"*Nein*! Don't," she said, folding her legs under her.

For a few moments, she stared in silence at the Kandinsky print. Then she turned to him.

"Everyone else wrote back—my Iran Air friends, your friends, even your mother!" Gaby said sharply.

"My mother?" Ayan said, surprised.

"Yes. We stay in touch. We've raised some money here in Germany for the free clinic she's started. I'm helping her, like Darioush."

Ma had kept him informed about Darioush's contact with her. Not a word about Gaby. Obviously, she was not considered to be his friend or to mean anything to him.

"So about your mother, I know a lot: her days, her life. But about her son, I know nothing," Gaby said. "I know he's found a new girlfriend, but not much else."

"I did try to reply," Ayan said. "None of my attempts sounded right. I couldn't think clearly when you left. I was lost."

"Don't lie about being so lost, empty, whatever!" Gaby said, sitting up angrily. "You connected with Fariba pretty quickly. I understand. I left. I hated being in Iran, was not myself—I understand all that. Life goes on and fills the places you occupied. Just don't give me any bullshit."

"Come on, Gaby . . . it was not like that at all."

"Here I was, writing down things so you would know exactly how I felt. I was so looking forward to sharing what was going on in my life with you, believing Darioush when he wrote and said I should return, that you missed me so much! Thinking a guy who said I meant everything to him would realize Tehran was making me crazy, realize I had to return home to become myself again. Give me time."

She turned away and dabbed her eyes.

"I felt abandoned. Rejected. I made a mistake."

"You know your problem, Ayan? You're insecure and needy," Gaby said, glaring at him.

"I know."

"And rush into any arms that'll hold you."

"Not true."

"And unfaithful," Gaby said, "and a liar!"

"OK, that's enough. That last part is unfair. I'm definitely not a liar."

"You are, and the truth hurts."

"I'm not the one who left. Not the one who said cruel things. I've forgiven you; you should do the same."

Gaby laughed.

"You have some fucking nerve," she said.

"You've not been with other men?"

"I was alone here. It's normal, no?" Gaby said, "Men ask me out; sometimes, I like them and accept. Mostly, they're just physical relationships. Not that important to me. It's not like you and Fariba. My Iran Air friends see everything, tell me everything."

"Well, your information is incorrect, Gaby. Fariba is a friend; that's it."

"You don't have to say that," Gaby said. "We both have different lives now. And come on—I've slaved over this meal—you better say you love it!"

"I've never moved on from you, Gaby! I understand that you went out with other men. I hate it but understand. As long as there's nobody serious."

He put his arms around her.

She pushed him away.

"Put the salad on the table for me," she said, "and open the bottle of Riesling in the fridge; the chicken's almost ready. I just need to put the finishing touches on the gravy."

"Is there? Someone else?"

Gaby looked at him.

"Yes, Ayan. Since you ask, there is somebody serious. I'm with someone now."

Of course! Women like Gaby always had somebody after them, Ayan thought. *Move forward, regardless, you have to keep going.* He had prepared himself for this.

"Who is he?"

"Somebody I grew up with; he's always been crazy about me. Now he's big and strong and handsome and rich and wants to marry me. My mother loves him."

"Not you, I can tell. So now, I'm not going to kill myself."

Gaby laughed.

"Well, he's asked me to marry him, and I'm thinking about it," she said. "He owns a plane. That's something to take seriously."

"Well, don't!"

"Sorry, your views don't figure in this calculation," Gaby said. "You can't just drop in and say things like that."

Cold words.

But her eyes and her tone told him he was still in with a chance.

There'd been nothing faked about her anger about Fariba; there was nothing platonic in the touch that was guiding him to the dinner table now.

"What did you write in the letters you didn't send me?" Gaby said as he pulled out a chair for her.

"How life felt without you, how Tehran now only looks grey and drab and impossible to survive in."

"No, that's not what you wrote. If you had, you'd have posted the letters. You probably wrote about how much you hated me for being a bitch."

They looked at each other and laughed.

"See? I'm right!" Gaby said. "I can see it in your face. Now you'd better start complimenting my cooking."

"You have to leave," Gaby said while she was brewing coffee after dinner. She looked at the clock on the kitchen wall. "Soon."

"Why?" Ayan said.

"I have a house guest."

"Your boyfriend?"

"No. A girl."

"So why can't I meet her?"

"It's complicated. She's a very private individual. I'll come to the Kempinski tomorrow morning. Be ready by 10:00 a.m. We'll have brunch, and then I have some art galleries I want you to see."

"Just a second before you kick me out," Ayan said. "I've bought you a present." He walked back to the coat closet in the living room and retrieved the Navitimer he'd picked up for Gaby at Geneva airport.

He watched her face as she unwrapped the box, and the watch's black dial, silver chronograph counters, and red second hand came into view.

"What's this!" Gaby said.

"You like it?" Ayan said, knowing that she'd always wanted this pilot's favorite, but anxious all the same.

"It's beautiful!" she said.

He slipped the watch onto her wrist.

But then it went very wrong.

The watch was off her wrist and back in the box, and the box was back in his hands, and she was moving away from him.

"I can't keep this; it's too much!" she said.

"But you like it, don't you? That was the idea! I can afford it, and I want you to have it!"

"You can't just walk in and think an expensive present will make things right! I'm not for sale!"

Her voice cut through him like the wind of a London winter.

"What! That's not what this is about! I was going to buy myself a Rolex Submariner and saw this watch and thought of you . . ."

"You shouldn't have spent all this money. It's not right."

"Please keep it," Ayan said, placing the watch on her kitchen table. He put his arms around her. "It is a selfish present but not in the way you think. When you're flying, you'll be looking at the Navitimer and might think of me. That's why I bought it—so you don't forget me."

"*Nein!* Take it away! And I'm not the one in the forgetting business," Gaby said, slipping out of his embrace.

"I've never forgotten you, Gaby. I will be in love with you forever."

"*Du Schmeichler!*"

She turned her back to him and walked to a window looking down on Carmerstrasse. She opened the window and lifted her face to the cold air.

Muffled chatter from the restaurant downstairs rose up to the room.

"It's a busy night for them," Gaby said.

"Yes," Ayan said.

They stood where they were for a while in silence, Gaby looking out towards the street, Ayan looking at her.

Trane's elegiac, bluesy saxophone drifted in from the living room.

He went over to her and turned her face towards his.

"What do you want from me, Ayan?" Gaby said, her hazel eyes intense. "After all this time. After all this silence?"

"Everything."

He tried to kiss her.

"No!" she said sharply. "Now go. Please. I'll see you tomorrow."

He heard the phone ringing as he entered his hotel room.

In two strides, he was across the room and cradling the telephone to his ear.

"Hi, it's me."

For one wild, churlish moment, he thought of saying, "Who?"

"Hi, Gaby," he said.

"I might be missing you."

"Come over then," Ayan said.

"Why?"

"Because I love you."

"I don't believe you."

"What else can I say . . . I used up all my words at your place."

"Find some more."

"I won't sleep without you by my side," Ayan said. He took a deep breath. His eyes scanned the George Grosz painting on the wall. "I'll lie awake for thousands of years, I'll watch civilizations crumble, and nothing will matter but that you're not by my side . . ."

"Any girl could warm your bed, and you'd be happy."

"Only you."

She was quiet for so long. Then, in a voice he strained to hear, she said, "You've been such a swine."

"I know."

"You deceived me. You said you couldn't live without me."

"I know."

"Why should I come to a bastard who's also a terrible singer?"

He felt himself starting to smile.

"Because he's longing for you, and so 'Tangled up in Blue.'"

Ayan paced the floor as he waited for her. He sat up. He lay down.

He could hardly believe the knock on his door an hour later.

He kissed her and held her close, throwing her overcoat on a chair, pulling off her blouse, her jeans, everything.

"You think I can come all the way in?" Gaby said, laughing. "And shut the door. This is not Khanom-eh Mohsen's rooftop. Somebody might actually see us."

"Let them," Ayan said. "We're in West Berlin. No one will care."

"It's still Germany—they'll want you to stop what you're doing till you pay for double occupancy!"

He carried her to the bed and placed her down gently.

"This what you want—isn't it? What you're so desperate for?" Gaby whispered as he kissed her thighs, her legs around him, her hands urging him, letting him know her desire was as great as his.

"You should be able to sleep now . . ." Gaby said, smiling.

"Yes, but tomorrow's too soon for goodbye," Ayan said.

"Why don't I drive you to Munich? I'm flying a charter out of there on Wednesday and can go down a few days earlier with you. We'll have more time together, and you can spend Sunday in Starnberg. If you want."

"Of course, I do! That's perfect! I'm booked in a hotel in Munich on Sunday night. I'll just advance the booking by a day."

"Great! We'll leave around 2:00 p.m., after I show you around Berlin; traffic will be light that time on a Saturday. It'll take us less than seven hours. Well, good night, again . . ."

"Gaby, wait—this guest of yours—she's Baader-Meinhof, isn't she?" Ayan said.

He hadn't wanted to open another front with Gaby earlier; but the sparse furnishings, the apartment that was not quite her, that room, the guest that required him gone— he knew what they meant.

"Yes. But she's just a teenager," Gaby said.

"You let Red Army terrorists come to your apartment!"

"I only let girls stay. And I meet them before, in the Dicke Wirtin bar downstairs. Usually they are hungry, lonely, no trouble at all. They arrive late and leave before I'm awake. They don't say much. And don't call them terrorists. Being Baader-Meinhof is the most meaningful thing they've done in their lives."

"How about the police?" Ayan asked. "What if they find out?"

"I'll just say they broke into my apartment. There are no records. Everybody is careful not to leave any evidence. I have house rules. I've thought through every contingency. I'm a pilot remember—always prepared, always worrying, always looking for a place to land in an emergency."

"Your things? Important papers? These terrorists have nothing to lose."

"All my valuable stuff is in Starnberg. Let them take what they want from here. I'm not attached to objects, anyway. You should know that. Not that anyone has ever taken anything; they're very grateful."

"Amazing! Nobody takes chances like that, like you're doing. I knew you were involved with these people. I'm just stunned at having been in the room, the place where it happens."

"Ayan, these girls are like Hamid: heroes against fascists, in the line of fire, brave fighters for something bigger than themselves who can't survive without our help. I'm prepared to do everything possible for people like them. I know you are too."

"I'm more cautious than you, Gaby, and definitely not as brave."

"You'll keep doing the right thing too," she said. "When people need your help, you'll not let them down. I want to believe that."

CHAPTER 15

Munich, West Germany, February 1978

"Want to fly?" Gaby said as they awoke in the Bayerischer Hof hotel in Munich on Sunday. "Come on! It'll be fun—you'll see everything from the air before we go to my parents' house for lunch."

"We can fly at such short notice?" Ayan said. "Just like that?"

He was tired. It had been a long Saturday of sightseeing and travel and intimidating confrontations with German police, particularly the random stop by the *Bundesgrenzschutz Gruppe* 9, the elite anti-terrorist group BGS G9, just before they reached Munich. Gaby's BMW 2002 was Baader-Meinhof's getaway car of choice; he looked like a Palestinian; enough said.

That was scary but brief. Gaby had her papers and flight credentials; he had letters from SA Group and Iran Power. The assault rifles that had been in their faces soon waved them on. The unpleasant business at the East German checkpoint was endless. There had been no face to argue with at the border, just a voice barking at him from behind a wall after he'd dropped his papers into an opening. For a while, he thought he might have to spend the night in a German prison.

He would have liked to take it easy this morning. Sleep in.

"Yes, we can fly today," Gaby said and picked up the phone. "I'm fairly sure Charlie isn't using his plane; now get up and get ready."

"Charlie? That's his name?" Ayan said, embracing Gaby—one hand on her breasts, the other slipping between her thighs.

Gaby put a finger to her lips and batted away his hands. She sat up.

"Karl-Heinz Mueller, bitte," she said into the mouthpiece, instantly transformed into an unfamiliar person, her expressions and gestures as foreign as her words and the sound of her voice.

It was startling to see Gaby in Germany, in her own environment. It brought upon a separation—a reminder that they were from different worlds. He'd felt a similar alienation in the art galleries of Charlottenberg yesterday and at the prosecco-laced lunch with her friends on Mommsenstrasse.

It must have been hard for Gaby, too, seeing how roughly he'd been treated by her countrymen, by both the *Landespolizei* and *Volkspolizei* for looking different—for being an Indian.

Ayan got up and began to shave, feeling anxious as Gaby chatted intimately with Charlie. He couldn't wait till they were alone again, just the two of them on common ground, on neutral cosmopolitan territory.

At Munich Airport's private jet terminal, Gaby took the controls of a white twin-engine de Havilland DHC-2 Beaver.

"I love Charlie's plane," she said. "Short take-off and landing, easy to maneuver . . . it's perfect for flying low and showing you around my home."

In minutes, they were over Lake Starnberg.

"See those trees by the water?" Gaby said. "I grew up playing under their shade. We had picnics; I stayed out all day reading; that boat dock is where we used to swim and sail from; we still do in summer."

Vacation homes with private marinas alternated with public beaches and recreation areas around the expansive lake. People were out for their Sunday walks. Swans, ducks, and gulls huddled close to shore.

"Nice place to grow up," Ayan said.

"I was lucky," Gaby said, picking up altitude.

The Bavarian Alps rose in a jagged and impressive sweep around them.

Suddenly, she banked sharply, dropping them low again, skimming the surface of the lake for a few seconds.

"Watch out!" Ayan yelled as she pointed the aircraft towards the shore.

He felt the plane straining into another steep ascent.

They didn't miss the treetops by much.

He raised his eyebrows at Gaby.

She had a smile on her face.

"We had miles to spare. I know what I'm doing," she said.

Then he was thrown back in his seat. The plane began a steep ascent. It was exhilarating. The Alpine peaks receded below them. Outside the cockpit, there was only the sun and defeated wisps of clouds.

For a moment, in the silence that enveloped them, he thought of not going back to Tehran. His heart lifted at the idea of just giving all that up and moving to Berlin to be with Gaby, sharing her life in beautiful, exciting Charlottenberg, and here, in Lake Starnberg.

Gaby moved her fingers rapidly over the switches on the control panel, concentrating on her aircraft, pulling him back into reality. Ayan sighed. How could he just arrive here, cap-in-hand, an immigrant looking for a job? She would quickly lose respect for him.

Suddenly, Operation Odysseus took on more importance. It was his road to independence, the only way he could join her here.

They covered the thirty-five kilometers from the airport to Lake Starnberg in just over fifteen minutes. He'd driven the fun, responsive car most of the way from West Berlin— but not this competently, not this fast.

"Ready to meet my parents?" Gaby said, downshifting and accelerating her BMW 2002 past the campervan ahead of them.

"Don't worry about me meeting your family," Ayan said. "I'm respectful and attentive. It's what we do in India. They'll love me. More than this Charlie fellow of yours."

Gaby laughed.

"Aha! Let's just wait and see about that," she said.

She smiled and touched Ayan's face.

"You know," she said, "I wasn't sure how I would feel when I saw you again. Then there you were at my door, and looked different, and I thought, where did all those lines around his eyes come from? And I felt moved and happy that you'd come."

"You took pity on me—wrinkled and old at twenty-eight."

"No," Gaby said. "You looked kinder. And still a little sexy."

"Well, here we are," she said, turning into a quiet lane and pulling into a gravel driveway.

"It looks like it belongs in the French countryside," Ayan said, looking up at a yellow-and-white three-story villa with twin gables.

"Yes, my mother loves everything Provencal. We have a white kitchen with terra-cotta floors; even the bathroom tiles are from the South of France!"

"Well, you undersold it." Gaby pointed to the second floor of a wing of the house that faced west.

"That's my room. I can see the lake. My parents have the first floor and patio. My brother Mathias is above them in the room with the balcony. We all have a little something special in our areas. You'll also like the garden. It's down those steps, past the columns between the hedge—and look, here is Papa."

A tall, dark-haired man with a round, cheerful face came forward to greet them.

"Hello!" Andreas Faber said, kissing Gaby.

"Papa, this is Ayan," Gaby said.

"Yes, yes, we've heard a lot about you," Andreas said, putting his arm around Ayan's shoulders. "From India, yes? I spent some good times in Bombay. Gaby, what do you think? Shall we sit in the garden for a while? We can come in when it gets cold."

Gaby nodded and took her father's arm. The three of them walked up the stairs and through a veranda into a hallway.

A lighter-haired, older version of Gaby stood inside: the same beautiful features, the same eyes.

"Ayan, meet Nina, my mother," Gaby said.

Ayan felt Nina's eyes running over him as he shook her hand—which was withdrawn quickly. She didn't look happy with what she saw.

He'd have to work on this one.

"I'm taking them to the garden; we'll eat there," Andreas told his wife.

He began to guide Ayan towards a door at the far end of the living room.

"No, Andreas!" Nina said. "It's too cold. We are eating in the conservatory. I have set the table there. Gaby, come help me in the kitchen. Why are you late? You were supposed to be here an hour ago!"

Gaby placed her hand on her mother's back and moved it in soothing circles.

"I took Ayan flying. It's not his fault. I insisted," she said. "Sorry!"

She kissed Nina and embraced her till her protests were quieted.

Mother and daughter went off to the kitchen walking hand-in-hand; so all was well, it appeared.

Andreas looked at Ayan and winked after they were gone.

"You see who's the boss here," he said, before shuffling off to bring some wine from the cellar.

The house suited its location near a lake. White walls and large picture windows brought in light, blurring the boundary between the living space and the garden outside. The warm heaviness of walnut cabinets and tables was offset by blue tablecloths, yellow and red throws, and terra-cotta tile.

Ayan wandered into the living room and moved towards the fireplace. He leaned towards the photographs on the mantelpiece, hands in his pocket, not wanting to touch anything in case Nina was watching.

She had looked at him like he was a swarthy intruder who might run off with the family silver.

He pivoted when a new voice said hello.

"Mathias?" Ayan said.

Gaby's younger brother had his father's strong face and cleft chin, a curly brown Afro, and scraggly sideburns that meandered down his cheeks before turning in towards his lips.

His handshake was surprisingly limp.

"Was that you listening to Queen upstairs?" Ayan said.

"Yeah," Mathias said, still looking at the floor.

"Freddie Mercury's voice covers such a range of octaves," Ayan said to get the conversation going. "More than perhaps any other rock singer."

"Yeah . . . sorry, my English is not so good," Mathias said, shrugging.

"No, your English is good, it's fine," Ayan said. "You probably know that Freddie Mercury was an Indian."

"No," Mathias said, "he was born in Zanzibar."

"Of Indian parents. He may have been born in Zanzibar, but he went to school near Bombay and formed his first band there. Besides Elvis and Little Richard and the others, he was also influenced by Lata Mangeshkar, a famous Indian Bollywood singer whose voice also extends over several octaves."

Damn, that sounded so fucking pedantic, Ayan thought.

"Cool," Mathias said. He shrugged again and went off toward the conservatory.

Ayan watched him sit down at the lunch table and butter a dinner roll.

Indifference is probably a win for me with this guy, Ayan thought.

He went out and joined the group assembling for the meal.

Nina and Andreas sat down at the ends of the dining table. Ayan was placed between Gaby, who sat next to her father, and Mathias, who sat on Nina's right.

They faced the gravel and rock garden outside. The sun was still out. Gaby had her hand in his. *I couldn't ask for much more*, Ayan thought.

An intimidating quantity of preserved meat filled the charcuterie plate at the center of the table. He was hungry, but definitely not for that—nor for the blood sausage that was placed in front of him.

He would concentrate on the spätzle—and maybe the pumpkin bread and the potato salad.

Andreas raised his Steinkrug and looked at Ayan.

"*Auf Iher Gesundheit!* To your good health!" he said.

"Say something," Gaby whispered.

Ayan rose.

"I'm so happy to be here, in the place Gaby treasures, and to meet the people who mean the most to her. She has talked about all of you with so much love. But she left out something. I'm going back to Tehran and telling everyone Gaby's mother is even more beautiful than she is!"

Nina looked up at Ayan. A brief smile lit up her face.

Mathias giggled and almost choked on his mouthful.

Gaby reached behind Ayan's back and punched her brother's shoulder.

"See, Mother," she said, "I told you! He's always flirting. I can't trust him—even with you!"

"I say he has good taste!" Andreas said, laughing.

An embarrassed flush colored Nina's pale cheeks.

"No, no, I'm so old." she said. "Now please start; the food is getting cold."

That was the most he got out of Nina. She busied herself with passing things around the table. Half an hour later, she was gone, saying she needed to rest.

Gaby followed after her to make sure she was all right.

Then Mathias disappeared after wolfing down his food.

Not the extended lunch Ayan had anticipated. Not like the ones he had grown up with in India or those long, leisurely meals that were the custom in Tehran.

At least Andreas was welcoming.

It was relaxing to talk to the well-travelled, congenial man. He knew Iran and India from his travelling days with Bayer.

Andreas made sure their Steinkrugs were never empty. The alcohol had different effects on them: Ayan found himself fighting sleep while Andreas became more energetic and talkative.

"Did you know that both German and Sanskrit have their roots in Indo-European languages?" Andreas said. "We have many similar words and concepts; both languages use three genders: masculine, feminine and neutral. English can't express the dimensions of thought and feeling like our languages can."

"I know about the root language being common but not these interesting details," Ayan said. *Perhaps here was an avenue to bond with Gaby's parents*, he thought, sitting up to concentrate as Andreas listed common words and talked about how European writers and philosophers had noted that a tendency to abstract thought, speculation, and imagery produced an affinity between Germans and Indians.

"Gaby hasn't talked to you about these things?"

"In generalities," Ayan said.

"But I'm surprised!" Andreas said. "I told her all this—when she said she had a friend from India. Multiple strands connect Germans and Indians at a sublime level. I have some books I think you'll find interesting . . ."

"Thank you. I look forward to reading them."

"They're important. People who understand this side of the German can understand the religious fervor Hitler generated in our psyche, how well he manipulated us through symbols and sermons."

Steinkrugs

"Yes, I've heard how many people were taken by Hitler's call to duty for the Fatherland," Ayan said. "From German colleagues at work."

"Charismatic gurus in India have always created cults and led intelligent people astray. So many do whatever their guru asks them to do. Am I right? I saw it with my own eyes when I was in India. Hitler preyed on the same common tendencies in our people."

I'm not sure I like where this conversation is going, Ayan thought.

"In the West," Andreas said, "they ask how a great, sophisticated culture like Germany could have allowed what happened to occur. We were following our guru, part of his cult, doing what he asked us to do, for the Fatherland."

"What about the brutality, the atrocities?"

"Yes, but atrocities were committed by both sides. Dresden, for example."

"You're not saying there's an equivalence, are you?" Ayan said. "There can never be an equivalence."

He looked around for Gaby. Where was she?

The intimacy in Andreas' expression evaporated. He pointed to the sky.

"It was a difficult time. Only He can weigh the scales," Andreas said. "But for us Germans, Dresden will never be forgotten. *Mehr braucht man nicht zu sagen!* Enough! Coffee? I'll go and make some."

Ayan had spoken too abruptly.

But Andreas had startled him into being rude. Yes, he was like so many of the people Ayan had interacted with at work: After dinner and a few drinks, Germans of his age often brought up the Third Reich, with undertones of justification, some with righteousness. But Andreas was Gaby's father. How could he think like this!

Gaby returned with the coffee.

"My father's taking a nap," she said. "His usual twenty minutes after lunch."

She moved the strudel out of Ayan's reach. "You've had enough food; you'll get fat. Drink your coffee and let's go down to the lake."

"You and your mother seem very close," Ayan said as they walked along the gravel path that circled around Lake Starnberg.

"I take care of her. She has these sudden mood swings and terrible headaches. I'm the only one she wants around when she's not feeling well."

"You're so much like her. Even your mannerisms are similar."

"I'm nothing like her!" Gaby said sharply. "I'm not throwing away my life like she did. She was a brilliant student at Heidelberg. Now she's like any other German hausfrau: focused only on her family and her church and, not surprisingly, deeply depressed. I am the opposite of her in every way!"

"Yes, yes, I understand," Ayan said. "I was talking about the physical resemblance. Anyway, your mother didn't seem too happy to see me."

"She was just upset that I ruined her Sunday plans. She missed the social events after church," Gaby said. "And she had a migraine."

"That's nice of you to say, but I could tell that she was uneasy around me."

"You can understand that, can't you? A strange foreign man coming home with her precious daughter?"

"Yes. Particularly a man with intentions."

"I see. And what if our intentions are different?" Gaby said smiling. She led him off the path, towards the lake.

"I'll persuade you. And her."

"Ayan, you are so far away from me now—in many ways. You're in Tehran, on your own journey to who knows where. I have a life here. I have to be near my mother."

"I'll find a way to link my journey with yours," Ayan said.

"It will be hard. Now come this way. I want to show you my favorite spots. Where I used to go to be alone and read."

She led him off the path, towards the lake.

As they were returning, Gaby stopped him at the gates that led to the garden.

She put her arms around him.

"I'm still not ready for you to leave, Ayan," she said. "I'll really miss you, and you're not so good at staying in touch."

"It's different now. I'll come and see you. All the time."

"Will you? You promise? I'll come sometimes too. I still get free tickets in my new job."

"You'll come back to Iran?"

"For a few days. Let's take turns. I'll come next. Let's go to Isfahan. I've always wanted to spend more time there."

"Isfahan it is. When?"

"I'll let you know. I have to check my schedule—but soon. My work is more predictable now."

Later, when they were in upstairs and in her bedroom, Gaby kissed him and tried to unbutton his shirt.

"Not here," Ayan said, "I can't."

"Come on—I want to. Now!" Gaby said.

She threw off her clothes and lay down on her bed.

"Still can't?" she said.

"You must have made a good impression on my father," Gaby said as they drove back to Munich a couple of hours later. "He doesn't usually part with one of his Steinkrugs."

"That was nice of him," Ayan said. "We had an interesting discussion."

"What about?"

"Corporate life, shared experiences, the past . . ."

"The past?"

"Yes."

"Oh. What about the past?"

Ayan looked at her. Her face was suddenly serious.

"Well, linguistic similarities, German history, perspective."

"He's been a good father to me," Gaby said. "And a wonderful husband to my mother."

Her shoulders were stiff, telling him they'd reached a red line.

She looked ahead.

Apparently, Gaby was willing to talk about her mother's shortcomings but not her father's darkness. Perhaps that compromise was too great to acknowledge.

He just knew he shouldn't say more.

"Stop tapping the dashboard!" Gaby said. "It's distracting."

"OK, I will," Ayan said.

"Were you singing?" Gaby said, her expression softening.

"Running on empty . . ." he sang.

"Is that what we're doing, babe?" she said, smiling at him, her clear soprano taking over, pitch perfect as she made up lines, singing in tune to Jackson Browne's song.

PART
FOUR

CHAPTER 16

Tehran, Iran, February 1978

Ayan walked along the railing cordoning off visitors outside the customs hall at Mehrabad Airport. Despite the modern facilities and the fashionable crowd, the smoke and traffic fumes reminded him he was back in a developing country.

This arrival in Tehran felt different, though. His life had changed in West Berlin. He looked around for Hamid, trying to suppress the Greek chorus telling him he was 3,000 miles from Gaby, warning him about that rich bastard Charlie—that he should worry because he'd crossed another bridge in Switzerland. To hell with all that! *I'm going to be happy*, he told himself.

And at some point, anywhere you live becomes home, and for now, Tehran was that. He was returning to familiar scenery, friends, and not a bad life.

Two small persons came crashing into him. Hamid appeared right behind them, out of breath from running after his sons. The three of them began to argue over the handling of Ayan's luggage. *Not even the Italians can match the charm of Iranians acting out their dialogue*, Ayan thought with amusement. There were expressions, shrugs, and a variety of other gestures. Finally, it was decided: Hamid relieved Ayan of his overcoat and duty-free shopping bag; Imran got the briefcase, which he hugged to his chest; Adil took over the luggage trolley; and the party made its way to the airport parking lot.

A tall, thin man was standing next to the Iran Power Mercedes.

Ayan recognized the hawkish profile of the unhinged thug who had led the angry chants in Hamid's mosque and promised to personally dismember the Shah.

"This is my good friend Hedayat," Hamid said.

Hedayat gave Ayan a cursory nod.

You're not that important, Hedayat's look communicated. *You're just another foreigner here to loot us.*

I hate you, too, you uneducated low-life, Ayan thought, brushing past Hedayat dismissively.

Hedayat opened the front passenger door and sat down.

"No! Get out!" Ayan said harshly. "Hamid, no one is allowed in this car besides you and me. You know that! I'll make an exception for your family, but that's it."

"I'm sorry, Ayan Agha," Hamid said. "I thought being the weekend, a Friday, it would be all right. We are taking Hedayat to a function in the mosque after dropping you home."

"He can take a bus or a taxi. He can't sit in an Iran Power car again. Is that clear?"

"Yes—I'm sorry. It won't happen again," Hamid said, leaning to Hedayat and explaining the situation.

Hedayat looked at Ayan with a sneer. He slammed the door of the car and spat contemptuously.

Several army trucks were parked on the road leading out from the airport. They reached Shahyad Square, and everywhere

Ayan looked, there were soldiers with AK-47s. Hamid's jaw was grinding. He looked nervous. What the fuck was going on? Ayan fought a sudden, overwhelming desire to turn around and leave Tehran, to go back to Germany and be with Gaby. He looked away from the bristling army presence and at the soaring Shahyad monument, then at the Alborz, still visible in the evening light.

The boys had been silent since his confrontation with Hedayat. *They don't deserve this*, Ayan thought and gave Imran a box of Suchard chocolates he'd picked up in duty-free. "Share this with your brother," he said, "and I'll tell you about my journey to Europe."

He began to spin tall tales about the trip, embellishing his stories to entertain the boys.

The younger boy paid attention, nodding encouragingly.

Adil, sitting with his father in front, lost interest after he'd coaxed a sizable number of the chocolates from Imran.

Finally, reacting to the escalating absurdity of Ayan's tales, Imran giggled and said, "You're making it all up. You're lying, I know you are!"

His hands continued to stuff chocolates in his mouth. "You're not a very good storyteller! Not like my mother."

"She's from Rasht," Hamid said, smiling into the rear-view mirror. "Rashtis tell a lot of stories; many foreigners have lived there."

Ayan ruffled Imran's hair. "Tell me one of your mother's stories."

He rested his head on the back of the seat. Outside, women in chadors hurried about, shepherding their children through narrow alleys in the side streets. There were more soldiers about—even a tank.

Fariba was waiting for him when they pulled into Khanom-eh Mohsen's driveway. He wasn't ready for this! Fuck! Fuck! Fucking fuck! Wasn't she supposed to come over tomorrow?

"I couldn't wait to welcome you home, Ayan *joon*," Fariba said, kissing him. She was wearing a black pantsuit, pearl earrings, and a long pearl necklace. Her hair was freshly styled.

Ayan felt a pang at seeing her dressed up for him.

She wiped her lipstick from his mouth. "I've cooked some *fesenjan* for you. It's in your kitchen. Khanom-eh Mohsen let me in."

"Good to see you, Fariba," Ayan said, giving her a hug. "I can't wait to attack your brilliant cooking. Thank you! I'm starving!"

A slight frown appeared on her face.

"Don't speak to me like that!"

"Like what?" he said, giving her a hug.

Fariba's large brown eyes looked at him pensively.

"Maybe you're tired. You must be. Shower and settle in," she said. "I'll heat the food."

"First a drink," Ayan said. "I'm one below par."

He made Fariba a screwdriver—not too much vodka, plenty of orange juice, just the way she liked it—and a dirty, dry, very strong martini for himself.

He lingered under the shower, martini within reach.

Please forgive me for what I'm about to tell you, my dear, dear Fariba.

He heard her hum along to "Dreams." She'd put on *Rumors*, her favorite album. They must have heard it a million times together.

Sadness and guilt overwhelmed him.

No good outcome was possible tonight.

He refreshed their drinks and chatted nervously as they ate.

Fariba's elegant *taarof* bought him time, and he was grateful.

She responded politely, listened attentively.

Till "Go Your Own Way."

"Dance with me," she said, rising from the table and putting out her hand.

She pulled him closer as he moved in time with her.

This is too uncomfortable, I can't do this to her, Ayan thought.

"Fariba . . ." Ayan hesitated and looked down to compose himself.

"Ayan—*joon* . . . what's the matter?" Fariba said.

"I saw Gaby, and we sort of, you know, got together again. We're back together . . ." he trailed off uncertainly.

She reeled.

It was as if he'd punched her in the chest.

She sat down, breathing heavily.

"You bastard!" she said, looking at the floor—then louder, looking at him, "you . . . you dirty, deceitful bastard!"

"Fariba, please, let me explain . . ."

She pushed his hand away and came at him, slapping him, trembling with rage.

Tears rolled down her cheeks.

"That bitch dumped you once, and I hope she dumps you again! I know she will. Because you're a pathetic man! I hate you, you bastard!"

She ran out onto the roof, came back to grab her purse and overcoat, and ran out again.

He chased after her.

"Fariba! Please! Don't go like this!"

She took off one of her high heels and threw it at him—and then the other.

"Don't come near me again!" she yelled. "Don't speak to me again, don't you dare ever look at me again!

He watched her run barefoot down Khanom-eh Mohsen's driveway.

As she roared off in her Fiat Spider, he thought, *Hours, days, months together. All disappearing.*

Just like that.

He felt guilty—and lonely. Far worse than he had feared he would.

But he knew he deserved this.

He went inside and tried to call Gaby. The operator said there was no answer.

"Please try again," Ayan said. *Gaby, baby, please pick up. I really need to hear your voice tonight.*

CHAPTER 17

"**Y**our new driver is waiting, outside the gate, like he should," Khanom-eh Mohsen said as Ayan came down the stairs on Sunday morning, after taking Saturday off to recover.

"Oh! Hamid's not here?" Ayan said, surprised.

Hamid never missed a day of work.

"This person is much better than that *dehati* who makes himself at home on my property."

"Don't get your hopes up," Ayan said. "Hamid is probably sick. He'll be back praying on your lawn tomorrow. By the way, here's the Drambuie you asked for from duty-free. Also, some chocolates—from Hamid!"

"You're an insolent but nice boy," Khanom-eh Mohsen said, putting down the bag Ayan gave her and walking with him down the driveway. "I saw Fariba run away in anger. Don't worry. These things happen. Girls are emotional. She will come back. Perhaps you've made up already."

"Goodbye, Khanom," Ayan said, frowning at her.

In her house, it was difficult to keep any sort of boundary around his personal life

"Where's Hamid?" he asked the slim, balding man who hurriedly snuffed out a cigarette and opened the rear door of the Iran Power Mercedes.

"I don't know, sir! Excuse me! It's my pleasure to drive you, sir!"

"I haven't seen you before," Ayan said as they started the commute to the factory. "Are you a new driver?"

"No, sir! I've worked in Iran Power for a long time, sir. I'm Colonel Hosseini's driver, Mehdi Shamshiri. I was driving his private cars, sir. That's why you haven't seen me."

"The Colonel shouldn't have to be inconvenienced on my behalf. Why didn't they send me a spare driver from the pool?"

"I don't know, sir. Excuse me, sir."

Mehdi was an excellent driver. Better than Hamid. His English was also surprisingly good.

"You are SAVAK, aren't you? The Colonel already has enough people spying on me."

Mehdi's nervous look into the rearview mirror confirmed it.

"No, sir! I'm just a driver," Mehdi said. "Don't worry about anything."

He smiled and made reassuring gestures with his hands.

"Don't worry about anything, sir," he repeated.

"I don't want anyone working for the Colonel coming to my house again. Do you understand?

The man now looked worried.

"No sir! Not SAVAK! Believe me!"

There was no point in continuing this conversation.

"Go via Pahlavi," Ayan said. "I need to pick up a newspaper."

"I'm happy to see you back, Ayan Agha," Hosseini said, timing his entry into Ayan's office with Amir Agha's tea tray, as usual."

He lifted both palms skyward, tilted his head, and smiled theatrically.

"'Ever since happiness heard your name, it has been running through the streets trying to find you . . .'"

"Colonel, we need to talk about Mehdi," Ayan said, dispensing with *taarof*.

"Yes, I've found you the best driver," Hosseini said, sitting down on the chair opposite Ayan's desk.

He directed Amir Agha to pour some tea for Ayan, making the old man nervous in completing a task he had already started to do.

"I'm very happy with Hamid," Ayan said, helping Amir Agha to mop up some of the tea that had spilt onto the tray.

"Hamid's disappeared," Hosseini said casually.

"That can't be," Ayan said, shocked. "He was just with me a couple of days ago."

"These people," Hosseini said. "They come, they go . . ."

"Hamid couldn't have gone anywhere!" Ayan said.

Hosseini shrugged. "I don't know," he said. "Anyway, let's talk about West Berlin; I heard it's a very interesting city."

What the fuck!

"Why West Berlin?" Ayan said.

"I took two calls for you: one from border control in Germany, the other from the counter-terrorism force. They wanted to confirm your identity."

"Oh," Ayan said, raising his eyebrows. "Really?"

"Yes. The German police were suspicious about you."

"That's interesting," Ayan said nonchalantly, breaking off a piece of lavash bread and deliberately adding a topping of feta cheese and caviar. "I was on holiday there." He squeezed a slice of lemon on top of his morsel and slid his tray towards Hosseini. "Some breakfast, Colonel?"

"No, thank you," Hosseini said. "Gaby has an apartment in Berlin. She spoke about it; perhaps I'll go and visit her too—also enjoy some moments with that beautiful lady, now that you are engaged to Fariba Khanom. With your permission, of course."

He made a mock bow.

This bastard needs a hard kick in the balls, Ayan thought. *Someday . . .*

"You need to be more careful, Colonel. You're crossing a line," Ayan said.

Hosseini looked reproachfully at Ayan.

"No need to get angry, Ayan Agha. Not at the person who helped you with those Germans. I didn't have to. You were not on official business."

Ayan sat back in his chair, shaking his head in disbelief.

"Colonel," he said, smiling sarcastically, "I have to hand it to you. You're a maestro."

Hosseini waved a hand in the air and shrugged. "I'm nothing. You are the smart person who gets a new Mercedes— and gets sent to Switzerland to do important things."

"I don't know what you mean," Ayan said.

Let Nader tell him, if he wanted to; perhaps he'd already done that, and Hosseini was just fishing for more. "I went to Germany, not Switzerland, to work with Hauser. I'm just a numbers man who does as he's told."

"No, Agha Ayan, you are an important person, who has been asked to do important things. That is why I've selected Mehdi to be your driver."

"I don't need your driver! I'll ask my staff to get me somebody from the pool till Hamid gets back. Don't worry about it."

"No worry at all. Mehdi speaks English, and he is a very good and safe driver. Keep him. My pleasure."

"No!" Ayan responded sharply. "It has to be Hamid. Now, if you'll excuse me, I have a lot of catching up to do."

"Agha Ayan," Hosseini said calmly, "Hamid is uneducated. It is not good for you to be driven around by somebody like him. It brings you down in the opinion of people. Mehdi is very intelligent. You will be able to pass time enjoyably with him."

"I'm happy with Hamid, so I am keeping him," Ayan said as the Colonel got up and started to walk out of his office.

Hosseini hustled back and sat down again.

He could move his bulk quickly when he wanted to.

"Agha Ayan," he said, placing both elbows on Ayan's desk. "Let me tell you something serious: We are concerned about people who are from the countryside who are unemployed—dissatisfied people who stay in Tehran to make trouble. Hamid has been seen in the company of these undesirables. He is under investigation. You know what I'm talking about?"

It had to be that loudmouth Hedayat and his braggadocio, Ayan thought. *Hamid was in the Colonel's sights because of him. How many times had he warned him to be careful!*

"Hamid is a simple person," Ayan said emphatically. "He is only interested in his family's welfare. He is very dedicated to our company and his job. I vouch for him."

"Agha Ayan. I'm sorry to tell you Hamid is already under arrest."

'What!" Ayan said, standing up. "Why? He's done nothing!"

Hosseini calmly examined his fingernails.

"What's happened? What have you done to Hamid?" Ayan said fiercely.

"Nothing!" the Colonel said, raising his palms outward and moving back in his chair.

He looked irritated and offended.

"He was supposed to be arrested, but he disappeared."

"Look, Colonel," Ayan said. "Hamid has been with me for a long time; he is more than a driver to me. I consider him to be a friend. I'm going to find out what you've done to him."

"Then you should have known that your driver is an insurgent, a communist, and a terrorist. You should have warned me. Why didn't you?" Hosseini said.

Ayan sidestepped the trap.

"I know nothing about all that."

"Ayan Agha, Hamid, who is totally unworthy of your friendship, corrupted a group of our workers. They went to Tabriz with him yesterday and engaged in illegal and immoral violence against the city. We have photographs of him and the others committing crimes in Tabriz. We were about to arrest Hamid, but somebody alerted him."

"That's unbelievable!" Ayan said.

"Hamid was not sick yesterday, as he told people here. He took part in an illegal demonstration; he belongs to a violent anti-government group that has committed many crimes against the State. We have captured many of the traitors; Hamid was one of the few who escaped. We will find him soon."

"I told Hamid I was taking a day off yesterday, so he probably used it as a chance to do some personal work. Hamid was not in any demonstration. He was with his family. I know it."

"I'm sorry, Agha Ayan. Hamid has deceived all of us."

Ayan came around to Hosseini's side of the desk and sat down next to him.

"Colonel, there's been a mistake. Hamid is very poor. His family will starve. Help him. Please."

"If there were no photographs and witnesses, but . . ."

"Give him another chance. I'll speak to him," Ayan pleaded, regretting his earlier aggression and rudeness.

"Let this be, Agha Ayan," Hosseini said. "Neither of us can help Hamid. He is finished. There are many people like him who try to block progress. Don't waste your time with useless people like him. Fortunately, Mehdi is available. Mehdi is a trained bodyguard, like drivers of other important people in this company. You're in good hands now."

He got up.

"It's easy to complain and cause unrest but very hard to build a country," Hosseini said. "We are pulling Iran into the modern world. That's why we have brought people like you to our country, so just take care of this." Hosseini swept his hand across the manufacturing activities outside Ayan's window. "And stay out of matters that don't concern you."

Where was Hamid? What was happening to the family? Ayan worried, even as he briefed the team in Nader's office on the work he'd done at SA's Stuttgart office.

There was only one way to find out: go to Hamid's house near the Bazaar. He would do that tonight.

It was freezing when he got home.

Ayan flicked the snowflakes off his hair and kicked the door shut. A draft blew in behind him, chilling him through his clothes. He switched on the lights, turned on the two-bar electric fire in the living room, and hung up his overcoat.

He thawed out in the shower, ate cheese toast and an apple for dinner, filled the Steinkrug Andreas had given him with two bottles of Heineken, and settled down at his desk. He'd call for a taxi at 9:00 p.m., when the traffic to the Bazaar would be manageable.

In the meanwhile, he had to write reports. The boss wanted everything by tomorrow. He'd been distracted in the meeting today: hesitant and uncertain about some details. The engineering department had poked holes in his plans to increase automation in his area, the deal he'd cut with SA Stuttgart, and his need to interrupt the production line for two days for the auditors' verification of inventory. It was the old war between finance and engineering. He'd get them next time. For now, he was on the spot.

Darioush called to see if he was coming to the Key Club later.

"Not tonight," Ayan said. "I have too much work."

"You should come. Speak to Hassan. I know I would have had to kill you if you had ruined my sister!"

"That was fast," Ayan said. "Who told you?"

"Doesn't matter," Darioush said. "Why did you sleep with Fariba if you were going to leave her?"

"I didn't plan any of this."

"You have a big problem, my friend."

"I know, but I didn't ruin Fariba, as you say. She had boyfriends in America and here, incidentally. It was a mutual thing with us."

"OK. Whatever you say. Perhaps you should have agreed on a *mu'tah* before you went too far: signed a contract, paid her a negotiated settlement, had your fun for however long, and then it would be over."

Ayan heard Darioush laugh.

"It's not funny Darioush! I'll meet Hassan tomorrow and try to explain things."

"Well, good luck with Hassan. It's not my problem except you've also screwed our doubles game. Hassan will never play with you again. It's your responsibility to find a replacement. And what's so important that you can't come by and say hello? Haven't seen you in a while."

"Work. Have to catch up."

"So? Work afterwards. You're an insomniac."

Mu'tah

"I also need to take care of something downtown."

"At this time? I wouldn't go there. It's still a mess from yesterday."

"Really?"

"Turn on the radio. There were protests all over the country yesterday. One hundred people were killed in Tabriz. Stay away from downtown for a few days. And come to the Key Club. I'm just heading over."

Ayan turned on the Sony short-wave radio his father had given him. It was already tuned to the BBC, the only reliable source of information around. The World Service had its interminable Africa program on. There couldn't be much of an emergency in Iran if farming conditions in the Rift Valley were getting this much play. At any rate, he wasn't going to the Key Club. He was going to keep at these reports and then take a taxi down to the Bazaar, as planned. He had to find out about Hamid—leave some money for the family, at the very least.

He was going to be busy for the next several days, and this was his only opportunity.

Ayan turned up the volume when the late news came on. Finally, the situation in Iran was mentioned. Forty days after the deaths in Qom, the newsreader said, at the customary remembrance, the *Arbaeen*, for the fallen yesterday, troops and tanks were brought out from a nearby base in Tabriz, and things had got out of hand. The Shah's forces had opened fire on the peaceful protestors, killing dozens of people.

The newsreader cut to a reporter in Qom, just a few miles south of the Iran Power factory, interviewing Ayatollah Shariatmadari. "The protestors were fighting injustice," the religious leader said. "Iran has never had free elections—just suffered interference from local moneymen and foreign powers. The laws are repugnant to Islam and public interest, and there is alcoholism, gambling, illicit sex, dishonor of women . . ."

Another correspondent in Tabriz came on. He sounded distant and urgent, as if reporting from a war zone. He began interviewing students who had joined in the protests. One of them had seen a machine gun volley shred his classmate's chest, and he angrily denounced the theft of national oil wealth by the Shah and his cronies, a fake economy that relied on imported goods and expertise, development projects that were just vessels for royal family corruption . . .

These complaints are just echoes of Hamid's grievances, Ayan thought. He turned down the volume on the transistor as the newscaster went on to provide a context for yesterday and for earlier political uprisings in Iran. It was not surprising that both self-serving and benevolent initiatives of the West seemed to lead to the same outcome—more trouble on the streets of Iran.

He already knew the answers to the questions raised by the BBC about the network that mobilized so many people and the fervor of the crowd. The imam in Hamid's mosque was surely not the only one exhorting his followers to gather strength for this *Arbaeen*, and Hamid was surely not the only one responding to Ayatollah Khomeini's taped calls for a jihad against the Pahlavis.

But it was still worrying to watch the protests gather strength.

He returned to his work, trying to ignore a sense of an unraveling.

CHAPTER 18

A yan called the Best Taxi Service fifteen minutes before he needed a car. They were based around the corner and maintained a sizeable fleet. No taxis were going to the Bazaar tonight, he was told. A promise to pay double got him a ride.

Everything looked the way it should on the way down. The press of Tehran life had washed over whatever had happened yesterday.

But it felt bizarre to be driving south so late in the evening, moving through familiar streets looking strange without traffic, moving so fast on this unreal mission.

The atmosphere became heavy and sullen as they approached the Bazaar.

The taxi driver stopped responding to Ayan's attempts at conversation.

This is a mistake, Ayan thought, tensing as they arrived at a roadblock, and gun-toting soldiers asked for identification.

He should have listened to Darioush.

A flashlight examined Ayan and the driver.

What was his business in the Bazaar at this time?

Visiting a friend, Ayan said.

The area is closed. Come in the morning.

It is an emergency, Ayan said. It will only take a few minutes. I am from Iran Power.

The flashlight glanced at Ayan's business card.

Wait here, he was told.

An obviously more-senior man arrived.

Iran Power?

Yes.

Good company. Very big.

Yes. Thank you.

You can go.

They were waved on.

Ayan directed the now reluctant taxi driver through the maze of alleys next to the Bazaar till he saw one that looked familiar. He asked the taxi driver to wait for fifteen minutes, quieting the man's grumbling with the promise of an extra hundred tomans, and walked down the alley to the building he'd seen Hamid enter.

It was towards the end of the cul-de-sac. A man was squatting on the stairs leading up to the rustic wooden door.

"Salam Agha," Ayan said to the scowling face. "Do you know Hamid?"

"No, mister. No Hamid here," the man replied, waving Ayan off.

Not surprising.

Ayan sat down next to him.

"Is Khanom Sholeh here? I have some money for the family."

The man stared at Ayan.

"I know she lives here. Call her. Tell her Ayan has come to see her."

He got up reluctantly and disappeared inside.

He returned with three other men, who surrounded Ayan and began to bark questions at him.

"Who are you?"

"What do you want?"

"No Hamid here. Don't cause problems! Leave immediately!"

Ayan smiled to defuse their aggression.

"I've come to help," he said with a reasonable face and voice. "Tell Khanom Sholeh that Ayan is here. She knows me."

The youngest of the four men stepped towards Ayan.

"We don't know anything about a Hamid or his family. Go!"

He shoved Ayan backwards.

Ayan bottled the desire to smack the little shit to the ground. An army patrol was nearby, and explanations might get difficult.

His designated bouncer pushed him again as Ayan walked back towards the taxi.

A mistake.

Ayan floored him with a rage-filled roundhouse.

The man forced himself up, looking surprised.

He staggered back towards his companions, who were half inside the building by now.

They urged him to move faster as Ayan came for him again.

Not fast enough.

Ayan managed to land a satisfying kick on the man's behind that sent him flying through the door of Hamid's building.

The door slammed shut.

Ayan kicked the door a few times.

Silence greeted his calls for the men to come out.

Ayan retreated, looking over his shoulder frequently, and worrying about the army patrol.

Thankfully, the soldiers had moved on.

He was getting back into the taxi when an old woman shuffled up to him and tugged at his jacket.

"Salaam Agha, I am Hamid's mother. I am sorry about these stupid men. My son has told me about you."

She looked like any number of chador-clad women around. But there was something familiar in her expression—enough to make Ayan reach into his coat and pull out the envelope with the money.

"Salaam Khanom," Ayan said. "I'm happy you came to me, because I have some money for the family. I know it's hard times. Please give it to Sholeh Khanom."

The old woman whisked the envelope from his hand and hid it somewhere under her chador, looking around furtively.

"*Kheili mamnoon,*" she said, smiling at Ayan and exposing gums mostly bereft of teeth.

"How is Hamid?"

She raised her eyebrows and clicked her tongue, signaling a negative. Then she turned and merged into the dark.

The taxi driver looked back at Ayan as they drove away from the Bazaar.

"Very dangerous here for foreigners," he said. "You should stay in Shemiran. Everybody's very angry in Tehran. Shah very bad; Amrika very bad! Israel very bad!"

Ayan nodded.

"Yes. I should stay in Shemiran," he said.

After they had driven some distance and no one was about, the driver stuck his neck out of the window, balled up his hand into a fist, and yelled, "*Marg bar Amrika! Marg bar Israel! Marg bar Shah!*"

Turning to Ayan again, he said, "I also hate everybody." He repeated the chants, then rolled up his window. "I only love some peoples: Persian peoples, Hindi peoples—peoples from India very good! I love Ayatollah Khomeini—I love him! He should be here! You love him too? That's why you came to Bazaar? To help somebody?"

"I love everybody, everybody," Ayan said.

The taxi driver beamed. "Hindi peoples very good, very good. But Hindi people very quiet; you like to fight?"

Ayan contemplated the back of the driver's head for a while.

"When fighting is needed," he said. "I fight."

The driver nodded his head approvingly.

"You a dangerous man," he said. "Very dangerous. Just like me."

The next evening, Ayan went out onto the roof to escape the reheated air of his apartment.

Khanom-eh Mohsen was walking home after her evening stroll. She believed in being outside during twilight, even in cold weather, and looked up at him.

"I saw your driver just now," she said. "The bad one. He turned away when I saw him. How strangely he behaved! What was he doing here at 6:30 p.m.?"

Ayan shook his head and shrugged.

He waited untill he heard the front door shut, then rushed out of the villa.

The street was busy with people coming home from work. There was no sign of Hamid. He completed a loop of the neighborhood—still no Hamid. *She must have imagined it,* Ayan thought.

A hundred yards before he got back home, his instincts made him move away from a dark cluster of trees and low bushes.

Hamid emerged from behind one of the trees. He was unshaven, and his clothes were dirty, but otherwise, he looked fine.

Ayan embraced him, relief breaching the reserve their relationship had dictated.

"I'm glad you're OK," he said.

"I came to thank you," Hamid said. "I have nobody else to turn to; without you, my family will starve. Thank you, thank you . . ." Hamid's eyes welled up.

Ayan wanted to say, *I warned you several times.*

A voice came out of the darkness asking Hamid to hurry.

"I'm here for you," Ayan said. "But Hosseini is determined to find you. You can't stay in Tehran."

"Yes, I know. They have arrested many people from our mosque. I'm sure they've been martyred," Hamid said, drying his eyes on his rough woolen sweater. "I am not in Tehran." He pointed to the bushes. "Hedayat is very clever. No one can find us. My wife's family is trying to find work for me in a small village near Rasht. In the meantime, whatever you can spare will be like a blessing from Allah."

Hamid took Ayan's hands in his and brought them to his heart. Then he was gone.

A motorcycle engine spat, and a light two-wheeler raced out of the bushes with Hamid holding on to Hedayat. They were both hunched forward against the cold, faces camouflaged in scarves.

And so it began.

Every Friday, soon after the Khanom returned from her evening constitutional at 6:30 p.m., Ayan walked the hundred yards to the left of the villa where the cluster of bushes provided cover for the fugitives. After some *taarof*, he pressed the money into Hamid's right hand, and they—for Hamid was always with Hedayat—would be off on Hedayat's motorcycle.

Ayan had been giving 1,000 tomans to Hamid each month to pay for the boys' schooling. That lifeline had to be increased significantly now that Hamid's salary had been cut off. He settled on 1,000 tomans every week. It was more than Hamid's salary as a driver for Iran Power, and he could spare the $600 a month it amounted to, if he cut back on things he didn't really need.

CHAPTER 19

old Friend [handwritten annotation]

"**I**f more people die in these kinds of protests, go straight to your bank and send all your money abroad," Darioush said as they drank the Macallan 18 from his personal bottle at the Key Club one night.

"You're not getting nervous, too, are you?" Ayan said. "Mr. Responsible, socially conscious, respected helper of all?"

"Business is down. Jobs are disappearing with all this inflation and rising interest rates. Now that we also have peasants, mullahs, students—everybody—losing their fear of the SAVAK and the Shah, everybody's making plans to move to LA or Toronto or wherever, if things get worse."

"Not you, though, you can't just get up and go. What about all your hotels?"

"Marco is a partner in most of them. He can run things till the hotels are sold. March 29 is a day I'm watching: the *Arbaeen* for the people killed in Tabriz. If the Shah can't control the crowds on that day, I'm gone."

"And visas? Do you have a Green Card or permanent residency somewhere?"

"Every country allows you in if you invest enough. I have money abroad and a real estate company in Beverly Hills, a multiple entry visa into the US, and also an offer of residency in Canada."

"Unfortunately," Ayan said, "I just have my Indian passport, no visas to work anywhere else, and a working man's savings account. I'll have to ride it out in Iran, for another year at least, till my bank account is fat enough to allow me to jump ship."

He fidgeted, playing percussion on the table, feeling that he should also be making some back-up plans that went beyond just waiting around till he had enough money. Did he really have to, though? Indians were well liked in Iran. Rich Iranians and Westerners fleeing would mean that he would be in greater demand. They would still need people to keep the lights switched on. He had enough on his mind. He didn't need to add a fast exit out of Iran to the list.

"Well, when you're ready, come to LA and join me," Darioush said. "You'll enjoy it: tennis, skiing, blondes."

"Gaby wants to stay in Germany. Perhaps I can get her to move somewhere else in Europe, but not to America. Most likely, I'll go to West Berlin and join her there. Start something of my own."

"So, this time, it's serious. On her side too?"

"Yes."

"Well, good. I'm also serious about somebody," Darioush said. "See that blonde dancing over there? She's Julie. Gaby brought her up here one day."

Ayan looked over at the dance floor.

Julie stood out in the changing sea of beautiful European women in their early twenties who worked as flight attendants for Iran Air. She was gorgeous and with somebody. But if Darioush wanted her, he would probably succeed. Not many women resisted him.

why

"Yes, I'm acquainted with Julie," Ayan said. "But what about your current wife—the good Chantal Brodeur?"

"Ayan, listen. I know that you and Chantal are friends, but she's really not been a wife to me for a long time. She's here now, but that's rare. She wanted property in Saint-Emilion, and I've bought her a hotel in the village. I buy her whatever she wants, and that's the only reason she stays with me. I'm going to make babies with happy, beautiful Julie. Look at her laugh! What a mother she'll make! I'm in love with her. Like you with Gaby!"

"There is a difference," Ayan said sarcastically. "I've actually spent time with Gaby."

"I just have a feeling about this girl, Ayan. She is the one. She doesn't know it yet, but she's going to be my next wife. Do me a favor. Come up to Shemiran on Thursday and bring her with you."

"I'll come, but alone," Ayan said. "I like your wife. I'm not getting in the middle of anything."

"OK, I'll find a way to invite Julie," Darioush said. "But it would easier for me if she came up with you. I need cover with Chantal. Do that for me. Now I'm going home. Some of us need sleep before a working day. See you on Thursday. If you survive tonight!"

Darioush smiled in the direction of Hassan, who was sitting with a couple at his usual table, just above the dance floor,

"It's time you two talked," he said, giving Ayan an encouraging squeeze on the shoulder.

Ayan had delayed the inevitable confrontation, but here was Hassan walking towards him, and then right by him, ignoring Ayan's outstretched hand.

So that's how it's going to be, Ayan thought, getting up to follow Hassan.

The man was understandably angry. But they were friends, and he needed to explain what he'd done.

He caught up to Hassan as he approached the coat check.

"Hassan, I need to say something to you," Ayan said.

Hassan collected his overcoat and tipped the attendant. He turned to Ayan with a hard expression.

"Go ahead," he said.

"I wanted to tell you about something that has happened—I met Gaby in Germany."

Ayan went through his story, Hassan's tight smile and unchanging expression making him nervous and garrulous.

Hassan soon held up his hand.

"I've heard you out," he said. "You've got to do what you've got to do. Fariba is an adult. She does as she pleases. But if she confirms that you took advantage of her, as I've heard, I will do whatever it is I have to do."

The coldness in Hassan's eyes left no room for appeal.

He brushed past Ayan, and the heavy door of the Key Club closed behind him.

He hadn't taken advantage of Fariba! She'd been an eager partner at every step in the escalation of their intimacy. He hadn't seduced an innocent. But how was Hassan to know that? Or take Ayan's side over family? Accept what he had done in this culture?

He understood Hassan's reaction, but that didn't soften the blow.

Gaby was so far away. Coming soon but not soon enough. He tried to picture her face. She materialized for a while, flying him around Lake Stanberger, her laughing eyes and dimples making light of his concern as she buzzed the tree line. Then the image faded, and he was back, standing alone at the door of the Key Club.

His life here was built on quicksand, he realized: on friendships that he couldn't really count on. Hassan had become an enemy in an instant. Nick, the CIA man, must be playing him. And Darioush was making plans to leave Iran.

A sudden nostalgia for Delhi, for familiar things, for *desi* voices and faces, took hold of Ayan as he walked out of the club, and he decided to visit the Indians he knew at the Iran Center for Management Studies.

He'd attended a few of their parties at the beautifully landscaped campus that meandered down the Alborz, and they'd complained he didn't spend enough time with them. There were reasons: Gaby found their ambitions too narrow and their loud confidence annoying; Fariba preferred the company of her Iranian circle; and unlike Darioush, Hassan, and Nick, the ICMS group were not sporting men. Well, tonight they may regret inviting him all those times, because he was on his way to crash their scene.

They would welcome him, he knew, as they would any other person like them from the subcontinent, and he would feel at home despite not seeing them for a while. It was not that late. They would still be hard at work, preparing for tomorrow's case studies. Or they should be. They were attending one of the best business schools in the world and aspired to be CEOs. Sleep was for middle-management types.

"Hey! Hey! Big shot! You've come just in time to help us with this finance case," Suresh, the leader of the Indian gang at ICMS, said when Ayan joined them in the vaulted space shared by students, who lived in a madrasa-style cluster of four rooms surrounding a courtyard.

"I'm here for purely selfish reasons," Ayan said, sitting down next to Suresh on the sofa. "I'm feeling homesick."

Rajiv and Deepak were flopped about, immersed in their reading. The Pakistani, Noor, a history major and the only non-engineer in the group, was sitting in an armchair, writing notes.

Noor got up and brought Ayan a plate of chicken curry and rice.

"I'm not in any state to really read this," Ayan said, flicking through the case study on IBM's capital structure.

"Come on, Ayan," Suresh said. "This is straight up your alley."

"If the professor calls on you tomorrow," Ayan said, putting down the case study and sampling the food, "just say a few words about cash flows under different scenarios, add some thoughts about the capital structure versus the discount rate, throw in points about volatility and tail risk, and an A is in the bag."

"That pays for your rice," Rajiv said with a smile. "Now give us something for the chicken."

"I'm not reading the damn case, but I'll share something with you that helped me ace exams, something to think about beyond tomorrow's case."

He told them about meeting Javed Khan in the Channel Islands, in the cram school Hadley Jones paid for to make sure its employees got through insanely competitive professional exams, and summarized his tips for storing the vast technical knowledge required and recalling it into working memory under the intense time pressure of examinations,

"We know all that stuff, Ayan," Suresh said. "Everybody does. Exams are not our problem. They are a month away. So, about tomorrow's case . . ."

He felt a little hurt. He'd shared something important with them. How he wished he'd met Javed earlier, in college, when his insights about time management and test technique would have made his endless hours of study so much more productive.

"OK, you fucking know-it-alls," Ayan said, looking through the case study again. "But I've had a lot to drink so

I'll be simplistic—and probably only directionally correct," Ayan said. "Interest rates are high and going higher; IBM's stock is cheap—it has sold off more than the market—so skew the capital structure towards fixed-rate debt . . ."

They chatted and joked as they discussed the case: the engineers challenging Ayan's lazy thinking and good naturedly pointing out his tiredness or alcohol-induced inconsistencies; Noor's philosophical leaning and exquisite manners elevating the sensibility and broadening the conversation of the confident and blunt graduates of the Indian Institutes of Technology, who just knew they were going to rule the world.

Ayan drew from the warmth of their company till the students switched off the common room lights and sent him back home. He got into bed listening to Chaurasia's mystical, haunting flute on the tape he'd borrowed from Deepak and drifted off to sleep thinking of the evocative smell of monsoon rain on Indian earth and the familiar, reassuring sound of dogs barking across the valley on a Himalayan night.

CHAPTER 20

Tehran, Iran, March 1978

Tehran soon returned to commerce and the business of life.

Nobody talked about the *Arbaeen* of Qom's fallen, the Ayatollah, or the deaths in Tabriz for a while. The BBC World Service moved on to other hot spots.

Jackie called from Beirut, said she knew about Tabriz, thanked Ayan for keeping her posted, but the situation wasn't urgent enough for her to score a Tehran assignment just yet.

It was ski season, and the slopes of Dizin and Shemshak took the place of the tennis courts, and après-ski at Cascades replaced evenings at the Key Club; both helped Ayan avoid Hassan and Fariba.

Work pressures remained insistent. He labored deep into most evenings to keep up with the fast-moving Qazvin expansion and Operation Odysseus. Chip, through Alpine Global, had already submitted invoices for millions of dollars, ostensibly for services related to Qazvin. It was difficult maintaining confidentiality with so much money washing through Iran Power's accounts. He'd caught the mention of NUFCOR SA, Nuclear Fuels Corporation of

South Africa, on some of the invoices—a surprising lapse by Hermann Gerber that would have caused a stir if Ayan hadn't whited it out.

The cost allocation study was also turning out to be the beast that he'd feared it would be. Ayan had hired Hadley Jones to help him. But the largely British team they'd assigned to Iran Power was having difficulty dealing with the stonewalling of the workers, worried that their slack time would be identified—and their supervisors, who were trying to game the Hadley Jones analysis to preserve the size of their departments. The project was aimed at improved decision-making, not cost cuts, but times were getting difficult, even in Iran. No one wanted to be out of a job in 1978, and Iranians could draw on deep reservoirs of cultural facility with obfuscation to protect their positions.

There had been a strike protesting the study while Ayan was in Europe, Hosseini had reported with amusement, and Ayan's name had been chanted, accompanied by unflattering epithets. The strike was cut short by the Colonel's call to the local police department and the arrival of a few squad cars. But Nader had been unhappy with the disruption, and Ayan lost many hours guiding the Hadley Jones team and playing peacemaker as they tried to analyze all the significant functions in Iran Power.

Time just rolled on, and before he knew it, he was on his way to the airport to meet Gaby for the weekend in Isfahan.

She walked briskly out of passport control, brushing loose strands of hair off her face as she scanned the area.

"Sorry, our flight was late," Gaby said, offering her cheeks for three quick kisses as Ayan ran up and hugged her. "We had a mechanical problem in Athens."

Ayan looked up at the information board above them. The light on the departure gate for their flight to Isfahan was flashing last call.

He grabbed Gaby's bags.

"Easy—I have heels on," Gaby said, holding his arm to slow him down. "And this is my territory, remember? They know me in Mehrabad Airport. I've sent a message. The flight will wait for us."

She smiled as they settled into their seats. "I had to time everything perfectly to get these days off, make the connections, and be here. And now, finally!"

She took in a deep breath, exhaled, and rested her head against his neck.

She looked up at him. "Hello again!" she said.

"I've been counting the minutes," Ayan said, his kiss letting her know how much he'd missed her.

"That's sweet. Nice to hear," she said.

She ran her hands through his hair and patted it back into place.

"So now that you've got me to yourself for three days, what are you going to do with me?"

"Well . . ." Ayan said, kissing her neck and moving down.

"Besides that," Gaby said, pushing his face away and fastening a couple of buttons on her shirt.

She shook her head and smiled.

"I've got a guide to give us a tour tomorrow," Ayan said. "It'll give us a sense of the city. We can do whatever we feel like after that."

"That sounds good," Gaby said. "You think it will be safe? I've heard that people in Isfahan are beginning to resent foreigners too."

"Things are quiet. Even the Americans, the ones they really hate here, are out and about: in the Bazaar, on the slopes, everywhere. Isfahan will be fine."

A member of the flight crew approached them once they had reached cruising altitude. He was in a pilot's uniform and held a bottle of champagne in his hand.

"Bahman!" Gaby exclaimed.

She jumped up from her window seat and crossed over Ayan's legs to embrace the handsome Iranian.

"Gaby *joon*! It's been a long time! I saw your name on the manifest. Welcome back to Iran."

He handed her the bottle of champagne as they exchanged kisses.

"Why didn't you tell me you were coming?" Bahman said. "You must spend a few days with me. Shahab is in the cockpit. Come immediately and sit in front with us."

Gaby turned to look at Ayan.

"Bahman, meet Ayan, my boyfriend."

"Hello, Ayan!" Bahman said with a smile, his face full of mischievous charm. "I'm sorry, but I'm taking Gaby away from you! Captain's orders!"

He winked and took Gaby by the arm.

"I'll be back in a second," Gaby said, and walked off with Bahman towards the front of the aircraft.

There was a physical closeness, an easy familiarity between them, that Ayan willed himself to ignore.

She's with me now, and that's what matters, he told himself and pulled out the in-flight magazine.

They were about to land when Gaby nudged him to get back into her seat.

"Shahab must be at the controls," Gaby said, wincing as the aircraft bounced a couple of times before its wheels settled on the tarmac. "That's not like Bahman."

"So he's super competent too," Ayan said. "Why am I not surprised?"

Gaby smiled. "He asked me to ditch you, you know, and spend the weekend with him."

"Of course, he did," Ayan responded. "Like any self-respecting Iranian man who finds himself with a beautiful woman. I suppose I'll have to be on the top of my game, or you'll run off with him."

"He's not your competition," Gaby said. "He's fabulous. I adore him, but I love you."

She gave him a lingering, mad-making kiss.

"So relax!" she said. "You've got even more lines around your eyes. I'll have to see you more often, take care of my worrying man."

They threw their luggage in their room in the classic wing of the Shah Abbas Hotel, put Bahman's champagne bottle in the mini bar, and raced to the Chehel-Sotoon restaurant to make the last seating.

An elegant maître d' guided them to a booth, his dignified and measured pace calming after an evening that had been full of hurry.

An elderly American couple lingered over coffee and dessert near them, looking at a guidebook. Some businessmen, seemingly talked out, wrapped up their meal at the other end of the restaurant. There was no one else around.

Ayan sat back and took a couple of deep breaths. *The Shah Abbas's reputation for luxury was well deserved*, he thought. The monumental lobby, their spacious room overlooking the garden courtyard, and now this architectural extravaganza they were dining in, somehow achieved a balance between grandeur and soothing comfort.

Large antique carpets everywhere, polished beige marble floors, porcelain vases, crystal chandeliers, latticed staircases, intricate mosaics, ornate fixtures . . . it could have been too much, but the overall effect felt right for where they were,

ARBaeen

and the fountains, greenery, and vast empty spaces provided a refuge from the hot, arid landscape that surrounded them.

"How are things at work—Nader, Hosseini, Hamid?" Gaby said after they had ordered.

"Hamid's gone underground."

He told her the story.

"Hamid and his family will make it with your help," Gaby said. "I want credit for it, too, for bringing out this side of you. Praise me."

"All hail," Ayan said. "But I would have done it anyway."

"Perhaps, but I made certain," Gaby said. "Bahman thinks the *Arbaeen* for Tabriz will be more intense than it was for Qom."

"Darioush is worried about it too. He's made plans to leave for LA."

"Shouldn't you be doing the same? Making plans to leave?"

"I have something in mind, not as specific as Darioush, but I am organizing myself."

Gaby leaned forward.

"Maybe speed things up," she said. "The pieces are falling into place in Iran as Professor Mehran predicted. Khomeini's tapes, Shariati's ideas, and newly emboldened mullahs are building energy for an explosion."

"That could be—does seem like it," Ayan said, not quite ready to match Gaby's concern.

"Ayan, you have a charismatic leader, a respected intellectual who's established a framework for revolution, and mullahs spreading the message. Watch out if you see the sharp edge of the sword."

"That would be people like Hedayat, Hamid's best friend," Ayan added.

"OK then! If you know that people are willing to kill for change and not just die at the hands of SAVAK and the army, everything's set. Why wait? Get the hell out!"

"I will, Gaby. Trust me, I will be long gone from Iran by the time the army, SAVAK, and the Americans succumb. I just need more time. No one besides your Bahman and the professor think it will happen anytime soon, if at all. Nick is optimistic."

"You think he knows more than Bahman? Mehran? Darioush?"

"Why should he? He's only with the CIA, the people who run the world," Ayan said.

"Come on, Ayan, he's just a slimy parasite! One of many in this town."

"He's my friend, Gaby."

"Why, no one knows."

"He's had a difficult run," Ayan said. "I appreciate his resilience."

Gaby grimaced.

"And you? How goes it in Germany?" Ayan asked, trying to dodge more scrutiny about his decision to stay on because everything he said would sound irrational unless he brought up Odysseus, which he couldn't do. *It was ironic,* he thought. *He couldn't talk to her about the one path that would allow them to live together wherever she wanted.*

"We've regrouped," Gaby said casually.

"What does that mean?" Ayan said.

"We were all focused on getting the prisoners freed from Stammheim for a long time. The loss of Baader and the others was hard, but the fight goes on."

"Gaby, those soldiers in Munich—the anti-terrorist force—looked like they meant business!"

"So do we. The new RAF is tough. Perhaps too tough. I'm not happy about the killings. That does bother me, Ayan.

A lot. But Schmidt is forcing our hand—throwing everything the government has at us."

"Exactly, Gaby! I'm selfish and don't want to lose you," Ayan said, reaching for her again.

"Baby, relax! I'm invisible," Gaby said. She moved her hand out of reach and slapped his lightly.

"I'm being reprimanded?"

"Yes," she said, smiling. "For being very foolish. Schmidt's SS are hunting for RAF commandos in communes and universities, harassing artists, journalists, people like that. They can't imagine a well-known Bavarian burgher's daughter with a great job as an ungrateful sympathizer of a terrorist group. So I am not to be worried about."

"Ulrike Meinhof was from an established family, had a good job. They got her."

"That was different. She was in front."

"So you're still only providing a safe house for women?" Ayan said hopefully.

"That and other things in the background."

"Like?"

"I sometimes arrange medical help for injured commandos through a doctor friend of mine. Do what I can."

"That's more involved than you're making it sound. You're further in. I knew this would happen!"

"Calm down! Everything is under control!" Gaby said.

After a silence, she reached over for his hand.

"Perhaps I should not be angry—I like that you worry about me," she said, kicking off her heels and rubbing his leg with her foot. "Let's talk about something else."

"Does your mother know you are visiting me?" Ayan said as they made their way outside to walk around the courtyard amidst flowerbeds of marigold and manicured rows of mop-headed trees.

"No. Why should she? It will just bring on another migraine," Gaby said, slipping her arm in his.

"Is she still trying to get you married to Charlie?"

"Yes. And now she's convinced my father too. They're always inviting Charlie over for dinner."

"Has my visit completely faded from their memory?"

"Mathias brings you up occasionally."

"I see. I thought he barely noticed I was there."

"Mathias talks about you when he wants to cause trouble and annoy my parents."

"Nice!"

"Try and understand it from their perspective. You are somebody from my past, my boyfriend in Iran, a person in a place that was part of my growing-up adventure."

"But you've told them I'm more. Much, much more . . ."

"I've hinted," Gaby said. "I'm working on them."

"So you say something nice about me, and they reply by saying something nice about Charlie. Is that how it is?"

Gaby laughed.

"Something like that."

Ayan stopped to contemplate the immense blue dome and the minarets of the Chahar Barg Madreseh that rose above the walls of the courtyard.

"Have you told Charlie about Baader-Meinhof?" he said as they resumed their stroll.

"No! Of course not!" Gaby said.

Ayan smiled.

"Don't look so pleased. That doesn't mean you have an advantage."

"It kind of does."

"What should tell you more is that I got on that plane and travelled thousands of miles to be with you. Now, look—there's Andromeda! Al-Sufi's little cloud . . . perhaps he stood right here a thousand years ago when he discovered it. Why not? He was in this city. Why not here in this magical garden. Andromeda looks like a little cloud from here, doesn't it? I've seen it from another perspective, from the sky . . ."

She turned to him. "On some days up there," she said, "I can see the whole world—countries merging into continents, giving way to oceans, then more land, glaciers, relentless rivers, endless plains—and on silent, star-filled nights like this, I feel a greater presence. Do you know what I mean?"

"I can imagine what that must feel like, looking out from the cockpit, 30,000 feet above earth."

"I sense a universal spirit, Ayan."

"Yes."

He put his arm around her.

They walked along the broad blue-tiled brook that formed one axis of the garden. A series of jets extended along its length, changing colors and competing for attention. The sound of the water splashing in the fountains and the tall palm trees spaced around the courtyard made the surrounding desert feel a world away. *Everything a caravan on the Silk Route would need was here*, Ayan thought. *Shelter from the blazing desert, food, drink, supplies, and inspiration . . .*

Gaby led him towards a pool. Ayan followed her gaze, losing his thoughts in the hypnotic patterns on the tile on the bottom, the water moving in concentric circles away from the base of the fountain.

"This is working, isn't it? Us?" Gaby said, looking at him. "In Berlin, Starnberger, and now here?"

"More than working," he said, "It's perfect."

Gaby smiled, looking away.

"What?" Ayan said.

"Nothing," Gaby said. "Just happy."

She shivered. The temperature in the desert night had dipped precipitously.

"Come on," Ayan said. "Let's go back inside."

She walked towards the window, toweling off after a shower, and looked down on the garden they had been in. The rays from the courtyard lamps, coming through the translucent drapes, traced patterns of light and shadows on the body Ayan had visualized for days, longed for . . .

Gaby slipped into the bed beside him, still damp.

He put his arms around her, hungry for her softness and her flavors and her smell. She allowed him to do what he wanted for not nearly long enough before she flung the covers off them. Then she was on top of him and leaned forward and did what she wanted to him.

"Open Bahman's champagne," Gaby said when Ayan brought over the cheese and fruit plate the hotel manager had left in the room to welcome them.

He passed her crackers with Camembert and cheddar and fed her grapes and dates as she sipped the Veuve Cliquot.

"Your father must get lonely up in the mountains by himself. And Padma, too, alone in Delhi," Gaby said.

"He likes being isolated in the Himalayas, where politicians can't bother him, and he can get on with running his little part of India," Ayan said. "And my mother keeps herself busy, too, as you know. She's surely exhausted by her hours, but lonely? Probably not—not with the number of patients she has to take care of."

"Still," Gaby said, "she must miss your father. And he, her."

Her words brought up the change in his father's mood when it had been time for Ayan to leave at summer's end—reminded him of the disturbing solitude in his father's eyes

as he'd followed the jeep taking his son on the day's journey
to the railhead for the train back to Delhi; he thought about
his father hiking ahead of everybody in the far reaches of
Pithoragarh, pipe in mouth, head down, lost in thought—
alone up there without his beloved Padma; he thought about
the exhaustion he'd seen on his mother's face when he'd
driven her home from the hospital at the end of her shift,
carrying on without her emotional support that was so far
away, high up in the Himalayan mountains.

"My parents were earning a living, giving their children
the best possible education, doing what has to be done," Ayan
said, feeling sad. "They sacrificed their time together. I was
a selfish teenager, unprepared to deal with adult problems."

"Well," Gaby said, "they got something out of it
too. Your father chose a life that he relates to, and your
mother was brave enough to have a career, chose a life
that doesn't revolve around just being a wife—that's one
of the reasons we get along, stayed in touch, and have
become friends."

She looked at Ayan, making him uncomfortable with
her searching gaze.

"It won't be easy for us either, Ayan," she said. "You
might be like your father—choose a path I can't join you on.
I'm in Germany; that may be hard for you to accept."

"We'll find a way, Gaby. I'm ready. I'm all in."

"Are you, Ayan? Really?" She sounded doubtful.

"Yes. Absolutely."

She was tired from the travel, Ayan could see. He
massaged her neck and shoulders. Gaby leaned back against
him, sighing in approval.

Minutes later, a cold liquid splashed on his chest, startling him. Ayan eased the now-empty champagne glass out
of Gaby's hand and settled her head on the pillow.

Watching her sleep, he made a decision. He would answer the uncertainty he'd seen in her eyes.

They spent the morning walking around the greatest square in the world: *Naqsh-e-Jahan.*

Their tour guide Samir—fleshy, henna-dyed hair, and perfumed—was well informed. He conjured up images of the past, when the Square, the *Maidan,* was simultaneously a polo field, meeting place, ceremonial ground for official functions, and renowned marketplace.

"This was the crossroads of civilization. To the east is the Mesopotamian Plain, to the north, the Caspian Sea, and to the south, the Persian Gulf. The plan was laid out 500 years before Versailles. It was the center of the empire that stretched from the Euphrates River in today's Iraq to the Oxus River in Afghanistan. Isfahan was bigger than London and more civilized than Paris, grander even than Istanbul—and this *Maidan* was the center of everything."

Ayan tried to concentrate on the Samir's words, but he was distracted by his mustache—divided into two neat sections, which moved separately as he enunciated his words—and his carefully manicured hands that sported a cocaine user's extra-long nail on his little finger.

Ayan looked away and rested his eyes on the Shah Mosque on the south side and the grander of its two domes, a masterpiece of Safavid architecture.

Eventually, Samir was done with his discourse, and they walked up to the mosque through the towering facade of the entrance gateway, finding themselves enveloped in radiant tile mosaics of an intense blue.

"You will feel the presence of God," Zora, Ayan's hairdresser, had told him when she had recommended the Shah's Mosque.

She was right. He was not a religious man but felt touched by a special force as he ventured further inward, towards the main prayer hall, past scholars sitting in isolated corners, preoccupied in study. He sat down on a bench, in awe of the majesty of his surroundings, beginning to understand the power of Islam.

Gaby was walking ahead with their guide, her head covered in a scarf, talking to him in hushed tones.

It should be here, Ayan thought. *I'm going to bring Gaby back and propose to her in this transcendent place. Tonight.*

He left Gaby with Samir, saying he needed some water and was off to get some refreshments for them.

"An Indian girl?" the fat Afghan merchant asked when Ayan walked into the most respectable looking jewelry shop in the Bazaar.

"No," Ayan said.

"A nice Persian lady then?" the merchant continued hopefully.

"No," Ayan said. "She's European."

"Then it has to be a diamond, a solitaire," the merchant said, wiping his forehead with a handkerchief. He looked disapproving but guided Ayan through his collection. "European girls must have a diamond engagement ring. They love all these traditions, but before you know—finis!" He smacked his hands together. "It's over! They run away and leave you. Anyhow, no problem, yours will stay, *Inshallah*. Just buy this one. *Khalas!* It's the best ring you can find in your price range."

Several hours later, as the sun began to set and the winter cold forced overcoats to be buttoned up, Ayan returned to the entrance portal of the Shah Mosque with Gaby.

It had been a long day of sightseeing, rattling along in Samir's old Paykan car and riding out Gaby's fury at the child labor in the carpet-weaving factory. She was tired, fought him about returning to the Maidan, relenting eventually when he came up with the argument that they had to attend the special Friday evening prayer in the greatest Shia mosque in the world.

"Gaby," he said when he had maneuvered her to a quiet spot at the entrance. He reached into his pocket. "I have something for you."

He knelt on the floor.

"Ayan!" Gaby said. "Wait! What are you doing!"

He took her left hand in his and slipped on the ring.

"To the long game . . . I want to play it too . . . with you . . . forever."

Gaby dropped to her knees beside Ayan. She looked at the ring on her finger and then at him with startled eyes.

He pulled her to him.

An usher emerged from the shadows.

"Excuse me, this is a religious place; you have to go outside," he said, pointing towards the *Maidan*.

Gaby sat down on the raised cement around the fountain just outside the entrance to the mosque.

Ayan joined her.

She turned and put her arms around him.

"You know I love you, Ayan," she said. "I want you. But I'm not sure that it's time for this just yet."

"It is! I'm sure."

"You're not rushing things?"

"No! It's settled in my mind."

"You will endure? The separations, the distance, our differences?"

"I promise."

Gaby looked at the ring again.

"Say yes!"

She nodded and smiled at him through sudden tears.

He jumped up and pulled her to him.

"OK then," she said, putting her arms around his neck. "Take me back to the hotel so I can call my parents."

Gaby wrapped herself tightly around him as they arrived at passport control in Mehrabad Airport for her flight back to Munich.

"That's enough. You have to come to Starnberger for more," she said, leaning back. "And to face the music."

"Yes, I'm a bit worried about that," Ayan said nervously.

She held up her left hand as she picked up her carry-on bag with her right. "You didn't think you could put a ring on a girl's finger without dealing with her family, did you?" she said smiling. "You have to help me calm my mother down."

"That will be two mothers who need calming down," Ayan said. The Fearsome Force in Delhi had not been thrilled by the news.

"And one father," Gaby said. "You should ask my father's permission; he won't say no, but you have to ask."

"At least one of the four was pleased," Ayan said.

"I was really touched when your father told me it was one of the happiest days of his life, that he was so happy we'd found each other. I can't wait to meet him," Gaby said. "And actually, your mother loves me. She was just shocked by our call from the blue."

PART
FIVE

CHAPTER 21

The moguls on the Shemshak piste had been particularly challenging, and Ayan fell hard. A late afternoon windstorm had blown away fresh powder, leaving the steep terrain icy. After several runs, Ayan's thighs burned, and his shoulders felt tired. He wasn't carving the ice aggressively with his edges, not turning at the right spots, not using his poles effectively, leaning away from the fall line, and generally making things difficult for himself. He took the ski lift up for one last run, not ready to deal with the tension caused by the visiting Chip de Groot's play for Darioush's new love, Julie, nor with the mood swings of Darioush's wife, Chantal, who had been drinking since lunch.

Within seconds of heading downhill, one of Ayan's skis caught an edge, and he went down, cursing and trying to protect himself from the ski that stayed on. He tumbled a long way before he managed to stop.

He righted himself and tried to sidestep up to retrieve his equipment, but his right knee gave way. The slopes were deserted. Everybody with any sense had given up and retreated to Cascades or left for Tehran.

Peyman

Fuck! How was he going to get down?

The answer appeared twenty agonizing, freezing minutes later. An Iranian man, skiing expertly, came flying towards him. His legs kicked up a cloud of snow and ice as he stopped and handed Ayan his missing ski and poles.

The Iranian introduced himself as Peyman and held out large, calloused hands with mistreated fingernails. He was skiing in ancient jeans and layers of battered woolens. But he was strong and clearly a man of the mountains.

Ayan was grateful for his support as Peyman helped him onto his skis and held him as they snow-ploughed in tandem to the base. He bore most of Ayan's weight down the treacherous terrain, escorted him to the entrance of Cascades, made light of Ayan's gratitude, and sped off towards the buses that seemed ready to depart in the adjacent parking lot.

You have done more than protect me physically, Ayan thought as he watched Peyman merge into the crowd. His friends were abandoning him, leaving town, being generally less reliable than he'd assumed. Every week, the clandestine operation with Hamid and Hedayat reminded him that he was living dangerously in an unstable place. This stranger, true spirit of this generous, caring nation, had left him fortified, made him feel he could survive a little longer here.

He limped into Cascades, asked a waiter for one of the cold compresses they kept in the freezer for skiing injuries, a common occurrence in Shemshak, and sat down with Chantal at Darioush's private table. He had developed a rapport with her over many conversations during such post-skiing afternoons, drinking together while Darioush went about his duties as a host. She was interesting—had wandered with *sadhus* in India and, like many French, responded enthusiastically to conversations that began with a bit of philosophy. But today, she was in a foul mood.

"See that slut sitting with Marco and your friend?" Chantal said, sliding her bottle of vodka towards Ayan with such force that he had to scramble to stop it from slipping off the table. "See her staring at Darioush? Fucking my husband with her eyes?"

Ayan poured himself a drink and contemplated Julie sitting by the bar next to Marco, Daroiush's business partner who was helping out with bartending duties. Several men were competing for the attention of the beauty with blonde hair, full lips, and insistent breasts. Chip was the most aggressive of them all, leaning forward to whisper something in Julie's ear, moving his body to the music that was playing, trying everything to get her to show an interest in him, it seemed.

But as Chantal had said, Julie's eyes were only for Darioush.

She was following him as he went about greeting visitors at different tables. It was an intimate, possessive gaze.

"You're going to do something about it?' Ayan asked Chantal.

"No! None of these short-term whores are worth the bother."

Chip came over a few minutes, frozen out by Julie.

"I'm glad you brought me here," he said to Ayan. "This is a cool après-ski place; I feel I'm back in Verbier."

"We planned it that way," Chantal said. "To feel like Europe." She held out her hand. "Hi, I'm Chantal Brodeur. The owner."

"Wow!" Chip said. "My lucky night. With the owner— the most beautiful woman in the room!"

Chantal smiled.

"You've said the magic words," she said. "You can sit with me. Ayan, go chat to Marco and make that bitch disappear while you're at it."

Ayan pushed himself up and walked with difficulty to the bar, still protecting his improving but tentative knee.

"How's Gaby?" Julie said as he sat on a stool next to her. "I haven't seen her in ages. I absolutely loved flying with her."

"Good. She was just in town."

"I heard she came to spend a weekend with you. It's the talk of Iran Air. Lucky man!"

Julie looked him up and down.

"Gaby can do a lot better. You must have hidden qualities."

"Unlike yours," Ayan said. "Which are very much in my face." He waved away the smoke from her cigarette. "Darioush is married," Ayan said. "You know that, don't you?"

"Not very married," Julie said. "His wife just left with your annoying Afrikaner friend."

The table in the alcove was empty.

"And you don't have to be a bastard to me. Be nice," Julie said, pausing to draw on her cigarette again. "Be on my side; I'm Gaby's friend. I've been on her crew many times; we've spent a lot of time together. I know all about you."

She laughed. "And your hidden qualities."

A short while later, Darioush came over, winked at Ayan, and took Julie by the hand. He looked around and slipped her behind a curtain separating the bar area from the supply room.

Ayan turned away quickly, but not before he saw one of Julie's legs bend around Darioush's hips.

There was the sound of rushed love making.

A few minutes later, they reappeared.

Darioush returned to his host duties.

Julie sat down beside Ayan, tucking her hair back into place.

Her look was insolent, mocking, happy.

Twenty minutes later, Chip was in the swimming pool outside the villa, thrown in by Darioush, who had caught him in bed with Chantal.

When Ayan and Marco came out to see what the noise was all about, Chip was standing beside the pool, naked, shivering, and warning Darioush to keep his distance.

A couple of Cascades bouncers had arrived and formed a restraining wall between the men as they exchanged angry words.

"Get this bastard off my property!" Darioush yelled when he saw Ayan.

"Fuck off, you dumb Iranian prick!" Chip shouted as he struggled into his clothes. "How the hell was I to know she was your wife?"

Chip drove the unmarked beige Range Rover Nader had provided for his use, concentrating on the unforgiving road back to Shemiran. Most skiers had already made their way down to Tehran; southbound traffic was light, but there was no telling when one would have to swerve to avoid an oncoming vehicle.

"Look, mate, I'm sorry," Chip said, taking in a long breath and sighing. His hair was wet from the pool; his lips were bloodied; his eye was swelling shut. He looked a mess. He shouldn't be driving. But there was no way Ayan could operate a vehicle with that knee.

"Caught with your fucking pants down!" Ayan said. "Just another day in Chip's world. You better come to my apartment and clean up before your flight."

"Cheers. I need a shower," Chip said. He turned to Ayan with his gap-toothed grin. "Honestly, I had no idea that Chantal was his wife." He laughed again. "Wife or no wife, man, she was so worth the punches I got! What a perfect, juicy body! We went at it hard. It didn't take a lot of talking to get her into bed. She came right away, shaking and screaming her head off! Your pal walked in just as his wife was in the middle of an orgasm with a stranger. In his own fucking bed! Can't say I blame him for thrashing me."

"Just thank your lucky stars Darioush had Julie on his hands, or you'd be dead right now, and I would be wondering what to tell Nader."

"Why are you sticking your neck out for Nader?" Chip said. "I was thinking, after our time playing squash, hanging out in Annabel's, skiing around Luc's chalet—now seeing your life here—that you're different from the Indians I know in London or Jo'burg: They're either scheming, unscrupulous bastards, only interested in making money twenty-four hours a day, or hired help who ask 'how high?' when they're ordered to jump. It makes no sense somebody like you is Nader's coolie."

"Go fuck yourself, you racist prick!"

"No, seriously, this is a risky business; everybody's interested and watching; don't think this purchase of yellowcake will remain a secret. I don't know what the payoff is for you, but it better be big to be involved in this thing, that's all I can say."

"They're taking care of me," Ayan said.

"I hope so. I've been doing this for a long time. I've got cover and contacts. People like Nader are off the books and will stay there. You're completely exposed. You have to protect yourself. Know that."

"Why didn't you tell me that in London?"

"I like you more now. We've had a few adventures together."

"I knew you were a fast-talking salesman when I first met you," Ayan said. "Anyway, I feel more comfortable now that we have our operation running relatively smoothly. Iranians move money by the billions every day for the fastest infrastructure buildout in history. What I'm doing won't get onto the radar. And why would anybody be interested in me? I'm just another financier."

"The money's being transferred from the account you set up," Chip pointed out. "Your signature is on our invoices."

"It's not illegal to buy yellowcake, is it?" Ayan said. "And I have nothing to do with what happens to it."

"The shipments have arrived in Iran, and they are not just in civilian hands; the centrifuge cascades are being assembled for refining. That's the part of Odysseus that is many times more complicated than finding the uranium—and why I'm in town. Now if you were any good at this game, we could find a role for you in that . . ."

"No! I don't need to wade any further in, thank you very much," Ayan interrupted.

"Yes. That's too big-time for you," Chip said. "Pity, though. It's where the real money is. Anyway, back to what I was saying: Watch yourself. You're the front man, as you know."

"You're really helping my morale," Ayan said.

"This yellowcake deal has your fingerprints all over it. Go for the maximum payoff and try not to get your head cut off. Don't assume you're half-in on something like Odysseus; you know what they say: If you don't know who the sucker is . . ."

"Thanks for that scintillating insight," Ayan said. "And this may surprise you—I may look stupid—but I do have a plan: I'm leaving Iran soon and starting a firm of my own in Europe."

"What kind of firm?" Chip said. "Can't be deal-making. You're not cut out for the transaction business."

"I'll leave the transaction business to you. You keep hustling for the next deal. I'm thinking of starting my own investment firm. No politics, no bullshit. Just perform, tie your compensation to a growing asset base, and be truly independent."

The idea of becoming an investor, beholden to nothing but his own track record of performance, was becoming more appealing to Ayan. He would be good at analyzing companies, assessing management, tearing apart balance sheets and cash flow statements. And if he performed, he could open up his own firm and manage money from pretty much anywhere—including Munich or West Berlin. He could live with Gaby wherever she wanted.

"Ask Luc about that—he may be able to help. Private banks in Geneva have a lot of discretionary assets they can send the way of a portfolio manager. You have any kind of track record managing money?"

"No, but I'm developing a strategy that will utilize what I've learnt."

"You'll need to put in your own money. No one will trust a beginner."

"I know. I'm trying to save up. You asked why I'm working for Nader. So now you know."

"What kinds of investments you thinking of making?" Chip said. "I have some loose change I may send your way."

"Worth a shot," Chip said after Ayan had explained his ideas about choosing investments and managing risk in a hedge fund. "Sounds better than the boring funds Luc sends my way. How much are you thinking of putting in?"

"One hundred thousand," Ayan said.

"Come on!" Chip said. "That's a joke. You want to attract attention, build a real track record; put in at least $1 million.

Then, between Luc and me, we can get you to $10 million. Definitely $5 million. Have balls."

"There's no chance of me having that kind of money," Ayan said.

"Why not?" Chip said. "Odysseus can get you to your $1 million if you play your cards right; it's peanuts in the scheme of things. You have to be careful, but that doesn't mean you should be in such a rush to leave Iran. They like Indians here. You guys are smart and easy to boss around."

Ayan saw a note on the table by his front door the next morning.

It listed a phone number starting with 41-22, the dialing code for Geneva. Written below was message in block letters:

PER OUR CONVERSATION TODAY—IN CASE OF SOS PERSONAL EMERGENCY ABROAD LEAVE MESSAGE—TTT LISA—PROVIDE CONTACT INFO.

Ayan folded Chip's note and returned it to its envelope. He placed the envelope inside his passport, his mind racing.

Chip had just brought back all the fall guy anxiety he'd felt in Geneva.

He put the passport back in the safe that was built into his closet. It was small and well camouflaged, tucked underneath the bottom shelf, with just enough room for a few documents and jewelry: a perfect hiding place for his passport, savings book, checks, and emergency cash.

He felt the need to examine his savings account book again.

The balance of $70,000 did not feel as substantial as it had earlier. It felt like a joke.

Like peanuts.

CHAPTER 22

Tehran, Iran, April 1978

Ayan left a relatively calm Tehran on March 20 to visit Gaby in Starnberger. He returned a week and a half later to find a bipolar city—made neurotic by the massive *Arbaeen* for the dead of Tabriz, more people gathering to mourn forty days later, more dying in Yazd, soldiers everywhere—but the wheels of Tehran life continuing to turn as if none of this were important . . .

"People close to the Shah say the real problem is that he's not the same man," Darioush explained when Ayan called him that evening. "Something's happened to him. He's become indecisive and detached. The mullahs and the wasters—students, the unemployed, the resentful—smell blood."

"Your red line's been crossed," Ayan said. "Are you really going to leave Iran now, as you said you would?"

"Yes. Time to get out."

"I don't believe it. You're not going to leave everything you have here."

"Believe it. Time's up. The end for people like us. I'm getting married to Julie, taking her to LA, and buying her a big house in Beverly Hills, where I will make love to her every day; we'll have four children—she's agreed to four, but I think we'll have more."

"And Chantal?"

"She's back running her hotel in Saint-Emilion. I've given Chantal more money than she'll be able to spend in a lifetime. Don't worry about her; worry about yourself. You'll also have to get out of here too—sooner than you think—and you have to be our first guest in LA."

"I'll take you up on that," Ayan said. "It will be lonely in Tehran without you, my friend."

"It's funny how these things work," Darioush said. "We meet at Club Veyssi; you run into Gaby on a flight, introduce her to Cascades; and one day, she walks into my restaurant with this girl I've waited for all my life. So of course, you have to be our first guest! In the meanwhile, do what I've made Marco do: transfer your money abroad and convert whatever you have here into dollar or sterling traveller's checks. It will be hard to get foreign currency soon."

Gunfire sounded in the distance as they talked on the telephone. Darkness had brought out the protestors in the southern parts of Tehran.

California sounded so appealing.

Ayan called Nick Stasney next.

He was still unconcerned.

"Like I told you before, leave it to SAVAK," Nick said. "The people who know are not losing sleep."

"Right. But you also said the US is focused on Russia, that there are too few of you in Iran to track what's happening here."

"I have no idea what you're talking about."

Nick hung up and called back.

"This is a secure line. Now listen to me, you stupid son of a bitch. We've allowed SAVAK to take responsibility for all domestic intelligence because they've earned it; they've been trained by us and Mossad. They're competent and tough. And this is the last time we're talking about this crap!"

"I'm so reassured by my super competent CIA friend!" Ayan said, his irony lost on the dead telephone line.

Ayan threw himself on his bed, jet-lagged and exhausted from the trip to Starnberger.

The weekend with Gaby's family had gone better than he'd expected. Probably because she'd told her parents that he would be transferred from Tehran to Munich by SA Group via an intercompany arrangement. They were not to worry. She was going to stay near home. Just stick with that story, Gaby had said when she picked him up at the airport.

But she was getting more involved with the RAF. There was no question about that. She had left him alone with her parents and driven to Munich, admitting later that the trip was to help commandos get onto her charter flight to the Canary Islands—from where they could make their way to Palestinian training camps or to the GDR.

She never lied when he asked her a question. Sometimes, he wished she did.

A knock on his door startled him out of his ruminations.

Ayan walked to his front door and looked out through his living room window. Hedayat was standing outside.

Damn! Ayan thought, realizing why he was here.

He'd given Hamid extra money to cover the one Friday he would be in Germany. Today was the thirty-first, also a Friday, and it was 8:00 p.m. He had missed this week's handout.

Ayan rustled around.

He could only find 500 tomans.

It would have to do.

"Where's Hamid?" Ayan asked as he stepped out onto the roof.

"He's been hurt. In Yazd. Hamid sent me to get the money. I've been waiting for you for more than an hour in the usual place."

Hedayat held out his hand, his insolent eyes scanning the flat over Ayan's shoulder.

Ayan closed the door behind him.

No need for this bastard to see how he lived.

"What happened? How badly is Hamid hurt?"

"Shot in shoulder by police during *Arbaeen*. Bullet has been cut out. He has to lie in bed for a few days, that's it."

"Who treated Hamid? Where?"

"A friend. He has worked in a hospital."

"A doctor?"

Hedayat shrugged. "Somebody who knows enough," he said, holding out his hand again. "I have to leave. Give me the money now."

"No! I'll give it to Sholeh or Hamid's mother. Not you. I don't know you. Now go! And don't come to my door again!"

Ayan turned and went into the flat, slamming the door behind him.

But he didn't hear the sound he expected.

He spun around.

Hedayat had blocked the door with his foot and was inside.

"Nice apartment," Hedayat said, scanning the living room. "So many nice things! I knew you foreigners were getting rich stealing from us!"

"Get out!" Ayan yelled, pushing Hedayat to the door.

Hedayat broke free and darted further into the living room.

Ayan charged at him and swung hard, connecting with Hedayat's jaw.

Hedayat fell against the entrance table.

Ayan grabbed the groaning man by the lapels of his scruffy coat and dragged him out of his apartment.

Khanom-eh Mohsen's lights were on downstairs.

It was a cold night. Hopefully, her windows were shut.

Ayan closed the door behind him, successfully this time, and waited by the window till he saw the bastard stagger away.

The next morning, he saw that a photograph had been slipped under his door. It was a Polaroid showing Ayan embracing Hamid.

The photograph was grainy and full of evening shadows, but their faces were unmistakable.

There was a second photograph attached by static to the first. This one showed Ayan handing money to Hamid.

He looked outside and saw a note that had not made it all the way under his door.

"Come tomorrow same place with 2,000 tomans, or many pictures like this go to SAVAK," the scrawled note said.

Hedayat must have returned at night.

Ayan hurried back inside and locked the door.

He shredded the note and photographs.

Damn it! This was serious. Hosseini couldn't be allowed to find out he was meeting with Hamid, supporting a fugitive wanted for terrorism and treason!

Ayan slammed his fist into the closest wall. How dare that son of a bitch try to blackmail him!

He should have been more careful.

But how could he have imagined an entrapment with Hamid involved? And there had been no warning, no sound or flash. This extortion was Hedayat acting alone, taking advantage of a convalescing Hamid. Nothing that could have been anticipated.

What now?

He should go to the Bazaar and give Hamid's money to his mother. She found him last time; she would find him again. Perhaps he could also speak to the imam of the mosque, get an update on Hamid, and ask him to keep Hedayat away.

The bastard had the photographs, so he couldn't be ignored.

I probably have to give him something on a regular basis too, Ayan realized. Nothing like the 2,000 tomans a week he was trying to squeeze out of him. No more than 500.

A man on the run like him wouldn't want to end a steady handout of any size.

Ayan put on his overcoat at 6:30 p.m. the next day and walked down to the usual handoff spot outside Khanom-eh Mohsen's house. It was dark and the street was quiet.

The Khanom's voice startled him from the other side of the road.

"Good evening, Ayan. A walk before dinner?"

"Yes."

"But today is Saturday. You walk only on Fridays, I've noticed."

"Perhaps you've missed me on other days, Khanom," Ayan said through his disquiet with her observation. "And aren't you usually inside by this time?"

"I was delayed. Well, time for me to go in; it is not safe to be alone in the dark," she said. Did she just glance towards the cluster of bushes and trees where he met Hamid and Hedayat?

Ayan waited till he heard the villa gate shut, and a few minutes more.

He saw Hedayat come out of the cover and beckon him. Ayan looked around. No one was about.

"Here," he said, walking up to Hedayat and holding out the envelope. "Take it and go.

You'll get the same next week."

Seconds later, a powerful arm reached out and jerked Ayan behind the growth.

He was hurled to the ground, and a bony knee pressed down on his chest.

Hedayat was on top of Ayan.

A giant of a man held his arms above his head.

"*Haramzadeh*! Where is the rest?" Hedayat said, holding the 500 tomans in Ayan's face. "I told you 2,000 tomans! Go and get another 1,500, or my friend here will break you into pieces!"

"Fuck off!" Ayan mumbled.

"What did you say?"

"Fuck you, your mother, and your father. I'm going to kill you," Ayan said, struggling to rise.

He succeeded in dislodging Hedayat and kicking him.

The giant pressed down on Ayan, immobilizing him.

Hedayat jumped back on top of Ayan and banged his fist repeatedly into Ayan's face. Blood streamed from Ayan's mouth. He could feel his eyes closing up.

"Enough! Somebody will hear," warned the giant.

Ayan was crumpled on the floor of his apartment when he regained consciousness.

His head was throbbing.

His body warned him not to move anything too fast.

He willed himself into a sitting position and rose carefully.

There was a great mess about. All the drawers of his desk had been emptied, and his clothes were on the floor.

Hedayat and his goon had ransacked his apartment.

Ayan walked to the front door and bolted it.

The key he kept by the entrance was gone. He'd have to get Khanom-eh Mohsen to change the lock. She wouldn't be happy, even if he were the one footing the bill.

His wallet was empty. They had taken the 1,000 tomans that had been there, as well as his driver's license and a list of telephone numbers. Both Nader's personal line at home and a direct line to Firouz Akhbari at the Ministry of Energy was on the list.

Fuck!

His safe!

Ayan reached below the bottom shelf of his closet. The safe was intact.

He entered his code and confirmed that his passport and bank papers were still there. Thank god!

Ayan gingerly set about restoring some order to his apartment.

He picked his scattered files off the floor and made to return the files to his briefcase. It was missing!

The briefcase was packed with confidential information he'd been using to develop a presentation for the upcoming board meeting: Iran Power's financial history, list of key clients, inter-company relationships in Germany, ties with the Ministry of Energy, descriptions of how the proposed expansion fit into the Shah's nuclear energy agenda.

They were now all in Hedayat's hands.

Ayan sank into the chair by his desk.

And saw the note.

It was written in broken English but was clear enough.

"You can't find us. We can find you. New rule now. You come Bazaar next Friday, 12 daytime. Leave 2,000 tomans in envelope on steps outside house you came first time and go.

You repeat every Friday same time. Nothing happen if you do. No mercy if you fail."

Ayan's hand was drawn to a stickiness at the back of his head as he contemplated the note. His fingertips returned a mottled red from the congealing blood. He ran his tongue lightly over his bruised lips and gums. Several places were sore and painful. He walked over to the mirror and looked at the damage. His eye was swollen; his lip was thick and still bleeding.

He would deal with the situation in the morning.

Right now, he had to rest.

He cleaned his cuts, swallowed a couple of aspirin, and lay down on his bed with a cold compress.

Mehdi was startled by his appearance the next morning but appeared to accept his excuse that it was a result of a skiing accident.

Ayan sent the driver off and called Nader's secretary to tell her he needed to see a doctor and would work from home for a couple of days.

He called the Best Taxi Service and booked a car for 11:00 a.m.

That would get him to the Bazaar in time for the mid-day *Dhuhr* prayer.

CHAPTER 23

Ayan asked the driver to wait and found his way into the Shah Mosque he had gone to with Hamid when Ma was visiting.

It was a weekday, so the passage was easy. He took off his shoes in the courtyard and washed his face, forearms, and feet, following the actions of the men around him. At the end of the *Dhuhr* prayer, he walked up to the imam, and looking into a face he remembered—a face of kindness and wisdom—he said, "I hope you remember me. Hamid was my driver. He introduced us before, when I was here with my mother. I give money every month to help Hamid and his family because they are in need. I want to be sure that the family is receiving my money and that they are well."

The imam looked at Ayan in surprise. Then his eyes showed recognition, and he smiled.

"It seems every time I see you, you are hurt," the imam said. "Be more careful, and please convey my regards to your mother."

He nodded at Ayan, turned away to say something to an assistant, and left.

The assistant took Ayan by the elbow and led him out of the mosque. He placed his index finger on his lips, discouraging conversation. "SAVAK," he whispered.

When they were alone in the courtyard, the assistant said, "The imam knows about your support and thanks you for what you are doing. It is truly blessed. But you must not come here again. It is too dangerous. *Asalamu alaikum*."

"*Walaikum Asalam*," Ayan replied. "But before you go, I also need help. One of your men has attacked me for no reason and stolen my property. His name is Hedayat. Please stop this crazy man. Tell him to return what he has stolen."

The assistant shrugged.

"I don't know," he said. "No Hedayat here. Don't come back. Dangerous for you. Dangerous for us."

"Hedayat is here! I've seen him in this mosque myself. You tell him to stay away from me, or I will keep coming back! I will bring people with me next time. I don't care how dangerous it is."

The assistant looked around. He put his hand on Ayan's back and walked him forward.

"Hedayat has not been seen for many days. He is foolish, not reliable. If we see him, we will counsel him. Go in peace. With the blessings of our imam. We pray that you will keep walking on the side of righteousness. May Allah watch over you."

Ayan got back into the taxi and guided the driver to Hamid's alley.

He was safe in the daylight. There were soldiers everywhere. And he had a lethal F-S fighting knife, a present from Nick. It would be his constant companion from now on.

One of the men who had challenged him last time was lolling about when he reached Hamid's doorstep.

He tensed when he saw Ayan approach.

"How's Hamid?" Ayan said.

The man looked towards the door, thought for a moment, and put his hand out.

"You came wrong day," he said. "Today Sunday. Give envelope and come on Friday next time."

"What is your name?"

"Toufan. Give money."

"And who am I?"

"Ayan Agha. Give money."

"Toufan Agha, I don't have any money for you. I'll come on Friday with the envelope. Today, I've come to enquire about Hamid and to make sure the money is reaching his family. You tell them inside that the money will only come in the future if I know Hamid is recovering. Is he?"

The man made a clicking sound, moved his eyebrows up, and tilted his head back.

Hamid was either not recovering, or he didn't know.

"Give money," Toufan repeated.

Ayan shook his head and walked slowly back to the taxi. He waited for several minutes, hoping Hamid's mother or somebody else from his family approached him again.

No one came.

But a cassette was outside his front door the next morning.

Sholeh's sobbing voice gave him the news. Hamid was now with Allah, Sholeh said. Her husband's wound had become infected, and there had been no place to take him for treatment.

Ayan had prepared himself for the worst because Hamid's journey was inexorably leading to this.

But it still hit hard.

He wept, for Hamid, for Sholeh, for Adil and Imran.

Hedayat had the sense not to reappear for a while.

*Perhaps the imam has spoken to him; perhaps he knows that I'll
be armed the next time he confronts me*, Ayan thought.

He made the trip down to the Bazaar every Friday. Hamid
was dead, but there was a connection between Sholeh and
this system. Her tape had confirmed that. He put 1,000
tomans in the envelope. Some of the money would reach her,
hopefully. Nothing extra for Hedayat. That bastard probably
stole most or all of the money; there was nothing Ayan could
do about that; but Hedayat would never get a single rial from
him directly.

The spring of 1978 came and went.

The sycamores of Pahlavi Avenue reclaimed the boulevard, their green foliage once again shielding pedestrians
from the early summer heat.

Ayan met Gaby in Mykonos, on the Caspian coast, and a
few weeks later, in Barcelona. She came to Tehran, and they
spent a few days with Darioush and Julie—hiking together in
the Alborz and water-skiing in Karaj just before the couple
left to live in LA.

Darioush's departure worried Gaby. Indians like him
were probably safe even if things unraveled, Ayan reassured
her. And he could leave quickly if he had to: His savings
could be transferred overnight to a numbered account in
Geneva, which he'd get down to opening on his next trip
to Europe, as Darioush had advised; it would take a moving
company under an hour to pack up and ship what he owned.

In response to her concern that he had his head in the
sand, Ayan took Gaby to Bank Melli, withdrew some of his
savings, and converted them into American Express traveller's checks that he kept in the safe in his apartment. And

he promised that he would soon start sending some of his things to her place in West Berlin.

He didn't ship his belongings, but he converted more of his money into traveller's checks every week or two—hesitant to carry too much to the American Express office at any one time.

Eventually, he had almost all his money in traveller's checks, and keeping them at home made him nervous. He rented a safe deposit box at his bank, and on one of her trips over, he added Gaby as a co-tenant and authorized signatory.

She objected, but he insisted.

She didn't want to play the *hausfrau* to his *mann*, she said. It was not the life she envisaged for them.

"I don't want your money," she said. "I can look after myself."

"Just fill in the paperwork and keep this duplicate key to the safe deposit box—in case Tehran traffic claims me— which it well might," he replied.

In Gaby's absence, Ayan concentrated on his Iran Power projects, bringing hours of work home and rarely going out in the evenings. The regular tennis game was long gone. With Hassan estranged and Darioush in LA, he settled for a game of singles now and then with Nick, or a hit with one of the professionals at Club Veyssi. The Key Club was still rocking, but it was not the same, frequented now by people he was trying to avoid.

But it was all right.

He was staying busy. He had the Indian gang at ICMS if he wanted company and Project Odysseus paving his way out of Tehran.

The summer rolled on.

Protestors mobilized by the mosque network created turmoil in several Iranian cities, but the conflict remained on the fringe of Tehran life till the army shot and killed one of Ayatollah Shariatmadri's supporters in front of him. Ayan breathed a sigh of relief when the Shah appeased the cleric by firing the head of SAVAK and implementing various reforms. The ayatollah asked his followers to abandon the streets and air their grievances in mosques, and it appeared that the Shah had found a balance between accommodation and enforcement that allowed life to go on as usual, at least in Iran Power.

But suddenly, in August 1978, the mood of appeasement and containment the Shah had struggled to achieve was shattered. Demonstrations in Isfahan were one day inexplicably, foolishly met with police gunfire. Many people died. Protests around the country reclaimed national and international attention. Martial law was declared.

Then the Cinema Rex in Abadan was set on fire and hundreds of people died. Gaby called. So did his parents. They urged Ayan to leave Iran.

Nick said not to worry. He told Ayan that religious students, targeting corrupt Western sites, were responsible for the Cinema Rex fire—not the government.

The country believed the opposition story, blamed SAVAK and the Shah, and the situation worsened noticeably.

The Shah's actions began to telegraph public signs of desperation, shocking Ayan, particularly when he made Sharif Emami, a man known to oppose the Shah's policies, the prime minister. Even that failed to quell unrest, and soon, on Friday, September 8, disaster struck during a peaceful protest in Jaleh Square, Tehran.

A crowd defied the ban on demonstrations the Shah had ordered in one of his strong man moods. The gathering, numbering in the thousands, mocked the Shah's authority, and their refusal to obey orders to disperse stuck a collective finger in the eye of heavily armed soldiers backed by tanks and helicopters.

Some reports said it was the professional agitators in the crowd who fired first. Others blamed the soldiers. But as the bullets rang out, and the blood of communists, students, soldiers, and anyone who happened to be in the wrong place mingled in Jaleh Square on that Black Friday, Iran changed irreversibly. The deaths shred all hopes for peace and unified the disparate groups forming the opposition to the Shah. The mullahs, possibly exaggerating the numbers of civilian casualties, succeeded in making the world acknowledge and condemn this state-sponsored brutality. Positions hardened.

A curfew was ordered. Judging by the sound of gunfire that Ayan heard from his rooftop practically every night, many people defied it. The main fighting seemed to be somewhere to the south. The BBC World Service confirmed the resulting nightly bloodshed.

Now everybody started to panic. Most Europeans and Americans Ayan knew packed up and left. The ones who stayed began to ask him to do their grocery shopping. It was too dangerous for whites to be in the streets.

It was an amazingly quick spiral down into chaos.

The rebellious mood began to infiltrate Iran Power. Hosseini still strutted about, but factory workers began to stroll into the executive building in groups, inspecting the halls they would have never dared enter in the past. Ayan's staff also seemed just a little slower to follow his instructions. A couple of them openly challenged him.

Nader, normally decisive and focused, seemed distracted, postponing meetings, waving Ayan away when he brought in updates on projects that were supposed to be so urgent. The only topic that got his attention was the business with Chip. The flow of money to Geneva continued unabated.

Nader told Ayan that an additional $50,000 would be deposited into his account as a December bonus. That would take his savings account balance from the $120,000 it had reached after the Nowruz bonus to $170,000.

Still far from the $1 million Chip said he needed but moving in the right direction.

Outside, it was a similar strange world of mixed signals. According to BBC reports, the Shah had managed to get Khomeini kicked out of Iraq in an effort to cut his communication lines with the revolutionaries. The Ayatollah arrived in a French suburb a few days later, and his supporters began to use Western infrastructure and newspapers to great advantage.

Nick Stasney told Ayan that the Shah was going to pull it off, negotiate a truce, find some sort of compromise, and perhaps create a Vatican-style state in Qom. Of course, true power would remain with the Pahlavis. There was no chance of an overthrow, he said.

The streets told a very different story. The protests grew larger as the cold season arrived.

The days grew short and bleak. The sycamores of Pahlavi Avenue lost their autumn colors and stood bare, and the October nights rang with gunshots.

International airlines began to cut back on flights into Tehran. That made it difficult to meet Gaby and forced Ayan's hand.

He decided he would leave at the end of March 1979, after Nowruz, when the big bonuses were paid. What he had by then would still be peanuts to Chip, but it would have to be enough. In the meanwhile, he would renew his visas for the UK and Germany. It seemed a sensible precaution.

Jackie called him and said she was making plans to come to Iran, finally. A major newspaper had commissioned her to report on the worsening situation. Would he help her get interviews?

He would, Ayan said. He would.

PART
SIX

CHAPTER 24

Tehran, Iran, October 1978

Nader called an impromptu management meeting at 4:00 p.m. on Monday to discuss changing staff attitudes, rising indiscipline, and the political unrest.

Where was Hosseini? Ayan wondered. He hadn't seen the Colonel since breakfast. The SAVAK man was usually invited to sit in on these meetings and would be the one taking the lead in these matters.

The CEO directed the conversation towards securing Iran Power operations around the country. They should expect to see armed military personnel on the premises within the week, Nader said, because he'd asked for help from the government security team that looked after oil fields.

Nader closed the meeting at 5:00 p.m. As was his custom, he stood at his door ushering them out—shaking each of their hands and wishing each a good evening.

Ayan held out his hand when it was his turn.

Nader pressed a piece of paper into his grip.

Ayan looked at Nader in surprise. Stern and serious eyes met his.

He rushed to his office and shut the door behind him.

The handwritten note from Nader said: "Call 0345678 at 7:00 p.m. Use a payphone. Critical. Nobody can know about this."

Ayan drew in a breath. This was about the Geneva operations. It had to be. More secrecy than usual, but these were unusual times.

He made the call from Club Veyssi's public phone. It was in a private corner of the clubhouse, and Ayan planned to get some exercise afterwards by playing with one of the pros; he might as well make the most of the evening.

Nader picked up after a couple of rings. He was in a restaurant or club, judging by the background noise.

"Ayan, what is wrong with you! Have you lost your mind?" Nader said.

"Excuse me?" Ayan said, his heart rate accelerating as Nader's fury erupted over the line.

"I mean, how foolish can you get? You! Of all people! We trusted you. Treated you like our own. Brought you into our inner circle. And you throw that in our faces—start supporting criminals who want to destroy our country!"

"Nader, I'm sorry, I have no idea what you are talking about."

They'd found out about Hamid and Hedayat! How was he going to explain this!

"People have been calling my private line saying they have confidential information about our company. I have received blackmail demands that Hosseini has investigated. He monitored the calls and arrested a student, a communist, who led us to his uncle—a friend of your driver Hamid—a man called Hedayat who confessed to SAVAK that it was you who gave him our secret information. Hosseini showed me photographs of you. He has a big file on you. What were you doing in the Shah Mosque? Why were you giving money to criminals? Have you gone insane? You raped a girl from a prominent family? Madness! People are being shot for far less than this!"

Ayan held on to a chair as his legs began to give way.

"I can explain—I was trapped . . . they stole . . . I never raped . . ."

"Too late for explanations. There is nothing I can do to help you. This call is only because of Firouz. He is a friend of your uncle's, he said. I gave you this job because of him, so I had to call him. He is as shocked as I am. He asked me to warn you because of old relationships. Give you a chance. Now pay attention to what I'm going to tell you. Hosseini is going to arrest you tonight. I know he's busy till 9:00 p.m. You have less than two hours. Disappear. It's your only chance. This telephone call never happened. It is going to be our last conversation."

"I can't just leave . . . please . . ." Ayan said, his voice thin and effete.

He knew he sounded pathetic.

Nader's voice softened. "Ayan, I know that this is a shock. But you don't have time. SAVAK is sparing no one these days. Ayan! Are you still there?"

Nader's sharp tone jolted him out of his shocked state.

"Ayan! I'm taking a risk by calling to warn you—on top of everything else I've done for you, all this money I've paid you," Nader said. "Now you have to do something for me. I'm moving my family to Germany. Our German partners have asked me to become the head of their Middle East and Africa Division. I can't be seen to have any involvement in Odysseus; if you are arrested, and I hope that you won't be, leave me out of it. Say your orders came directly from the Atomic Energy Organization of Iran. They have received the material from South Africa and are satisfied with the execution of

Odysseus. I will make sure that somebody in AEOI will put in a good word for you."

"But what about the paper trail?" Ayan said. The ground was shifting fast, but the situation was clarifying. "Your signature is on the invoices."

"You opened the account in Geneva and physically transferred the assets. I signed invoices for consulting services that you put in front of me. I sent you to Geneva specifically to confirm the legitimacy of the whole process. You allowed irregularities that have cost millions of dollars."

"Yes, but . . ."

"Ayan! Be smart! I will be in a position of influence in Germany soon. Think about what that can mean for you if you behave correctly. Find a way to the airport immediately. Your exit visa is still valid—I checked. Go home to India. Air India is still flying out of Iran. If you can't get on a plane, drive across the border. Now move! I don't know what will happen if SAVAK gets you."

The line went dead.

Yezdi, the junior pro, waiting on the tennis court outside, was looking at Ayan with a frown, shrugging with impatience and pointing to the night lights that he'd turned on.

Ayan apologized to the pro, paid him for the hour, and sprinted to his car.

He ran right back into the pro shop.

His phone at home was surely tapped.

He had to call Nick. There was no one else he could lean on.

"Nick!" Ayan said as soon as he heard his voice. "I have an emergency. I have to leave town fast. No, I can't give you the details—just that I have to be out of Iran right after I transfer my money tomorrow morning. I need a place to hide out for tonight. Can I stay in your basement?"

"I don't want to get caught up in any trouble, Ayan, I have a family to take care of. What the fuck did you do?"

"I'll tell you when we meet."

Silence.

"Nick! I don't have time! Are we friends or not? Come on, man! This is the time to step up. You said nobody comes down to your basement. It's only for tonight."

"OK. Use the street entrance and go straight down to the basement. I'll take some sandwiches down there and wait for you. Is it a woman you've got pregnant? You've not had a road accident, killed somebody, have you? Tell me so I'm prepared."

"Neither. Work related. I'll fill you in. You're a lifesaver. I won't forget this. Thanks. See you at 8:30 p.m. Wait, can you do one more thing? Can you call a few people? Tell them my plans have changed?"

He made Nick repeat the contact numbers he gave him for Gaby in West Berlin and Starnberger, for Jackie in London, and his parents in Delhi.

Who else should he reach on the local line available at the club?

The Indian Embassy, he decided.

He found the general number in one of the directories stacked next to the phone.

"Call tomorrow morning after 10:00 a.m. No one is here now," the person who answered his call to the Indian Embassy said.

"You're there!" Ayan said, "I need help, it's an emergency!"

"I'm just the guard, sir."

"You must take a message—I'm an Indian citizen being wrongly arrested."

"I can take a short message, sir. Please wait, I will get a notepad."

It was five minutes before he returned, another five minutes to take down the message.

"Somebody will call you in the morning. Number, please?"

Ayan gave him the home number in Delhi.

"Local number in Iran is required, sir."

"I just told you I'm being wrongly arrested tonight! No one is going to answer my local number tomorrow!"

"Local number is required, sir."

Ayan slammed the receiver and raced home.

It was 7:45 p.m. by the time he walked into his apartment. He had to be out of here in half an hour. No later.

He retrieved his papers and money from the safe and checked his passport. Nader was right. His exit visa was good till December 20.

Chip's note had fallen out of his passport as he'd been flicking through it to find the right page for the exit visa. He'd call the number on it from Nick's place.

He pulled out the navy blazer he always wore when he travelled, placed his passport and wallet in the right inner pocket, and secured the button. He put his checkbook and savings account passbook in the left inside pocket, all the cash he had at home—700 tomans—in one flap pocket, and his address book in the other. He draped the blazer over his desk chair.

His safe deposit key!

He felt inside the safe and dropped the small key into his trouser pocket.

He pulled down a suitcase and his Pan Am flight bag from the top shelf of the cupboard and started throwing his clothes and whatever else that was nearby into them. He took Gaby's picture out of the frame by his bed, placed it in his family album, and added it to the pile.

He had to take his papers—where were they?

He found his degrees, transcripts, birth certificate . . .

It was going to be difficult to zip up his luggage.

He sat on his suitcase and struggled. The zip began to give way.

He started throwing clothes out of the suitcase.

And didn't hear the front door open.

Just heard a voice from hell say:

"'. . . O caravan master, my burden has fallen—O God where is Your help? . . . Friend! Do not blame me: my sodden eyes, ashes on my head . . . Dread and woes . . . What can I say? The tricks of fate, I neglected . . .'"

Ayan spun around.

Hosseini stood in his doorway.

"Colonel! How did you get into my apartment?" Ayan said, feeling sweat dampen his shirt.

It was just 8:15 p.m.! Nader had the timing wrong, and now he was fucked!

"I knocked and rang your bell. Nobody answered, so I used the keys your landlady gave me," the Colonel said, picking up the phone and returning it to the cradle.

He looked around the apartment.

"Going somewhere?"

"Yes, soon—to Europe, to see Gaby—I was just getting my luggage organized."

"Oh yes, Gaby. Beautiful Gaby. I would be packing, too, if she were mine and waiting for me."

"You've not barged into my apartment to talk about Gaby, I'm sure," Ayan said, trying to compose himself.

"Agha Ayan," the Colonel said, sighing as he sat down on the desk chair. "This is a very difficult moment for me."

He took out a paper from the breast pocket of his jacket and flattened it on the desk.

"Read this," he said, slapping the paper with one hand and massaging his forehead with the other. "I did not expect this from you. I'm very disappointed."

Ayan walked over to his desk and picked up the document.

It was a warrant for his arrest, signed by a magistrate.

The three pages accused him of supporting armed insurgency to overthrow the sovereign government, sponsoring deadly violence against state property and personnel, theft of Iran Power funds, corruption, and moral turpitude.

"Is this a joke? It has to be!" Ayan said, reaching for his desk, trying to steady himself. He was in some increasingly nightmarish, fictional world.

"There is another matter," Hosseini said, shaking his head. "Khanom Fariba's family says you raped her. She was an innocent girl, and you ruined her. You are lucky that she has refused to sign the charge. So far."

"Rape? Another lie! She came to me!" The words escaped Ayan.

It would have been better to deny everything.

He felt dizzy.

"That is a problem for another time. The charges the magistrate has signed are already enough to end everything for you. They had assigned some difficult people from SAVAK to arrest you, Agha Ayan, but I wanted to save you from that—because of our relationship, the friendship I still feel for you, despite everything wrong you've done. I told my colleagues that I would handle it."

Hosseini's face showed regret, not anger.

Perhaps he still had a chance with the Colonel!

Ayan placed a hand on Hosseini's forearm.

"Colonel," he said, "I haven't done anything wrong, please believe me!"

"I will try to help you," Hosseini said, patting Ayan's hand. "I am now your best friend in Iran. If you listen to my advice, you may survive. But that is for the next days. Tonight, I have to take you in. You've made bad mistakes, and SAVAK has many questions for you to answer."

"Colonel, come on, we both know this makes no sense. You have to help me!"

"There is nothing I can do right now. My hands are tied—by your own regrettable actions."

"Can't you give me some time? Just twenty-four hours. Let me take care of a few things. Surely, you can get me that time?"

Hosseini sat back and held up the warrant. "Sorry. You have been arrested." He looked around the apartment. "I'm glad Khanom-eh Mohsen informed us you had come home in a hurry and seemed to be packing . . ."

That fucking woman! How did she know! Was she spying on him through the fucking window?

"Before we go, I need your passport."

Ayan struggled to recover a semblance of calm.

"I don't have my passport with me," Ayan said. "It's with the Indian Embassy; they're adding some more pages."

It was a reasonable excuse. He had to keep his passport.

"Do you have a receipt?" Hosseini said, his manner becoming official.

"I do. It's in the office."

"Excuse me for doubting you. It's my job."

Hosseini got up and walked towards Ayan's closet. He knelt and felt underneath the bottom shelf.

"Khanom-eh Mohsen also told me about this safe. I have her master key. Your landlady has been very helpful. She is a patriot who loves Shah and what he is doing. Unlike you, who have acted disgracefully and deceitfully."

Savak [handwritten]

He should have known! He could kill that woman! Always solicitous, always ingratiating, and spying for Hosseini all this time!

Hosseini pushed himself up and held out his hand. "Your passport? Where is it?" he said.

"I told you that it's with the Indian Embassy."

Hosseini walked over to the suitcase and the Pan Am bag. He emptied their contents onto the floor. "Agents are going to search this place thoroughly tomorrow; they'll find everything. It's better to give your passport to me if you want to see it again."

Hosseini moved towards his closet and started throwing things that were still hanging or folded onto the ground. He was thorough and fast. It did not take him long to rifle through the mess and then reach behind Ayan for his blazer.

"Agha Ayan, I see everything. Your eyes told me you were lying. Lying to me is a very bad idea. I can't help you if you lie."

"Sorry, you surprised me; I'm disoriented."

"It's understandable. But I need you to be truthful from now on. Agreed?"

"Yes."

Hosseini glanced at his passport, money, and banking documents, and put them as well as Ayan's cash into his coat pockets.

Ayan fought the urge to check his trouser pocket. *Don't even look down!* he told himself. He'd just bought more traveller's checks. He had $100,000 in the safe deposit box—just $20,000 in his bank account, thank god! The key was going to stay where it was. Hosseini wasn't going to frisk him, was he? Pat him down and put his hands in his trousers? Let him try!

"Come on then," Hosseini said. "I have what I need. Come as you are. Let's go."

What should he do now? Think! Once he was in SAVAK's hands—no! Anything but that!

"I'm not going anywhere with you," Ayan said. "I'm an Indian citizen; you can't just come in here and take me away. I want to speak to the embassy."

Hosseini looked at his watch. "Let's see," he said. "On the one hand, we have a person who has funded treasonous, seditious activities and presided over the disappearance of millions of dollars of company money; accused of the most serious charges of threatening state security, theft, and corruption; and of raping an Iranian girl from the most respectable family. On the other hand, we have tens of thousands of Indians earning their living in Iran, billions in trade between the countries, export of all that Indian wheat to Iran, heavy Indian dependence on Iranian oil. India will never take the side of your kind of criminal against us. Let's not waste time."

Ayan braced himself, his muscles tensing, his fingers involuntarily curling into fists. He was not disappearing into a SAVAK rat hole. He had done nothing wrong, had just been stupid, trusted the wrong people . . . allowed himself to be blackmailed and compromised . . . been stupid! Stupid! Stupid! But he'd never advocated revolution, violence, nothing of that sort. And what was the nonsense about theft of Iran Power assets and corruption? He had no power to move money; the documents in Geneva stated that clearly! What did these people think? He wasn't some dispensable piece of trash. He had friends, connections, here and in India. Who were they to do this to him! He looked at his tormentor. Hosseini was out of shape, smaller than him, and alone. He could take this guy down and run.

"I'm not going," Ayan said, deciding. "You have no proof of anything. Give me back my passport. You have no right to do this!"

"Agha Ayan, be reasonable. I've taken the trouble to come here myself. I've spared you the rough experience of being arrested by policemen. Now come with me."

Hosseini pointed towards the door.

What were the risks, really? He'd heard Hosseini carried the standard SAVAK SIG Sauer semi-automatic 220 and a copper knuckle-duster. But getting them out would take time. Hosseini would never expect him to be violent. But he had to get closer.

He walked slowly towards the Colonel. "OK. I will come with you and put my fate in your hands."

He reached out to shake Hosseini's hand.

It went exactly to plan.

A left hook, a kick into his groin, another fist into his face, and the SAVAK man lay unconscious on the floor.

Ayan retrieved his passport, banking documents, and cash from Hosseini's pocket, grabbed his car keys, and raced out of his apartment.

This was it. No turning back now. He would ditch the Iran Power Mercedes somewhere, take a taxi to Nick's, be in Bank Melli when it opened at 9:00 a.m., retrieve his traveller's checks and the rest of his cash, and be out of this country by tomorrow.

He flew down the steps.

The last thing he saw before he lost consciousness were the headlights of an unfamiliar car parked in Khanom-eh Mohsen's driveway.

CHAPTER 25

Ayan tried to push the foot off, but the weight on his face was relentless.

He was lying on Khanom-eh Mohsen's driveway. A huge Iranian with crude features stood above him, twisting his shoe on Ayan's face as if he were extinguishing a cigarette.

Hosseini's voice said, "That's enough, get him up."

The Colonel had a handkerchief pressed to his mouth.

"Stupid mistake, Agha Ayan, thinking I was alone. But you've done so many stupid things. Now I see how you got yourself into this situation. Come on! I've had enough of this nonsense! Let's go!"

Hosseini's burly companion snuggled his AK-47 under his right elbow, handcuffed Ayan, and shoved him into the front seat of the car. Hosseini got into the back seat, directly behind Ayan and tied a scarf around his eyes.

Ayan's head jerked backward as Hosseini pulled it into a tight blindfold. He saw rays of light streaking down an endless dark road. I have to fight, stay alert, he told himself as he heard the boot of the car open and shut and the key turn in the ignition.

"Where are we going?" Ayan said, "Where are you taking me? I have a right to know!"

"Shut up!" the driver said, slamming his elbow into Ayan's chest.

His face hit the dashboard as he doubled over from the unexpected blow. Blood began to trickle down his chin.

Hosseini pulled Ayan back into his seat.

He told the driver to back off.

"Agha Ayan," he said, "don't speak unless we ask you a question. Understand?"

Ayan nodded—furious, defenseless, not wanting to be hit again.

They drove for twenty minutes or so. For a while, he knew exactly where they were, but soon, the turns down various roads and alleys disoriented him. The car stopped. He heard a gate opening. They drove in. The gate slammed shut.

"Agha Ayan," Hosseini said as they pulled up, "I am delivering you to the care of Captain Salehi. I advise you to cooperate with him."

"Where are we? Where are you going? Colonel! Please! You can't leave me here!"

Ayan tried to turn his head towards Hosseini in the back seat, but it was too painful.

"Salehi and I are a team. We just have different jobs. I will be informed of all developments."

Ayan was led out of the car and up some stairs. Then down two flights of stairs and into an area that smelled like a toilet.

The blindfold came off.

He was standing in a tiny, windowless cell. The walls were plastered in a dull, two-tone brown. A single neon light flickered on the ceiling. A tattered rug was thrown on the cement floor. A wooden plank, folding out from the wall, was the bed.

The driver who had roughed him was there. He came up to Ayan, threw him face down onto the plank, took off the handcuffs, and walked out, locking the cell door behind him.

"Wait!" Ayan yelled, struggling to his feet. "You can't keep me in this filthy place! Come back!"

The man's footsteps receded. Another door some distance away slammed shut. And then there was silence.

Ayan shook the bars of the cell door.

"Hey! Driver! Guard!"

Silence. Deep. Absolute.

"Help!"

Silence.

"Help me! Don't leave me here!"

Silence.

"Please!"

Ayan banged the walls and shook the cell door and screamed till his voice was a hoarse whisper.

He needed water desperately. The cell was freezing. Every part of his body ached.

He lay down on the plank. That relentless light was directly on him.

How had it come to this?

He had stayed in this country too long, been greedy, got dragged into other people's business, slipped into fetid waters. He could be with Gaby right now. She'd asked him to join her in Germany. Several times. He should have gone to her with the $120,000 he'd saved.

But no, he had to be a big shot. Arrive as a somebody.

Gaby wouldn't have cared how much he had.

It was his fucking pride.

What was he now?

Hosseini had his checkbook and statement. His deposit box key was also gone.

The bastard couldn't just walk away with his money in Bank Melli, could he? It was a world-class bank with international standards and controls. They wouldn't allow unauthorized withdrawals, and his signature was hard to copy. Nor would they let a non-registered person walk in and open his safe deposit box, even if they had his key.

Most people wouldn't even know what the key was for—it was unmarked and nondescript.

But the Colonel might know. The fucker knew everything. He would freeze his account and seal his deposit box at the very least.

What a miserable, fucked-up, son-of-a-bitch hole he'd dug for himself!

The hard surface of the plank made it difficult to lie comfortably in any position. Ayan picked up the filthy rug. His stomach retched as its rank smell enveloped him. But he had to endure it. He covered himself with it. It was too damn cold.

He woke up desperate to go to the bathroom, tried once again to yell for attention, and was forced to relieve himself against a wall in the corner of his cell. His stream, dark yellow with dehydration, made its way down the pitch of the cell and out into the narrow drain outside.

Sometime in the endless night, he must have fallen asleep because he heard a voice telling him to wake up.

The unforgiving surface he lay on and cold night had not helped his aching body. Sitting up was difficult.

An elderly man with genial features stood in his cell holding a paper plate and a metal cup.

"Good morning, Ayan Agha; it's time for breakfast."

"Thank you," Ayan said, grateful for the man's politeness.

The man placed the plate of lavash bread and feta cheese and cup of black tea on the plank.

"Agha, what time is it?" Ayan asked.

"6:00 a.m."

Ayan took a sip of the tea. The hot liquid sent a rejuvenating shiver through him.

"What's your name?" Ayan asked.

"Aref," the man answered.

"Quiet! No talking!" a voice down the hall barked.

"That is Agha Davood," Aref whispered, placing a finger on his lips. "He is in charge of you. I just make the food here."

He looked towards the angry voice, put on a strict face, and left the cell, locking the door from the outside with deliberate noise.

Then he disappeared, and everything was bleak again.

Ayan ate the bread and cheese and lay back on the bed. His eyes locked on the infernal light in his ceiling. There was a camera lens in the fixture. He was sure of it.

The cell door opened again. A beefy man came in holding a black garbage bag in one hand and a grey plastic bag in the other.

"Put what you are wearing in this bag."

It was the voice that had ordered silence a few minutes before.

Davood.

He was as tall as Ayan and significantly more muscular. He had two deep lines between his eyes, and a testosterone-fired moustache.

Ayan did as he was told.

"All your clothes! Into the black bag. Now!"

Ayan took off his underwear and placed it in the black garbage bag.

He stood naked and shivering and humiliated.

"Wear this."

Davood threw the grey plastic bag he was carrying at Ayan.

The bag contained a pair of baggy pajamas, a sleeveless vest, and rubber slippers.

"Agha Davood," Ayan said. "It's very cold in here. Can I have a blanket?"

"Where do you think you are? In the Sheraton?" Davood sneered.

He waved dismissively and turned to leave.

"Wait! At least take me to the bathroom. I need to go urgently," Ayan said.

Davood looked exasperated. Reluctantly, he took a scarf off his wrist, blindfolded and handcuffed Ayan, and led him out of the cell.

They turned to the right. After about fifty steps, they stopped in a place that smelled even worse than his cell.

Davood stopped and took off the blindfold.

Ayan faced a urinal, a squatting-style toilet, and a few feet away, a shower stall.

"Five minutes," Davood growled, took off Ayan's handcuffs and stepped away.

Ayan overheard him talking with two other people whose voices were unfamiliar. He used the primitive toilet and stepped into the shower. He still had a couple of minutes.

Davood pulled him right out.

"Who said you could bathe? Back to your cell. Immediately!"

"Get your fucking hands off me!" Ayan yelled, pushing Davood away instinctively.

Another man—Davood's twin, it seemed—stormed in and pointed his AK-47 at Ayan.

That resolved things instantly.

Ayan raised his hands and allowed himself to be handcuffed and blindfolded.

He lay down on the plank in his cell, his teeth chattering. He reached for the disgusting rug and covered himself with it again. What he would give to have his overcoat with him now! And his electric heater.

The overcoat Ma had found for him, that had kept him warm all over the world, must still be on the floor of his apartment where Hosseini had thrown it. The electric heater must still be on. Perhaps it would start a fire. That would serve his treacherous landlady right! When had she started informing on him? Probably right from the start—as soon as he'd moved in. That's how Hosseini knew so much about his comings and goings, and about Gaby.

He rubbed his hands and felt an unfamiliar emptiness on his wrist. What had happened to his grandfather's Jaeger? Hosseini must have taken it. And the Pan Am bag with his photographs, transcripts, diplomas, and references. The son of a bitch had taken them, as well as his checkbook, passport, and wallet, probably also his safe deposit key—pretty much everything he had.

Not that it mattered right now. All he wanted was an ointment for his wounds, a couple of aspirin for his exploding head, a long hot shower, and a comfortable bed in a dark room.

It was hard to believe that, a few hours ago, all those things had been so readily available. He would have been back at work by now. Wouldn't people wonder what had happened to him? He had three meetings scheduled for today, including Brauer from the Hamburg bank trying to undercut its way into Iran Power's business. Nobody else had Brauer's telephone number. What would they tell him when he showed up? Hadley Jones would be in at noon to give him an update on the cost allocation study. And Ayan had called a team meeting at 3:00 p.m.

Nader would probably tell them that he had to leave on an urgent business trip. Or perhaps, he would say that Ayan had left the company, left Iran suddenly, like so many other expatriates.

Everything would be believed at a time when things were changing by the day.

He had to shake himself out of this funk.

Come on. He had to believe that Nick had made the calls. Gaby would be on her way to Tehran soon. She wouldn't let them make him disappear. His parents were probably already swinging into action. His father must be working his contacts in the Ministry of External Affairs, his mother harassing everybody all the time, Uncle Vikram pressuring his pal Firouz Akbari to use his influence with the Shah.

Hosseini and SAVAK would soon find out that he was not somebody they could kidnap and humiliate with impunity.

Who the hell were they to treat him this way!

"Get up! Come with me!"

Ayan swung his legs down and put on his slippers, trying to shake off the doze he had fallen into.

"Hurry up!" Davood yanked him off the bed and hand-cuffed him. The blindfold came on.

They turned left out of his cell this time.

"Climb these steps!"

After ten steps, they came to a landing, veered right, and climbed five more. They walked to the end of a corridor and entered a room.

"Wait here," Davood said.

The blindfold and handcuffs came off.

Ayan found himself in a rectangular room with white walls and a grey linoleum floor. A basic wooden table stood in the center of the room with a chair on either side. A tray with a teapot and two small glasses sat on the table. The dark brown curtains on both windows were drawn. An incongruous chandelier provided a pleasant glow after the fluorescent nightmare in his cell. Radiators under the windows had heated the room to a comfortable temperature. There was a door on the far side, similar to the one he had come through. A round electric clock above the door indicated that it was 10:00 a.m.

The door opened, and a short, stocky man walked in. His uniform and prominent moustache squared with the image of a Persian army man. His chest was a riot of medals. The insignia on his hat marked him as a SAVAK official.

"Good morning, Agha Ayan," he said in a surprisingly deep voice. "I am Captain Salehi."

"Good morning," Ayan said, meeting a firm handshake.

"You have rested, I hope?" the Captain asked.

"I've had better nights," Ayan said.

"Yes, yes, I know. It's unfortunate," Salehi said.

He had an educated manner and seemed reassuringly reasonable.

"Perhaps we can resolve your situation soon. Please sit down."

The Captain sat on one side of a plain table and motioned to the chair on the other side. He placed a leather folder in front of him, unzipped it deliberately, and poured tea into the two glasses.

Salehi placed one glass in front of Ayan.

"We are going to get to know each other very well," he said with a broad smile, taking a sip from his glass and motioning to Ayan to do the same.

"Now let's get started."

Salehi took out a legal sized pad from his folder and moved it towards Ayan.

"Write down your background on this—your history—
as well as your activities in Iran. Use this pen. State what you
have been doing, your experiences, who you have spent time
with here, everything. Give me all the details right up to last
night. It will be to your advantage to leave nothing out. I will
come back in one hour, at eleven o'clock."

The Captain stood up.

This was ridiculous!

"Everybody knows my background. Hosseini definitely
does," Ayan said. "And this situation is uncalled for! People
must be looking for me. I shouldn't be here!"

The Captain sat down again and brought his face into
Ayan's. His smile was gone.

"Next time you say his name, you will say Colonel
Hosseini! You understand? He is worth ten of you.
Nobody cares for you. Nobody even knows where you
are. And nobody will find out. You are under arrest for
very serious crimes. Understand that I have a job to do.
It is in your interest to make it easy. Please provide the
information."

He tapped on the pad and stood up again.

"I've done nothing!" Ayan said. "You have no proof of
anything! I am not some poor Iranian you picked up off the
streets. I want to talk to the Indian Embassy. There are rules.
Who do you guys think you are!"

The Captain pointed to the notepad.

"I will be back in one hour."

Ayan flung the notepad and pen to the floor, damned if he
was going to write anything down.

He got up and walked about, drawing the curtains on
the window nearest him. It was protected by iron bars on
the inside and boarded on the outside, as was the other
window. He tried the door on the far side, the one Salehi

used. It was locked. It had a peephole. A dark cloth on the other side covered it.

What can they do if I refuse to cooperate? Ayan thought, sitting down again. This whole bizarre situation—Nader's warning call, Hosseini stealing up to his apartment and arresting him, the humiliating treatment by Hosseini's driver and Davood, the miserable conditions, and now this little dictator, Hosseini's enforcer, ordering him about—was some hideous farce, a travesty, that surely couldn't continue.

They had nothing on him.

Fuck Salehi.

The waiting became tedious. All Ayan could hear was the sound of his breathing and the whir of the electric clock. He closed his heavy eyes.

Salehi walked in precisely at 11:00 a.m.

"What's this?" he said, pointing to the notepad on the floor. "Pick it up immediately!"

Ayan shook himself awake.

"Pick it up, I say, pick it up now!" Salehi shouted. His eyes bulged, and the veins stood out on his neck.

Ayan ignored him, staring straight ahead in silent protest.

"Davood!" Salehi yelled.

Davood pushed the door open and came towards Ayan. Salehi raised his hand, halting the guard's advance.

"Last chance," he said to Ayan.

"For what?" Ayan said. "If something happens with this maniac pointing his gun at me, if there is an accident, you will be in more trouble than you can handle, and you know it! Stop ordering me about and threatening me."

Salehi gathered himself.

He smiled.

"OK. It looks like you are not in the right frame of mind today. We will try again when you are in a more cooperative mood."

He nodded at Davood and left.

"Wait! Where are you going?" Ayan said. "You have to talk to me. Tell me what's going on. You can't keep me here. This is bullshit!"

"Shut up!" Davood said, yanking Ayan up from his chair and wrenching his hands behind him. The handcuffs came on again.

"Fuck you, asshole! That hurt!" Ayan yelled as his head snapped back, and he was plunged into darkness by Davood's blindfold.

He braced himself for the inevitable blow.

It came as a slap that made him stagger.

He had not expected that affront.

A punch he could take. Had taken many.

A slap said you are my dog. My bitch. I can do what I want to you.

"I'm going to report you—miserable bastard!" Ayan yelled and charged in the direction of Davood's presence. He could smell the bastard, even if he couldn't see anything. "I'm going to fuck you up!"

He hit a wall and heard Davood laugh.

Ayan was soon back in his dank, disgusting cell, dragged and pushed there by Davood and Davood No. 2—who threw in a few punches of his own along the way.

He sat down on the plank, his head pounding and his ears ringing, his hand stinging from a burn. One of the fucking Davoods had stubbed out his cigarette on it.

In minutes, he was freezing and throwing up from the smell and cold and the misery.

He lay down and pulled the rug over him. It reeked of sweat and vomit and shit and piss, but it stopped the shaking in his body. He couldn't stay here! It was impossible! He had to get out of this hellhole!

How?

He screamed at his helplessness. He jumped up and pounded the unforgiving walls, shook the iron bars that locked him in, and screamed till he was voiceless. He fell back on the plank and reached for the foul rug again.

—too many American movies

CHAPTER 26

Hours passed, and Ayan heard and saw no one.

He felt sticky and rank. Was it just yesterday that he'd got out of his comfortable bed and stepped into his own shower?

What a shower that had been! Hot water raining down on him, powerful jets massaging his legs and back, his feet sinking into the thick floor mat as he toweled himself dry . . .

He got up carefully. Many parts of him hurt, most of all his burnt hand, but he had to exercise. He found a relatively clean spot and jogged in place till his feet complained about the hard floor and the thin rubber slippers. He did pushups on his plank bed till his arms gave way. He lay down again, the endorphins lifting his mood.

Not for long.

Who was he kidding? His situation was bad.

How would Gaby find him here? Nobody would. And Hosseini was right: The Indian Embassy wouldn't push too hard on his behalf, not with the charges against him; and even if they could be made to bother with his situation, if his parents harassed them and got the ambassador involved, what clout would Indian diplomats have when SAVAK had thumbed its nose at the CIA—taken absolute control of domestic operations as Nick had said?

He was in a SAVAK unsafe house. The only escape was political pressure from home. But they were a Congress family, with ties to yesterday's news—to Indira Gandhi—and had no associations with the ruling Janata Party. There was no meaningful political lever his family could pull, nothing they could do to force SAVAK to free him.

He lay about listlessly, drifting in and out of sleep, not knowing the hour, waking up each time to rising desolation. He thought of Gaby constantly, of making love to her in Darioush's living room that last time, while Darioush and Julie stepped out to pick up dinner for them; of how he had wanted to go on and on, but Gaby had laughed and pushed him off, nervous about their host's imminent return, then left for Munich on the night flight.

He ached for her with all his being and despaired, entombed in filth, caged like an animal, hungry and thirsty . . .

Random thoughts circled in his brain. Silence and isolation gave them voice and acceleration, oppressing him beyond bearing. His chest tightened. The walls of the cell began to close in on him.

The light—the fucking flickering light!

He thrust his fist at whoever was looking at him, gave them the finger.

I'm losing my mind, Ayan thought.

He got up and paced restlessly.

He grabbed the bars of the cell door and shook them again and screamed till he had no legs and had to sit down.

He had to focus on something that wouldn't make him feel so completely helpless.

Think about Ma's compulsory Indian philosophy sessions on Sundays, he told himself, the Bhagavad Gita and the *Tat Tvam Asi* teachings of the *Chandogya Upanishad* that had made such an impression on him. Think about the "Hymn of Creation" in the *Rig Veda* that had given him solace before, returning to him from the ages, from mystics 3,000 years ago, resonating with him.

He repeated a small section of Basham's translation that he remembered because it was Ma's favorite:

"'Then even nothingness was not, nor existence . . . Then there were neither death nor immortality . . . That One breathed windlessly and self-sustaining. There was than One, and there was no other. At first, there was only darkness wrapped in darkness. All this was unillumined water. That One which came to be, enclosed in nothing, arose at last, born of the power of heat. In the beginning, desire descended on it—that was the primal seed . . .'"

He found the words comforting him in this miserable place, telling him not to worry because this life of his, this collection of atoms, was so insignificant in the travel of time . . .

Then he tried to breathe slowly, deeply: *Lie on your back and breathe into your abdomen,* he told himself, *then chest, then shoulders and neck and head till you are full of air—hold for a few seconds, exhale—repeat; withdraw your consciousness from this place, and center it on your breathing . . . focus, focus, concentrate on your breathing, dammit!*

It was a relief to hear another human, even if it was Davood.

Desperate for any connection, Ayan made an effort to engage him when he arrived to take him for the second of two trips to the toilet allowed each day.

But the surly Iranian restricted his communication to rough commands.

He marched Ayan, handcuffed and blindfolded, to the toilet, and afterwards, allowed him to wash his hands and face.

It had been almost thirty-six hours since he had brushed his teeth. Ayan swilled some of the soapy water and gagged but persevered; he had to wash out his mouth.

The next relief from the monotony and silence came at 5:00 p.m.

Dinnertime, Aref informed him. He could go to the toilet once more after that. The next time would be after breakfast at 6:00 a.m.

He placed a tray on the plank and passed Ayan a plastic bottle, keeping an eye out for Davood, who was talking to someone on a telephone.

"I cooked the food myself," Aref said. "And I've brought you extra water for the night. Please eat. I have to leave in a few minutes."

Normally, a plate of lentils over rice was comfort food: dal—with ginger, garlic, tomatoes, turmeric, green chilies, cumin, served with steamed basmati rice and vegetable curry; or the equally delicious Persian version, *adas polow*—saffron rice with lentils, raisins, dates, and unnamed spices. What lay before Ayan was bland: unsalted beans thrown on undercooked rice. Aref was no chef.

"*Merci*, Aref Agha," Ayan said, hiding the bottle behind the leg of the plank furthest from the entrance and eating the slop slowly, trying to extend the time in Aref's company.

"Aref Agha, you are a kind man," he said. "Would it be possible for you to bring me a toothbrush and some toothpaste?"

"We don't have any, Ayan Agha—no toothbrush or anything. But don't worry, you can bathe on Friday morning."

"What! Once a week only?"

"It is not good to bathe too often. Bad for your skin and hair."

"I'm sorry, I have to wash myself every day. I will speak to Davood."

"Better not. Perhaps he will say you cannot bathe at all."

Aref looked behind him.

Davood was some distance away, still talking on the telephone.

He came forward and sat beside Ayan on the plank.

"This work is very hard. Everyday, I work! Everyday! But I have four children to support," he whispered. "And six grandchildren."

"How old are they? What are their names?"

Aref extended the fingers of his left hand with his right as he counted his children's names and ages: He had three girls, and one boy—*who must be terribly spoilt*, Ayan thought. He repeated the process with his grandchildren: naming them while pulling on a finger. But his memory failed him after three. He kept working his index finger to remind himself, then gave up with a grin, massaged his forehead, and said, "Agha, they say you are unmarried. Why? It is better to have a family life."

"I am married," Ayan found himself saying. "To a beautiful woman." He liked the words as he spoke them, the future and permanence they implied. "She's German. From Bavaria."

"But the report says that you live in Iran alone."

"She used to be here. Her job took her to Munich. She is a pilot."

"It would have been better if you lived together. If she had been with you, she would have kept you out of this trouble. Wives are wise. But foreign women do what they want. They work, they go when they want, where they please. Now you both must suffer."

"Aref Agha, what they say is not true. I have done nothing wrong. This imprisonment is unjust. It is a mistake."

"Everybody who is brought here says the same thing. You all say you've done nothing, committed no crimes. I have seen the feet, the bodies of prisoners when they deny and protest. Eventually, everyone confesses. As I tell everyone, admit your misdeeds and ask for leniency. Accept your punishment. Why prolong the suffering?"

"Amazing! What kind of place is this?"

"You are in a special house. We only have important prisoners here: only one prisoner, one judge, two guards, and me, who takes care of everybody's needs. You are asked questions. You answer and confess. Agha Salehi decides your fate: who sees another sun, who lives, whose journey ends here. Agha Davood carries out his orders. He also has a very heavy hand. It will take me two months to recover if he decides to beat me, which he surely will, if I stand here talking to you."

Aref picked up the tray even though Ayan was not quite finished. "*Khodahafez. Inshallah*, I will bring you breakfast at 6:00 a.m. tomorrow," he said, locking the cell as he shuffled off.

Ayan heard him offering his salaams to Davood, who grunted in response, apparently still engrossed in his telephone conversation.

Davood escorted Ayan to the toilet and then made another call.

Back in his cell, Ayan listened to Davood's voice, willing him to keep on talking, dreading the silence that would return soon.

Not that he hadn't spent hours by himself before; during summer vacations, waiting for the blistering Delhi afternoons to end and for outdoor play to become possible again, he'd whiled away oceans of time—lying close to the cool air from the fan behind the moist *khus* grass mats, reading and daydreaming, enjoying the smell of wood and freshly tilled earth released from the vetiver roots that had reached deep into the soil.

The memory of that perfume came to him now and mingled with other reminders of India's summer: the fragrance of the jasmine flowers in his mother's hair; the taste of *nimbu paani*, fire-roasted *bhutta* flavored with salt, *masala*, and lime; and his favorite, sliced Alphonso mangoes.

He remembered the games of *pitthu*: the satisfying sound of a tennis ball knocking down the seven stones and the laughter of his brother and sister as they raced to restack them.

Ayan sat up against the wall as images of growing up with his siblings raced through his mind. He hadn't spent much time with Jaya and Shiv these last few years; but despite their separate lives, despite unshared adventures, triumphs and disappointments, he still felt viscerally close to them—needed to hug Jaya now, couldn't bear the thought of not seeing her again, needed Shiv to tell him what to do, how to survive this, because Shiv would surely know . . .

Breakfast was the next time his isolation would end: almost eleven hours to go. He wasn't thinking clearly and knew he had to. He had to be smart and tough. If only he could put on his running shoes, begin jogging, and get into his long-distance rhythm—ideas would percolate, and some clarity of what to do next would emerge. That always happened.

He tried the running in place and push-up combination, but was wiped out too soon and fell back on the plank, alternating between lying on one side, then the other, his feet pulled up against his chest, his eyes closed to block out the suffocating walls, the neon light, and the bars that kept him in this dungeon.

He had to come up with a plan to cope with this situation.

He slowly accepted reality.

Salehi was in control.

He'd derailed their interaction yesterday by refusing to provide the background information he'd asked for. Tomorrow, or whenever he saw him again, he would write down everything: about the South African deal, Nader, Chip, the Ministry of Energy, the Atomic Energy program, Iran Power's expansion, the reason he helped Hamid, Hedayat's aggression and blackmail—he would write it all down on that fucking notepad.

He mapped out what specifically he would disclose and the exact words he would use, pacing up and down the cell as evening probably turned to night and then into morning.

He was still awake when Aref arrived with breakfast.

CHAPTER 27

I t was embarrassing, looking and smelling like a vagrant in front of Salehi.

"Good morning, Ayan Agha. Are we in a better mood today?" Salehi said, offering his hand.

"Good morning, Captain Salehi. Yes. I have decided to do as you say and write down everything, even though it will repeat what you know already know about me."

Salehi beamed and pointed to the desk.

"Very good. Please start. I will be back."

"Yes, I know, in one hour."

Ayan sat down at the desk, scanning the room, enjoying the feeling of space. He stretched his arms and breathed deeply. The warmth in the air worked its way into his bones. He rested his face in his left hand, running his fingers over a stubble that foretold a thick beard, picked up the Bic ballpoint Hosseini had provided, and began to write.

"My name is Ayan Pathak. I arrived in Iran in January 1976 to work as a financial and strategic business consultant with

Hadley Jones, the leading management advisory firm in the world.

My plan was to leave Iran after a six-month assignment. However, the head of Iran Power, Mr. Nader Oveissi, offered me the job of chief financial officer after I was introduced to him by Mr. Firouz Akhbari, deputy director of the Ministry of Energy. Mr. Akhbari, who is closely connected to the Shah, is a friend and business partner of my uncle, Vikram Rai, CEO of Benton Larson, the largest tea company in India.

It seemed like a good opportunity, and Mr. Akhbari and Mr. Oveissi convinced me that it was better to pursue a business career in Iran rather than in the West. The Shah had great plans to develop Iran into a world power and raise the standard of living of its citizens, and Iran Power was to be an important contributor to both. I believed in the Shah's strategy to uplift his people and was impressed by the professionalism of Iran Power, and I accepted the job in March 1976.

In the two and a half years since I took the job, Iran Power has grown its revenues by 75 percent, its earnings by 110 percent. It provides energy to 40 percent of Iranians and facilitates GDP growth by providing low cost and reliable electricity to Iranian companies. It is now viewed as a strategic national business, and it is one of the cornerstones of the Shah's plans to develop the nuclear energy industry.

I have worked hard to help deliver these impressive results that have benefited so many Iranians. I have benefitted, too, and for that, I am grateful. I was given a senior position in this great company and rewarded generously for doing my job well, as can be seen in my performance evaluation and personnel records.

It is inconceivable that I would do anything to harm Iran Power and let down the people who placed their trust in me. It is inconceivable that I would seek to undermine the government that gave me a second home.

2020

That's not who I am. My parents work hard every day to help the poor people of India: one as a doctor in a free hospital, open to all; the other as government officer providing justice and development to remote districts. They taught me through example: work hard, be excellent at whatever you choose to do, and help those in distress. These are ideas I stand for. Not corruption, theft, insurrection, or plotting to overthrow the regime.

I did help my driver Hamid. His family of five live in two rooms. They are desperately poor. I have come to know his family, and they are simple people, warm and generous, who readily share the little they have. Hamid was a simple man who was influenced by the wrong people and got into trouble, lost his job, and was threatened with arrest. He is now dead.

I warned Hamid, who was a very decent and honorable man, several times. I reminded him about the good things the Shah was doing. I failed to convince him. But I had to help his young sons—they had to have food and pay their school fees. That's all I did.

I have made mistakes. I allowed the rogue Hedayat to trap me. He is a friend of Hamid's who pushed him to the extreme and blackmailed me. I also followed some orders in Iran Power that I should have questioned.

These are not crimes that deserve imprisonment in conditions fit only for animals. They are actions of the heart, faults of gullibility and perhaps excessive personal ambition. I stand ready to explain more to secure the freedom that has been unjustly taken from me" . . . etc., etc.

so will you

It was a good document. It was detailed and accurate.

Salehi didn't think so.

He ripped out the sheets from the notepad, crumpled them into a ball, and hurled them to the floor.

"This is a waste of my time. I am not interested in your lies and self-praise," he said.

Ayan sat up in his chair.

"It has the details, the specifics you wanted! They can all be checked. It's the truth, I swear!"

Salehi held up his hand.

"I ask the questions; you answer."

"Sure, Captain Salehi; I will answer any question you want."

"Good. Where is the $5 million?

"Excuse me?"

"Don't play games. Where is the money you stole from the account in Geneva?"

"I didn't steal anything! I had no power to transfer money out of it. Look at the documents and talk to the banker Luc Bossard in Geneva."

Salehi leaned back in his chair, flicked off some fluff from his jacket sleeve, and looked at Ayan with a sardonic smile.

"I have the documents. They say you opened the account. You authorized unlimited transfers out of it by unnamed persons. Nobody else was involved."

"Of course, other people were involved. I was only following direct orders."

He thought of telling Salehi everything. Compromise Nader too. Why should he remain free, living in his luxurious villa, while he was in this dungeon? Nader had forced him to go to Geneva and sign the papers by leaving no doubt that he would fire him if he refused. He should suffer now.

Still, Nader had helped him. He had taken a real risk by warning him. If he'd gone straight to the airport, perhaps he could have got a flight out. The warning was worth something. So was the $120,000 that he had as a result of bonuses Nader had paid to him. It was enough to buy a house in Europe and a car and still leave something to live on while he started over. Not enough to start a money management business, but not nothing either.

I'm going to protect Nader, Ayan decided. *I'll throw that slick banker Bossard to the wolves instead.*

"Mr. Luc Bossard prepared the paperwork. All I did was sign."

"Even if this is true, why did you sign an illegal document?"

"I had authority from the board to open bank accounts."

"Not a numbered account in Geneva with no other signatory but yourself!"

Ayan shifted uneasily. Salehi had started with the area where his actions had placed him on the shakiest ground.

"As I said, Mr. Bossard assured me that this was a common practice. He represents Iran Power in many matters."

"He forced you to do something wrong? How? Did he have a gun? You received a special bonus, didn't you? That's why you did this. And to set up a way to steal millions of dollars of Iran Power and government assets."

"Yes, I did receive a special bonus because I implemented a policy important to the government and my company. I didn't steal anything! If money has gone missing, Luc Bossard is the one who took it."

"You're lying! I know people like you. You're the kind of person who will do anything for money. You're a common thief."

Ayan leapt up.

"I'm not lying! Ask Luc Bossard! He planned everything!"

"Sit down! Don't move from that chair! Mr. Bossard can't say anything because of Swiss banking secrecy rules. We've asked him already. We also spoke to Mr. Nader Oveissi. He says that you were solely responsible for the Geneva account and the movement of assets. And frankly, we believe Mr. Oveissi. Everybody in Iran will accept his word rather

Nader
Oveissi

than yours. He's a leader of the business community. You're a foreigner who's admitted to doing anything for money."

"I've admitted to nothing of the sort! Don't put words in my mouth! The account I set up was used to help the Atomic Energy Agency of Iran purchase uranium, and you know it, since you know everything. As I had no contacts in that organization or any idea of its strategy or operations, I must have been following orders! Why would I dream up something like this? It's absurd!"

"It's not the account that is the main issue, it's the fact that it was set up to allow fraud. You alone did that. To make money. You were not happy with the very generous salary from Iran Power. Mr. Oveissi said that you were always looking for special projects that could earn you bonuses. You have admitted that you are available for hire, like a common prostitute. Now let's get to the main problem. Money has gone missing from the account in Geneva. More has been paid out than the value of what has been received. Five million dollars have disappeared. The auditors have confirmed the discrepancy. Mr. Oveissi, Mr. Bossard, and we believe that it was you who stole it."

No wonder Nader made the phone call to him, to get him to run and not get caught or be questioned like this. Nader had pocketed millions with Luc's help, probably using the provision that allowed Luc discretion to transfer up to $10 million.

"I warned against allowing Luc Bossard to move money at his discretion. It is in my due diligence files. I can prove it."

"Anybody can write anything in a file. And still the question remains: Why did you open the account that allows such things? Everybody was depending on your expertise."

"Luc Bossard is a corrupt man. Ask him where the $5 million is. He is the thief," Ayan said, shoulders slumping, knowing that he would never be able to prove this, that not one of these bastards would believe him.

"Making slanderous statements against a good man is not going to help you. Giving the money back will." Salehi banged the table hard for emphasis.

"I did not take any money! How many times do I have to repeat myself? I have no idea what you're talking about!"

"Let's not waste time. Just give the money back, and I will help you. So will Colonel Hosseini."

"I don't have it. I never touched one cent from that account."

"Very well. I am recording that you have refused to return the money you stole."

"You can record whatever you like; I never stole it. Arrest Nader Oveissi and Luc Bossard. Ask them for the money. They have it."

"Let's move on. Tell me about your friendship with Hedayat."

"Friend? Did you say friend! He's my enemy!"

"Then why did you give him secret Iran Power papers that allowed him to ask for blackmail through his nephew— papers that detail private company information and identify confidential national plans for nuclear energy?"

"I didn't! He stole my briefcase!"

Ayan felt like a child denying bad behavior to an authority who had already condemned him.

"Agha Ayan, you give sensitive, valuable information and large sums of money to a member of the *Tudeh* party, a religious fanatic, a terrorist who has killed three of my colleagues, and you expect mercy from me?"

"Captain, I doubt that Hedayat is both a member of the *Tudeh* party and a religious fanatic. But no matter, I hate Hedayat more than you do. I would love to see you put a bullet through his heart."

"We have already. His nephew has also departed this world. Now back to you. Money is a powerful drug. It has made many men, wiser than both of us, do immoral, stupid things. In your case, it made you turn against the people who welcomed you into their country, made you conspire to overthrow the government by giving money to insurgents— and also secret, valuable information that was entrusted to your care. This information is now available for anybody to buy on the street: traitors, anti-Shah anarchists, foreigners. All because you are a whore!"

"Oh, fuck off!" Ayan said, unable to control himself.

"No! You fuck off! You fuck fuck!" Salehi said.

"I am trying my best to answer your questions. Why are you insulting me? How does that help you?"

"I don't need your help. I have shown that you are guilty of the most treasonous, seditious charges. Now tell me why you raped Fariba Khanom? You have a girlfriend; there are so many foreign girls in Tehran; why victimize an innocent Persian girl from a nice family?"

"I'm not commenting on another false accusation."

Even after their painful breakup, Fariba would never sign any damn paper accusing him of raping her. She would never do that. She never lied. She had been the initiator the first time they made love and many times after that.

"Answer my question!"

"Why? You obviously only believe the sound of your own voice."

"Answer!"

"We were both lonely. We became close friends. It was mutual."

"Hassan Agha, her brother, says that you seduced her with a promise of marriage."

Ayan stopped the words, "I didn't." He felt tired. This was hopeless. He threw up his hands.

"Captain Salehi, why are we talking? Just make up anything about me, like those other charges, like this fictitious assault, and put it in your file. You are not interested in anything I have to say."

Salehi's features softened. "Ayan Agha, come with me. I want to show you something."

He followed Salehi to the door on the far side of the room. They entered a sparsely furnished bedroom suite with an attached bathroom. It was heated and looked clean. The bed had a mattress, sheets, blankets, and pillows. There was nightstand with some books and magazines and a desk with a chair. A small black and white Sony TV sat on a table facing a sofa.

"Ayan Agha, I use this room during the day sometimes, but vacate it for prisoners who cooperate with us. The choice is yours."

"Captain Salehi, I'm cooperating. I'm telling the truth. There is nothing more I can do."

"Yes, there is. Wait here."

Salehi crossed back into the interrogation room and returned with the notepad and ballpoint pen. He pointed an index finger and said, "Stop the lies. Write down how you plotted with Hamid, Hedayat, and the others to carry out the orders of the imam of the Tehran mosque to overthrow His Imperial Majesty."

The index finger tapped on the notepad a few more times.

"Write down exactly how you stole $5 million from Iran Power via the account in Geneva that you opened. Tell me where the money is."

Ayan opened his mouth to protest, but the captain held up his hand sternly. His stony expression said, "Don't even think about saying anything."

"Also write down how many times you raped the most virtuous daughter of one of our most respected industrialists.

Confess that you are a man of greed and vice, and you will stop at nothing to get your way. Write all that down, and I may show you some mercy."

"Certainly not!" Ayan said. "I'm not going to write any of that down because they are shameless lies that all of you are spinning for god-knows-what purpose! And there is no rape charge. Show me where it is!"

"Very well, then we are finished here."

Salehi walked Ayan out of the cozy room and said, "Davood! Take this gentleman back to his cell."

Davood sauntered in with his AK-47 slung across his chest and began to untie the blindfold from his wrist.

"Wait! I don't want to go back there!" Ayan said.

He wanted desperately to stay here in this warm, clean room. He had to find a way to stay out of that pit below!

"Captain Salehi, Agha, please, the crimes all carry the death penalty. Who in their right mind would ever sign their own death warrant—even if guilty, which I most certainly am not!"

Salehi came up to Ayan and put a hand on his shoulder.

"We have discretion. Confess and I will move you up into this room. We can talk about how you can help us to recover the money; perhaps we will need you to bait some insurgents. There are many ways to improve your file."

"Sorry, Captain. I know that if I confess to these lies, I am done for."

"As I said, Ayan Agha, I have discretion. We have time but not unlimited time. I have restrained Davood. Perhaps I have been too soft."

Salehi started walking back towards the paradise on the other side of the door.

The brutish Davood immediately handcuffed and blindfolded Ayan.

"Come on, Captain, don't send me down to that sewer," Ayan said. "If you are more reasonable, guide me a little. I would like to cooperate with you."

"Let me guide you. Confess in writing to every one of the crimes I mentioned. Exactly like I said. Nothing progresses before that."

Salehi had eliminated all shades of grey, all possible compromise. It was all or nothing: your head on a plate or rot away—if Davood doesn't finish you off first.

Well, he was not going to commit suicide by admitting to such serious offences, to doing things he hadn't done, to capital crimes.

Ayan walked back to his cell and lay down on the plank.

He gave in, gave up; there was no way forward.

CHAPTER 28

He knew it was Friday because he was allowed to bathe.

The water was shockingly cold, but he stayed in the shower until the allotted sliver of soap was gone.

Back in his cell, feeling clean in a change of clothes and swallowing to dilute the taste of soap in his mouth, Ayan sat dreaming of toothpaste and the jets of hot water in his Shemiran apartment.

Salehi had not called for him in a couple of days.

There was nothing to do but wait for his next move.

And wait.

Ayan's sense of self leeched out with the hours as Friday dragged into Saturday, and then Sunday and Monday. Sometimes, he felt that he might die from lying inside the locked box, just stop breathing and expire, or give into lurking madness.

He began to doubt that he existed.

Day and night were the same in the merciless fluorescent light.

He continued to exercise— countless pushups and
sit-ups, jogging in place, and yoga stretches. Then he was
tired and had to be still, and after he recovered, it became
unbearable again.

Exercise was an erratic refuge. So was sleep.

He was forced to find other ways to escape from his
surroundings. He had become better at concentrating on
deepening and slowing his breathing. That helped.

So did methodically recalling memories. He pushed
himself to see color and detail in his recollections, the faces
of people, their expressions and words, the conditions of the
light and weather at the time, the sounds and smells, his
emotions. . . and he tried to organize them chronologically,
going back to the earliest and eliminating the negatives, so
he'd be left with only the happy ones.

But sometimes, the images would blur, and dates would
elude him, and he would wonder if everything in his head
was just a half-remembered dream.

He found himself speaking to Gaby; he had so much to
tell her. It helped to hear his own voice and know he still lived.

He told her about birthdays, family holidays, about
recovering from early failure in school, failing at cricket,
then finding tennis; about close friendships, a few betrayals,
and intense relationships that had faded as locations changed
and time marched on, and why did it have to be that way?
He spoke of gestures that showed—more than any words—
what he meant to his parents, and how he'd been a taker of
their love and sacrifice and was going to find a way to atone
for his selfishness . . .

He would vary the topics he brought up with Gaby,
depending on his mood.

During the day, after breakfast, he talked about encounters that raised him above mediocrity. He told her more

about his passions and his career. At night, after his evening meal, he discussed the books that gave him a sense of a wider world and acceptance of imperfect souls, made him feel he, too, was made for adventure and travel to distant lands—where he would test himself, meet the brilliant and the accomplished, explore different cultures and ideas, and, of course, fall madly, recklessly in love.

He tried to recreate for Gaby how he'd felt reading about Sara Miles and Henry, Julian Sorel and Mme de Renal, Harry Street and Helen, about Settembrini and Naphtha, and felt he was surely losing his mind because he was empty in minutes, and nothing was in colors, and everything had faded . . .

Before he slept, he recounted tales about summer holidays. *They were the best part of the year*, Ayan told Gaby, describing the family trip to Kashmir: the riverside stops to cool the engine of the car and give their Alsatian Caesar a break; the visits to distant relatives along the way; the séance that one of them—aunt Sharda or perhaps Sarla—had held when, despite his skepticism, the hair on the back of his neck had risen as the coin on the board started moving, independently, it seemed, revealing all kinds of family secrets. The winters on the farm in Hansi, where he discovered Elvis and became a lifelong fan, because his cousins from Calcutta had somehow managed to get hold of RCA records. They rode tractors though the fields, chewing on sugar cane, hurled themselves down huge bales of cotton, played cricket and croquet and *pitthu*, and, in the evenings, chatted with local farmers who stopped by to smoke the hookah on the large *gaddhi* laid out in the large reception room—their distinctive smell of sweat, and tobacco filling the air, and their ribald jokes skewering the victim du jour, usually Shashi, a friend from Delhi who authoritatively aired his inexpert views. Then there were the summers in the mountains: How he had looked forward to the arrival of the tiffin man every morning with his éclairs and cream cakes! He told Gaby about boisterous card games, the Spaghetti Westerns at the Picture Palace in Mussoorie—his favorite then and now was *The Good, the Bad and the Ugly*—rowing across the lake in Nainital, and riding horses up the hill to their hotel. He fell off once, he said, when his horse took off in an unexpected gallop, and the broken ankle that resulted had forced him to learn bridge and billiards; he'd become a favorite victim of the drunks who never left the Boathouse Club and looked forward to his arrival—his pocket money and inevitable defeat subsidized quite a few bar bills.

Or he would talk about sports—about his father's perseverance to convince him to take up tennis, the family game, and how his Wimbledon and Davis Cup-playing uncle and cousin inspired him; he talked about running, how it lifted his spirits, starting with those early morning jogs to Teen Murti accompanied by his neighbor Joseph that got him hooked; then running at night in Regents Park and hearing the big cats in the London zoo, running in the Alborz mountains with the Hash House Harriers, *running along Lake Starnberg with you and Mathias . . . Gaby . . . baby, I don't know if I can hold on much longer. I feel myself slipping away . . .*

CHAPTER 29

Breakfast didn't arrive on Tuesday morning.

Ayan called out for Aref Agha. His hunger and thirst would soon bring on a migraine that would make everything infinitely worse.

Eventually, Davood unlocked the cell door and ordered him to get up.

"What's this, where are you taking me?" Ayan said, disoriented by the change in the morning routine.

No answer, just a grunt and a shove out of the cell. The blindfold and handcuffs were put on.

Davood grabbed his elbow and pushed him to the left, as usual. The direction they were heading meant that he was going to see Salehi. He didn't feel ready for the encounter.

Davood stopped after a few paces. He pushed Ayan into a cell that smelled worse than his own.

"What are you doing?" Ayan yelled as Davood threw him down onto a bed with a metal frame and iron springs.

Davood's fist slammed into Ayan's jaw, knocking him out.

He awoke to find himself naked, his arms extended above his head and his legs spread wide, his limbs secured tightly to the bed frame. The only thing he could move was his head.

Aref was standing in the corner, avoiding his eyes.

Davood held a thick electric cable in his hands.

As soon as he saw Ayan was awake, Davood drew his arm back and brought the knotted cable down on his feet.

Ayan felt his arches burn as the immense hurt from the blow rocked through him and exploded in his head.

The cable whipped down on his right arch, then his left.

Ayan shook his head from side to side and screamed, the pain escalating with each hit.

The lashing stopped. Ayan lifted his head to look at the damage and turned away from the swollen mess.

But Davood was just catching his breath. He started the whipping again, and again, and nothing in Ayan's life had hurt as much.

That was before Davood grabbed his left hand, took out a pocketknife, and dug it under the nail of his small finger.

"Stop! Please stop!" Ayan mouthed, his voice rising to a shriek. He tried to pull his hand away, praying, hoping that he would faint.

There's no way he could survive another stab.

But Davood was relentless, lifting each finger, drawing blood under each nail, separating the nails from his nail bed, a look of concentration on his face.

Then Davood punched him full on in the testicles. Ayan's body jerked forward, convulsing with dry heaves, nothing left in his stomach but bile.

"Clean him up," Davood ordered Aref, then left the cell.

"Ayan Agha, I told you to confess, see what he has done to you," Aref said.

Ayan, barely conscious, was dimly aware that Aref had covered him with a washcloth, unshackled him, and rinsed his hands and feet with water.

Aref went out and returned with a tray of ice, compressing his feet and then each nail till the blood coagulated. He took out a tube and squeezed some ointment on his cuts and under his nails. "Thank god he left the nails on your fingers! They will heal, so will your feet. The soles don't bleed with this, but there will be a lot of swelling. I will bring some ice for them and put some more ointment on your fingers this afternoon at 5:00 p.m. Normally, he stops with the feet the first time. They are in a hurry with you. Be thankful he didn't shock you. This bed is connected to an electric current. I have seen what they do to men, Agha Ayan, and even to a few women. They shock their genitals and stick electric prods inserted inside them. Then they get cooked to death, very slowly, on this very bed. Be thankful and cooperate!"

Aref brought in a pair of rubber slippers that were many times too large for Ayan. His swollen feet barely fit into them.

Ayan shuffled into Salehi's office the next morning. He kept his head down. He did not want Salehi to see the defeat in his eyes.

"Davood tells me that you are ready to sign; is that true? I hope that I'm not wasting my time again," Salehi said.

Ayan stayed silent. He knew that he could not go through another session with Davood.

"Here are four pages, one for each crime. Initial each line and sign at the bottom."

Ayan glanced at the papers. The first three pages listed the charges: seditious conspiracy, financing revolutionaries, theft of corporate assets; the fourth page brought up the rape. Each page had two paragraphs—the charge, his name, and then a statement: I hereby admit, freely and readily, to being guilty of this crime in its entirety.

There were lines for his signature, the date, and the signature of the witnessing official.

Ayan picked up the ballpoint pen in the gap between his right thumb and index finger, protecting his blackened fingertips.

What did it matter if he signed these documents? He was never going to leave this place.

He slowly initialed and signed the charges.

Salehi checked each sheet before opening one of the desk drawers and taking out a seal that he stamped on the witness line.

He put the documents into a manila file.

"Good!" he said, smiling. "All that's left is recovering the $5 million you stole. Write down where it is."

Salehi leaned in and moved the notepad towards Ayan.

"I don't know. I told you that I never touched the account. Perhaps Nader will know. Luc Bossard will, for sure. Ask them."

Salehi walked around to Ayan's side of the table and squeezed his shoulder. He smiled. "Return the money and things will go well for you. I told you that if you signed, I would move you up here, to the nice room. I will. But first, I need that money."

"I would give it to you if I knew anything about it."

"Liar!" Salehi shouted, moving back across from Ayan. "Liar! Mr. Oveissi, Luc Bossard—they all say that you have it. I believe them, not you, a confessed criminal."

"I swear! I am telling the truth. I don't have it."

"Last chance."

"I don't know, I don't know, I don't have it, I never had it . . ." Ayan said, looking up at Salehi, choking back his desperation, trying to stay composed.

Salehi walked to the door.

"Finish him," he said to Davood.

"I'm not going anywhere," Ayan said, feeling immensely tired as Davood put on the cuffs and blindfold and tried to shove him out of the room.

He threw himself onto the floor.

The carpet was soft and warm.

Davood kicked him.

"Get up! Get up now!"

"I'm not going anywhere. I don't care what you do."

Davood kicked him again and yelled for Aref.

He arrived with Davood No. 2.

Shortly after, Ayan smelled fresh air for the first time in days and felt the sun on his skin. But the freezing air made light of his vest and pajamas, and his body began to shake and cramp.

Aref and the two Davoods dragged his dead weight along. His oversized slippers and swollen feet caught on some bricks and came off.

He was pushed up against a wall. His legs gave way and he fell forward, passing out as his head hit stone.

Then he was awake, soaked with cold water, hanging by outstretched arms, his feet grazing the ground but unable to support him.

"Is the coward tied up properly?" Davood asked.

Aref and the other Davood grunted in the affirmative.

He heard two men walk away and the one-two crack of an AK-47 being cocked.

Ayan turned his head away.

He thought of the Ganges, running cold and fast—of the time he'd had lowered himself into the waters, helping his father empty the urn carrying his grandfather's ashes, the urn his father had kept in his lap, arms around it, throughout the long, hot, and dusty journey to Haridwar, a reconciliation after death that hadn't been possible in life because a proud son had defied a proud father and married for love.

He saw Gaby's image rise from the eternal river, saw her in that Isfahan *Maidan*, breathing deeply, making him nervous as she considered the ring he'd placed on her hand. He saw her smiling and whispering "yes." He heard the burst of gunfire, and a dark sadness overwhelmed him.

CHAPTER 30

"Leave him hanging there, trembling like a beaten dog," Davood said. "The cold will kill him by the morning. My bullets are too good for him."

He came up to Ayan and kicked him in the groin.

"Remember where the stolen money is. It won't save your useless life, but I might shoot you and end this quickly."

Three sets of footsteps receded. A door opened and shut.

Humiliated and ashamed by the fear and desperation he'd shown, Ayan felt his arms would be wrenched out of their sockets any minute. How much longer could he stand this? He wanted nothing more than to be back in his cell, on his plank, under his filthy rug.

It was dark when Aref cut him free.

"Brother, I told you to cooperate so many times, many, many times," he said, covering Ayan with a blanket and reviving him with tea and bread. "Now very bad. Davood Agha has left, and a car has come for you."

"A car?" Ayan said, shrinking back as Aref helped him to his feet and guided him somewhere. "Why?"

"More questioning somewhere. Very bad. You must get dressed now. Put on these clothes." Aref held up the shirt, blazer, and jeans Ayan had been wearing when he was arrested. "Here are your shoes, but I think they will not fit."

Ayan reflexively followed Aref's instructions.

His clothes were very loose, his shoes too small for his battered and swollen feet.

Aref helped him into the giant rubber slippers again, put on the handcuffs and blindfolds, and led him up the stairs and back into the cold air.

"Sit with him in the back. I'll drive," Ayan heard a voice tell Aref.

He was ushered into a car. They got onto a highway and drove for half an hour or so before making an exit onto a quiet street. The car pulled over.

"Agha Ayan, I say goodbye to you," Aref said, helping Ayan out of the car. He took off Ayan's blindfold.

Hosseini stood in front of him.

The Colonel nodded at Ayan and held out his hand towards Aref.

Aref passed him the keys to Ayan's handcuffs.

"Thank you, Aref Agha," Hosseini said, taking Ayan by the arm. "Tell Davood Agha I will have him back by 5:00 a.m."

A figure emerged from the darkness as Aref and the other guard drove off.

"Gaby!" Ayan yelled, sensing her presence before he saw her. He ran forward, tripping on the large slippers and falling to the ground.

"Wait a little, my love," he heard Hosseini say. "I can't bear for this to end. I wish I could have you for myself just a little longer."

Ayan pushed himself up to see Hosseini restraining Gaby.

"Leave her alone!" he yelled.

Hosseini waved him off with a sneer.

"Gaby *joon*—hear the words of Hafez, for he speaks of love much better than I: 'Lest my long service the beloved remember not: O morning breeze, remind my lover of our old pledges. In a hundred years, if you happen upon my dust my decayed bones will rise, dancing from the clay . . .'"

Hosseini pulled Gaby towards him and tried to kiss her.

Gaby looked at Ayan with concern.

Seeing Gaby with Hosseini, in his arms, shredded whatever was left in Ayan. He closed his eyes.

He didn't see Gaby resist, push the Colonel away, and run towards him.

Gaby fell on Ayan, embracing him.

"Ayan! Baby! Oh my god!"

She glared at Hosseini.

"What have you done to him!" she yelled. "Liar! You said he was OK!"

"Be calm, Gaby *joon*," Hosseini said.

"He's been burned, he's bleeding everywhere!"

Hosseini's face hardened. "Be happy this confessed criminal is alive! It is only because of me, because I am bewitched and unable to resist you, Gaby *joon*." He looked at his watch. "Now I advise you not to waste time. It is already 9:00 p.m., and the curfew starts soon. You have till 5:00 a.m to do what you want—again, because of me. Every policeman in Iran will be looking for him in the morning. I will not be able to save him again. So I suggest we complete our business."

Hosseini lifted a hardtop Samsonite briefcase and took out Ayan's passport and checkbook.

He tossed the passport to Gaby and waved the check-book at Ayan.

"I have reached an understanding with Agha Oveissi," Hosseini said. "He has been very generous. Now it is your turn to take care of Agha Salehi. He will be unhappy. This will help to soothe his anger."

Hosseini tore out some checks, tucked the checkbook into an inside coat pocket, and walked over with his Glock drawn.

"Free him," he said to Gaby, handing her the handcuff keys. "Make him sign these checks. Here is a pen. Use the briefcase as support."

Hosseini stepped back, keeping his gun trained on Ayan.

One check was made out to Salehi, the others to cash. They added up to 142,900 tomans—$20,000. All the cash Ayan had left in his Bank Melli account.

At least he still had the traveller's checks. Gaby could retrieve them with her key.

Ayan signed the check reluctantly and slowly, his fingers barely able to grip the pen.

"Now one of you open the briefcase," Hosseini said.

Ayan tried, but his swollen fingers were too inept.

"You do it," Hosseini said to Gaby. "Quickly. Time's passing, and I may change my mind about all this."

Gaby hurriedly complied.

The Samsonite snapped open.

It was packed with American Express traveller's checks.

"Sign every one," Hosseini said. "Payable to cash." He walked closer to Ayan. "Show me your signature each time. If it doesn't match the one on the check, I will do what Agha Davood is waiting to do."

Ayan looked at Gaby.

"Ayan, he knew, he insisted . . ." she said, shrugging, her face unhappy.

"Come on! Come on!" Hosseini said, seeing Ayan hesitate. His gun arm moved up a couple of notches.

"Sign them! Sign the damn checks! It's only fucking money! Let's go!" Gaby yelled at Ayan.

"Don't look at me like that! I swear, if anything other than 'thank you' comes out of your mouth, I will slam this car into a wall," Gaby said as she accelerated a grey Paykan, straining it to capacity.

"Thank you," Ayan managed to get out, without words of his own, in complete shock.

He turned his eyes away from her to his hands, nursing his fingertips.

Gaby broke the silence.

"You heard Hosseini. We have to move quickly. Here's the plan: we—the two of us plus your parents, they're here too—are on an Air India flight at 1:00 a.m. It goes to Bombay, not Delhi, but we all have seats out of Iran, which is impossible these days. I've got our tickets and enough cash. Bahman is waiting for us at the Air India counter. He's going to walk us through immigration. Your exit visa is valid; we're going to be fine; but Bahman's there, just in case; he knows everybody; this is his car, by the way."

"I don't have anything on me," Ayan said. "Not even a pair of shoes."

In the rush to escape Hosseini, he'd left his rubber slippers by the roadside.

"My god!" Gaby said. "Look at your feet! How can you even walk! Fucking, fucking bastards! We have to get you some shoes, stop this bleeding; you can't go to the airport looking like that."

"The only place that's open is the tennis club," Ayan said. "Somebody's usually there till 10:00 p.m. They stock extra-large tennis keds and have a first aid kit, but it means going backwards."

"*Scheisse!*" Gaby exclaimed. "OK. No choice! Give me directions."

"Your parents have been camping out in the Indian Embassy, pushing as much as they can," Gaby said as they drove to Club Veyssi. "But nothing was happening. Hosseini's the only one who returned my phone calls. Who is Jackie Ashton Smith by the way?"

"A friend, a reporter; why?"

"She's been writing about you. Her articles about your arrest by SAVAK put Hosseini under a lot of pressure—helped me convince him to release you. That and the traveller's checks. I'm sorry, Ayan, I felt terrible, knew how much your savings meant to you, but he had your records, found out you'd withdrawn a lot of money from your bank. He said it was cash stolen from Iran Power, and he had to recover it."

"He's a fucking liar! I never stole anything!" Ayan said.

"I know, I know, but I had to do something! I was so worried about you! And it worked, didn't it? I was right, wasn't I?"

"Yes, Gaby . . . thank you, I wasn't going to last much longer . . ."

"You should thank Jackie too. How did she find out about your situation?"

"Same way you did, probably. Nick. I left a few numbers with him. I told you Nick was my friend."

"I almost put the phone down when that American called."

"Glad you didn't."

"He said that you were in serious trouble, that I had to move fast if I wanted to see you again. All the details he had, his urgency, made me believe him. That's what made me get on the plane last Wednesday."

A rush of gratitude overwhelmed Ayan. He swallowed to compose himself but couldn't.

Nick had delivered when he didn't have to, and so had Jackie. And how was it possible he was with Gaby again!

"Ayan, baby, it's OK, you're OK now," Gaby said, pulling over and embracing him. "Where can I kiss you? Where? You're broken everywhere . . ."

They raced to the airport after a brief pause at Club Veyssi, driving past his villa in Shemiran.

Had he really lived there for two years? It seemed far removed, a fading unreal dream.

He was leaving Tehran with no money and no possessions, just the clothes he had on and these size-thirteen tennis shoes he would never use once the swelling subsided, if it ever subsided.

They passed Bohemia on Pahlavi, shuttered, his hairdresser Zora long gone home. He would have liked to say goodbye to her, he thought irrationally.

Then they were downtown and minutes from Nick's place.

Brother, we'll meet again someday, he thought. *I won't doubt your friendship ever again.*

The Paykan turned towards Mehrabad Airport. The Bazaar was not far away. He must keep getting money to Hamid's wife. There had to be a way. He would find it.

CHAPTER 31

Gaby parked Bahman's Paykan in the Iran Air employee lot, minutes from the departure terminal.

The airport was packed with locals and foreigners trying to leave Tehran, but it was not hard to locate the Air India counter. Dozens of Indians were congregating around Area 3, refusing to queue, as usual.

"There's Bahman," Gaby said, waving towards the uniformed Iran Air captain, who was talking to an Air India staffer standing at a counter that was not in service.

"You can check in here," Bahman said, kissing Gaby and smiling at Ayan in greeting, sounding cheerful even as his worried eyes told a different story.

"You are looking very weak," he said to Ayan. "I'm going to get you out of here. Get you back home to India where your parents can care for you. I have already escorted them past immigration. They are waiting for you."

"Give me your passports," Bahman said after they had been checked in. "Follow me. I'll speak. Don't say anything unless I ask you."

Bahman surveyed the lines.

"This way," he said. "I know this official."

Gaby and Ayan fell in behind Bahman as he went through an elaborate *taarof* with the stocky, mustachioed immigration man.

Bahman pointed to Gaby and Ayan as he handed over their passports.

Ayan heard Bahman promoting Gaby to captain in Lufthansa and introducing Ayan as an old friend and financial director of a big company.

The official checked Gaby's passport, stamped it in few seconds, and handed it back to Bahman. He paused to dab his brow and mouth with a small towel on his desk and turned towards Ayan.

Ayan put his hands in his pockets as the man looked at him, then his photograph, then back at him.

"Iran Power? Very good company, very important."

He smiled approvingly at Ayan and then at Bahman. Looking at some list, his expression changed to confusion. He dabbed his face again and said, "This exit visa has been cancelled, but your passport shows that it is OK." He looked at Bahman and said, "Wait here, I will check in the office."

Ayan felt his pulse quicken.

Gaby clamped her hand on his forearm.

Bahman leaned towards the immigration officer.

"Ehmad Agha," he said, "our flight is leaving soon; the exit visa in the passport is fine, no? Just stamp it, and we will be on our way."

"I'm sorry, Bahman Agha, it's forbidden to override the list without the supervisor's signature. I'll be right back. Don't worry, the flight doesn't board for another hour."

He dropped from his chair and walked towards a cabin about fifty yards away, taking his towel with him.

"What do we do?" Gaby asked Bahman.

"I don't know. We have to wait now."

"We can't just wait," Ayan said. "Hosseini has played us; we're sitting ducks with all the police in this place."

"He's right," said Gaby. "Damn it!"

"Give it a few minutes," Bahman said. "It might just be a mistake."

"OK. Five minutes," Gaby said.

Bahman said, "And after that? What are we going to do?"

Ayan said, "We have to get out of here, get to somewhere safe, think about what's next later."

Bahman tapped his fingers on Ehmad's desk. The five minutes passed. "I'm going to see what's happening," Bahman said.

He returned with Ehmad shortly afterwards.

"I'm sorry, Agha Ayan," Ehmad said. "This matter can only be resolved in the immigration office. Your exit visa was actually cancelled just today, and your name is on the no-fly list. No problem, somebody from Iran Power can get this resolved in no time. *Khodahafez.*"

Ehmad handed Ayan's passport back to Bahman, climbed back on his chair and beckoned the next passenger in line.

"I have an idea," Bahman said as they walked back into the lobby. "Why don't you go to Bandar Abbas, my hometown? It's on the Gulf—my brother can get you on a boat to Khasab in Oman. It is very near."

"How will we get through immigration in Bandar Abbas?" Ayan said.

"My brother will help you. There are fishing and trading boats that go back and forth between Bandar Abbas and Khasab, no customs, no immigration. Bander Abbas is about fourteen hours away, maybe less if you drive fast. Take my car. You have some money? Here, I have some cash, take it."

Bahman emptied his wallet into Gaby's hands.

"Bahman, I have money," Gaby said. "This is too much, you've given me too much!"

"Take it, Gaby *joon*. You have a long journey ahead. I'm going to call my brother now and ask him to inquire about boats to Khasab. He will find you one by the time you arrive tomorrow."

"It's 11:30 p.m., the curfew starts in thirty minutes," Ayan said. "And somebody should probably tell my parents what's going on."

"Hate to add to the complications, but Hosseini has seen us in your car. He probably has the license number," Gaby said. "And my suitcase has been checked in."

"Let me see, let me see," Bahman said snapping his fingers. "OK, wait here, I will ask my friend Golshan—she's working tonight. Gaby, you remember her? She's been with Iran Air forever. Take her car; I'll drop her home. My brother will get Golshan's car back to Tehran from Bandar Abbas soon enough. Don't worry about your suitcase, Gaby, I'll pick it up from Air India and send it to you wherever you are; Ayan, I will tell your parents that you've taken a different flight and will join them in India in a day or two. What else? What else! The curfew! Damn! OK—check into Hotel Faraz—it's ten minutes away. Sorry, it's pretty bad, but nobody will look for you there. Get on the road at five in the morning, after the curfew lifts. You'll be in Bandar Abbas by the evening. Hosseini won't be looking for a beaten-up car like Golshan's."

"Love you, you're a great friend," Gaby said, kissing Bahman on both cheeks, then one more time before she got into the driver's seat in Golshan's white Chevy Iran.

Ayan held out his hand. Bahman pulled him into an embrace.

"I'll never forget this," Ayan said.

"It's nothing—for Gaby, I'll do anything."

Bahman slammed his hand on the top of the car. "Now go! See you somewhere, wherever, soon!"

Ayan lingered in the small, but to him, beyond luxurious, shower of the Hotel Faraz—both hands wrapped in a shower cap to protect his wounds—and brushed his teeth for the first time in over a week.

He got into bed.

Gaby was curled up near the edge.

"Come in," Ayan said. "You're going to fall off."

She stayed where she was.

He reached over to touch her shoulder.

"No!" she said sharply, moving even further away.

"I'll sleep on the ground. I don't want you to be uncomfortable," Ayan said, throwing a pillow to the floor and lying down on carpet over parquet. He was used to lying on wood. This was a big improvement from last night.

"Do what you want. Now please! We have to drive for hours tomorrow. Let's get some sleep!"

Ayan stayed awake, startled by Gaby's hostility.

"It's that bastard, isn't it?" he said.

She didn't reply.

"I'm sorry, but I can't get that image out of my mind, Gaby—of Hosseini touching you."

"Stop it, Ayan!"

"What did he do to you?"

A pillow hit him, then her shoes, her jewelry, her watch.

Gaby sat on the side of her bed, her arm raised, a glass of water ready to be hurled at him.

"I don't care what state you're in, I'll fucking kill you if you don't stop right now!" she said.

"Gaby, please . . . I was just concerned . . . that's the kind of man he is . . ."

"Just leave me the hell alone!"

They left the hotel at 5:00 a.m., filled the tank, and drove south. The window Hosseini had given them to escape had closed, and the hunt for them was probably on.

Gaby was at the wheel, driving fast, but not too fast. With the make-up she'd borrowed from Golshan and the hijab another friend of Bahman had organized, she would pass for an Iranian.

People were already reporting to work through the factory gates when they passed the Iran Power complex. They flew through the yellow-brown terrain, bypassing the holy city of Qom, thoughts focused on the run ahead.

At 7:15 a.m., they were in Kashan, the town of carpets and silks. The ruins and remnants of caravanserai on the Silk Road flew by on the way to Isfahan, which they reached at 9:30 a.m.

Ayan threw himself into the business of navigating. His body hurt from the recent abuse; what was worse was thinking about Gaby and that son of a bitch Hosseini.

Gaby was exhausted, but there was no way he could drive with his hands in the state they were.

Route 71 stretched out for miles straight ahead of them. Sand dunes and shrub extended to the horizon on both sides of the road. They were alone except for the occasional truck or car.

Ayan rolled down the window. It was hot but dry, and the sun felt good on his face after freezing Tehran.

They reached the heart of the desert by 3:00 p.m., nearing Yazd, when Gaby, who had been very quiet, suddenly said, "I'm going to pull over. We need to talk."

"OK . . ." Ayan said.

She guided the Chevy to the shoulder and switched off the ignition.

Her expression was not promising.

"I've told you everything about my life in Germany," Gaby said.

"Yes."

"Now you better tell me everything. What happened? Why the hell did they do this to you?"

Ayan put his head back on the seat.

"It's a long story, and you won't like it—but know that I did everything so I could be near you, never stole anything, didn't hurt anybody . . ."

He told her about Odysseus. Forced the words out. What did it matter now?

She shook her head often as his tale unfolded, Ayan noticed uneasily.

"So I'm with a fucking nuclear arms dealer," Gaby said when he'd finished.

"No! Well, not exactly," Ayan said hesitatingly. "More like you are with Baader-Meinhof, on the periphery . . ."

Gaby turned to him.

"You know damn well that's different!" she said. "I don't do it for money!" Ayan, I've spent the last week—endless days with Hosseini—listening to the horrible things he said about you, working him to release you, putting up with his disgusting advances, promising to go with him, all the time wondering where you were, what was happening to you, if I would ever see you again. And right now, I'm wondering if it has all been worthwhile."

"Odysseus was the only option I had," Ayan said. "Gaby, you have to believe that."

"Don't pretend it was for me! I've been begging you to leave and come live in Germany! Why the hell didn't you? You know I don't give a damn about your money, status— any of that bullshit!"

"Gaby . . . I didn't want to be a burden, wanted to . . ."

"You were greedy and wanted more and more . . ."

"No! Just enough to be independent . . . be free, live life the way I want, the way I imagined . . ."

"So you admit that your Odysseus was all about yourself— the way you wanted to live—and nothing to do with me!"

I've admitted to being guilty of so many crimes, Ayan thought wearily, *signed my own death warrant—I'll admit to anything you want me to.*

"You are a greedy, selfish man."

"I've made mistakes, Gaby. But you're wrong! Odysseus was about you. Everything is about you."

"More talk I don't believe!"

She got out of the car, slammed the door, and strode into the desert.

Ayan tried to catch her, but his swollen feet made him fall far behind.

They were some distance from the car by the time she stopped and sat down on a dune.

He came up and threw himself beside her.

He looked up at the clear blue sky. Hawks circled above, banking and swooping on thermals.

The wind was the only sound in the desolation.

He turned towards Gaby.

She was draining sand through her fingers and watching it fly away. Her face was drawn, and she had purple shadows under her eyes.

He hated himself for what he'd put her through, for exposing her to Hosseini's brutishness.

"Gaby," he said, touching her arm, not knowing how to make amends.

"What?" she said sharply.

"A few hours ago, I was against a wall, sure they were going to execute me. I thought about my life and what it was all about, and I saw only you." He paused to compose himself. "I saw only your face, Gaby, and reached out for a hand to hold. Yours. No matter what's happened, what you think of me— and I have made terrible decisions—no matter how all this works out and how many years go by, I know that you will still be the one I'll be thinking of when my time is up. Nothing matters more than you."

Gaby looked at him for a long while. She ran her fingers over the bruises on his forehead and around his eyes, then leaned forward and kissed him gently on the lips.

"We have a long way to go," she said.

They were in Sirjan by 7:00 p.m. and Bandar Abbas by 10:00 p.m. At midnight, they saw a flashing light as they followed Bahman's brother, Jahangir, down to the water.

"That is Alireza," Jahangir said. "He has a strong boat and is a very good mariner. Our family has known him for a long time. You can trust him. He will get you both to Khasab. May Allah watch over your journey. *Khodahafez.*"

THE END

Author's Note

This work of fiction draws on my experience during the 1970s, when I lived and worked in Iran and Europe. While the novel generally follows the timeline of historical events, all characters, entities, and situations are imaginary.

The metaphors of the labyrinth and the wind, recurring motifs in the poetry of W.B. Yeats, represent themes in this novel: yearning and the quest for personal truth, ungovernable forces and flux, randomness and realization, and the anarchy and violence accompanying political upheaval.

For those interested in learning more about Iran, the Shah's nuclear ambitions, the Indian perspective under British rule and after Independence, and the urban guerilla movement in Germany, Hamid Dabashi's *Iran: A People Interrupted*, The Nuclear Threat Initiative (NTI) on *Iran's Nuclear Program Timeline and History*, Nirad C. Chaudhuri's *The Autobiography of an Unknown Indian*, Pavan K. Varma's *Being Indian*, and Stefan Aust's *Baader-Meinhof: The Inside Story of the R.A.F.*, are good places to start.

Acknowledgements

To my wife and best friend Shaila: all my love and gratitude for your inexhaustible patience. This book has benefited from your innumerable readings, invaluable suggestions, and superb literary perspective in matters large and small.

Thank you to my daughters: Tara June, your artistic sensibility and contemporary insights helped me bring the characters to life; Pia Halley, your instinct for compelling storytelling and narrative pacing helped me bring the plot to life; and to my son-in-law, Dr. Trevin Stratton: your cinematic lens was invaluable in bringing 1970s Tehran into focus.

Thank you also to Sheila Ajit Prasad, Mohini Chowdhry, Ramesh and Roda Sarin, Indra Chaudhri, Dalip Khosla, and absent friends from your remarkable generation, for sharing the stories of your fascinating lives; to Adil and Imran Trehan, and Aditya and Nikhil Pathak, the inspirations for Hamid's sons; to my sister Malini Chopra, my brother Sanjiv Misra, their spouses, and our wonderful cousins, for decades of companionship and affection; and to Kartikeya Rao and my other nephews and nieces for their enthusiasm and support.

This novel was shaped during workshop sessions at Stanford with Nancy Packer and Lynn Stegner. I am grateful for their guidance and for the comments and encouragement of fellow students who became part of my writing group, particularly Laura Svienty, Shanda Bahles and Greg Biles.

Thanks to Shaheen Rehman and Ahmad Shirazi for keeping me on track in passages about Islam and Iran, and to Martina Stamm and Fritz Bathelt for help on matters German.

To my publisher, Mike Sager, thank you for all your advice and for making this a reality.

About the Author

Madhav Misra was a senior financial executive in Tehran during the 1970s. He witnessed the Iranian Revolution unfold and evacuated out of the country on one of the last flights in December, 1978. He was born in Lucknow, India and graduated from St. Stephen's College, Delhi, and Columbia University, New York. In addition to Tehran, he has lived and worked in London, New York City, and San Francisco. He and his wife now divide their time between Marin County, California, Maui, Hawaii, and the Himalayan foothills. *Labyrinth of the Wind* is his first novel.

About the Publisher

The Sager Group was founded in 1984. In 2012 it was chartered as a multimedia content brand, with the intent of empowering those who create art—an umbrella beneath which makers can pursue, and profit from, their craft directly, without gatekeepers. TSG publishes books; ministers to artists and provides modest grants; and produces documentary, feature, and commercial films. By harnessing the means of production, The Sager Group helps artists help themselves. For more information, please see TheSagerGroup.net.

More Books from The Sager Group

The Swamp: Deceipt and Corruption in the CIA
An Elizabeth Petrov Thriller (Book 1)
by Jeff Grant

Chains of Nobility: Brotherhood of the Mamluks (Book 1)
by Brad Graft

A Lion's Share: Brotherhood of the Mamluks (Book 2)
by Brad Graft

The Living and the Dead
by Brian Mockenhaupt

Three Days in Gettysburg
by Brian Mockenhaupt

Miss Havilland: A Novel
by Gay Daly

The Orphan's Daughter: A Novel
by Jan Cherubin

Lifeboat No. 8: Surviving the Titanic
by Elizabeth Kaye

Shaman: The Mysterious Life and Impeccable Death of Carlos Castaneda
by Mike Sager

Hunting Marlon Brando: A True Story
by Mike Sager

Artifex Te Adiuva

Written in
A Beaurocraters
a Banken + Bond Book

Made in the USA
Las Vegas, NV
13 January 2021